CASES IN INVESTMENTS

SECOND
EDITION

CASES IN INVESTMENTS

EDWARD A
MOSES
University of North Florida

DILIP D
KARE
University of North Florida

DONALD J
THOMPSON, II
Georgia State University

WEST PUBLISHING

St. Paul ■ New York
Los Angeles
San Francisco

Interior Design ■ Melinda Grosser for *silk*
Composition ■ G&S Typesetters
Copyediting ■ Robert K. Burdette
Artwork ■ Rolin Graphics

COPYRIGHT ©1982   By WEST PUBLISHING COMPANY
COPYRIGHT ©1989   By WEST PUBLISHING COMPANY
                     50 W. Kellogg Boulevard
                     P.O. Box 64526
                     St. Paul, MN 55164-1003

Printed in the United States of America

96 95 94 93 92 91 90 89 8 7 6 5 4 3 2 1 0

Library of Congress Cataloging-in-Publication Data

Moses, Edward A.
    Cases in investments / Edward A. Moses, Dilip D. Kare, Donald J.
Thompson, II.—2nd ed.
        p.   cm.
    Includes bibliographical references and index.
    ISBN 0-314-48128-1
    1. Investments—Case studies. I. Kare, Dilip D. II. Thompson,
Donald J. III. Title.
HG4521.M8535   1989
332.6—dc19   88-28263
                                                            CIP

To my wife, Susan
E.A.M.

■

To the memory of my
father, Damodar
D.D.K.

■

To my children, David
and Laura
D.J.T.

Contents

PART FOUR

Other Investments 159

PART FIVE

Portfolio Management 177

Preface

This second edition of *Cases in Investments* is written with same purpose in mind as the first edition. The 33 cases in this casebook present investment situations that can be used to allow the students to relate theories and concepts to "real world" situations. It is our feeling that the use of cases increases the student's interest, enhances knowledge and improves the ability of the professor to illustrate specific points throughout the course. The diversity of cases within each part insures the casebook's compatibility with nearly all investments texts and allows professors to select cases most appropriate for their courses whether they are at the undergraduate or graduate level. All of the cases are written from the viewpoint of an investor or advisor and directly involve the student in the decision making process.

The Second Edition

A significant number of new cases is included in the second edition. In addition, almost all of the remaining cases have been revised and updated. These changes are necessary because of the dramatic theoretical and institutional changes that have occurred in security markets since the first edition. For example, the stock market "crash" of October 19, 1987 and the Tax Reform Act of 1986 represent changes in the investment environment that have been incorporated in appropriate cases.

Questions are included at the end of each case to guide the student and provide a basis for class discussion. While the cases center around specific topics (see the subtitles in the Contents), many of the cases contain financial data that allows the professor the opportunity to assign students additional areas of investigation beyond those suggested by the questions.

Accompanying Materials

The *Instructor's Manual* accompanying the casebook is designed to provide the professor with a comprehensive and convenient instructional aid. For each case there is a detailed teaching note that contains the case objectives, an assessment of the degree of difficulty of the case, a suggested classroom approach to the case, and a comprehensive analysis of each of the questions at the end of the case. In addition, a cross-reference table to a number of leading graduate and undergraduate level investments texts has been included in order to help the professor coordinate text assignments and case selections.

Diskettes with Lotus 1-2-3 worksheets, written by Dilip D. Kare, accompany the casebook. There is a student's diskette and a professor's diskette. The professor's diskette has the data for solutions to the case questions on the diskette while the student's version requires the student to supply the data. The worksheets have been prepared for those cases which lend themselves to computer applications. A copy of each of the diskettes can be obtained by the professor directly from West Publishing Company.

Acknowledgements

We are grateful to a number of people for making contributions to this casebook. The students who suffered through earlier versions of the cases deserve recognition. Their comments and suggestions, from a student's perspective, have been incorporated into the final product. We are also appreciative of the help of John M. Cheney, E. Theodore Veit, and Arthur L. Schwartz, Jr. for their contribution to the first edition of the casebook. We would like to thank John M. Cheney and Wallace W. Reiff for allowing us to include their excellent case in this casebook.

We would also like to thank Graciela N. Salinas and Linda Crickenberger for their research assistance and M. Leanna Payne for her great job of typing. Finally, we want to express our appreciation to West Publishing Company, especially Richard Fenton, Nancy Roth, Esther Craig, and Francine DeZiel for their help and contributions in bringing this casebook to life.

Edward A. Moses
Donald J. Thompson, II
Dilip D. Kare

CASES IN INVESTMENTS

The Investment
Environment

PART

ONE

CASE

1

George Thomas (Security Markets and Transactions)

George Thomas, an engineering Ph.D., has been working for one of the world's largest integrated oil companies for two years. Before taking this position he taught petroleum engineering in a state university for five years. George is thirty-three years old, married, and has two children, ages eight and ten. He has been able to accumulate some savings, owns adequate life insurance, and has a small amount of equity in his home. George's wife works full-time as a school librarian.

George's mother died recently, leaving him and his sister an estate valued at approximately $500,000 after inheritance taxes. Half of the estate is a small apartment complex in Chicago, and the other half comprises common stocks. When the estate was being divided, George's sister expressed a strong desire to have the apartment complex. She was recently divorced and felt that, in addition to providing income, management of the apartment complex would occupy her time. George reluctantly agreed to accept the securities as his share of the inheritance.

In talking with the attorney for the estate, George indicated that he was completely ignorant about common stocks. He felt a need for expert advice about managing the inherited securities. The attorney suggested that he consult Professor Barry Tucker, a member of the finance faculty at a local university. Professor Tucker taught investment courses at the university and had done consulting work for the attorney's firm in the past.

At their first meeting Professor Tucker suggested that George had at least two alternatives. He could personally manage the assets, making all of the buy-and-sell decisions himself, or he could have the portfolio managed by a private investment counselor or the trust department of a bank. Professor Tucker explained that, even with professional management, George could influence the buy-and-sell decision-making process if he desired. Tucker suggested that, as a

3

first step, George develop some understanding of the investment environment. Tucker offered to prepare a summary of the inherited portfolio.

To get this information, Tucker visited the local office of the brokerage firm George's mother had used in making her stock transactions. The stockbroker, Mr. Green, was very cooperative and provided Professor Tucker with the necessary information. This information is shown in Table 1.1.

Mr. Green pointed out that George's mother had been an active investor in the stock market. An inveterate "tape watcher," she had spent at least a part of every business day in the brokerage office. Mrs. Thomas never placed market orders when buying or selling securities; rather, she always instructed him to place limit orders that were "good till cancelled" (GTC). She never sold stocks short or bought stocks on margin.

According to Green, Mrs. Thomas always bought in round lots to avoid paying an odd-lot differential. After May 1, 1975, when all commission charges became negotiable, she continually threatened to take her business to a discount broker if Green did not lower his commissions. Since Green wanted to keep the account, he tried to give Mrs. Thomas a reduced commission on her trades. Realizing that he could not compete with the discount brokers' lower commissions, he tried to explain the advantages of dealing with a large retail brokerage firm. Mrs. Thomas countered that she was willing to give up some of those advantages to secure a 30 to 40 percent reduction in commission expenses.

■ QUESTIONS

1. Describe in general terms the investment objectives that might be appropriate for George Thomas. Is the portfolio shown in Table 1.1 consistent with these objectives?

2. What is the total expected dividend income in 1988 from the inherited portfolio? What is the expected dividend yield for the portfolio on current market value?

3. Briefly compare the characteristics of the New York Stock Exchange, American Stock Exchange, over-the-counter market, and regional exchanges.

4. What reasons might Mrs. Thomas have had for placing limit orders that were open (GTC)? What other types of orders might she have placed?

5. Distinguish between trades in round lots and those in odd lots. What is an odd-lot differential?

6. What is meant by "buying on margin"? How does buying on margin increase the investor's risk? What is a maintenance call?

7. Describe the procedure for selling stock short. What is the short-seller's responsibility with respect to cash dividends paid on the stock?

8. What services could Mr. Green's firm provide that might not be available from a discount brokerage firm?

TABLE 1.1 | George Thomas
Selected Portfolio Information as of 6/30/87

No. Shares	Name	Market Price per Share	Indicated Annual Cash Dividends per Share	Market*
200	American Tel. & Tel.	$ 27⅝	$1.20	NY, B, C, M, P, Ph
300	Charter Medical 'B'	30	.24	AS, P
400	Crawford & Co.	25¾	.58	OTC
400	EG&G Inc.	34½	.56	NY, B, M, Ph, P
500	Fieldcrest Cannon	34	.68	NY, M
200	G. Heilman Brewing	26⅝	.60	NY, M, P
300	General Electric	54⅜	1.32	NY, B, C, M, P, Ph
300	General Motors	82⅝	5.00	NY, B, C, M, P, Ph, T, Mo
200	Genuine Parts	37⅛	.92	NY, M
600	Hilton Hotels	88⅞	1.80	NY, B, M, P, Ph
100	IBM	162½	4.40	NY, B, C, M, P, Ph
200	Media General	38⅞	.34	AS
200	Moore Corp., Ltd.	25½	.72	NY, M, Mo, T
200	Oxford Industries	16½	.50	NY, M
500	Pacific Gas & Electric	20⅛	1.92	NY, B, C, M, P, Ph, Vc
500	Philadelphia Electric	21⅛	2.20	NY, B, C, M, P, Ph
200	Procter & Gamble	98	2.70	NY, B, C, M, P, Ph
200	Pub. Service of New Mexico	32¾	2.92	NY, B, M
300	Purolator Courier	36¾	0.00	NY, B, M, Ph
300	Upjohn Co.	45¼	.60	NY, B, C, M, P, Ph
200	Wang Labs.	15⅞	.16	AS, B, M, P, Ph

Source: Reprinted by permission of the Standard & Poor's Corporation.

*The market abbreviations are the same as those used in the July 1987 Standard & Poor's *Stock Guide* and are defined as follows:

AS — American	NY — New York
B — Boston	P — Pacific
C — Cincinnati	Ph — Philadelphia
M — Midwest	T — Toronto
Mo— Montreal	OTC— NASDAQ
Vc — Vancouver	

The *Midland Inquirer*
(Stock Market Indexes)

Henry Teaford, a brand-new business school graduate, was recently hired as an assistant to George Law, the business editor of the *Midland Inquirer*. Henry's first job was to secure the information for the *Midland Inquirer* Oil Index and write a short column for the Tuesday through Saturday editions of the *Inquirer*, describing the activities of the seven stocks composing the index. A typical column is shown in Table 2.1.

In reality, Henry had to do little to prepare the column. A local brokerage firm telephoned the *Inquirer* each afternoon with the closing calculations for the index, the total number of shares traded for each of the index stocks, and any unusual activity in these stocks. This process had been going on for over fifty years, and both the brokerage firm and the newspaper appeared satisfied with the arrangement.

Henry had taken a course in investments while in college, and he was familiar with the calculation procedures for the popular market measures such as the Dow Jones averages and the Standard & Poor's indexes. Upon being given this assignment, Henry had asked Mr. Law how the Oil Index was calculated. Law did not know and suggested that Henry call Jack Gamble at the brokerage firm. Gamble reported that the index was calculated in exactly the same manner as the Dow Jones averages—all capitalization changes were handled on a divisor-adjusted basis. On December 31, 1987, the divisor for the index was 1.4238, and changes in the divisor occurred only with capitalization changes affecting 10 percent or more of a firm's outstanding shares.

Henry recalled that his college professor had pointed out a number of weaknesses in the Dow Jones averages and had seemed to prefer value-weighted arithmetic indexes, such as those calculated by the Standard & Poor's Corporation (S&P). In reviewing his notes from the investments class, Henry found the general formula for the S&P Industrial Index:

$$\frac{(\text{current market price}_i \times \text{current outstanding shares}_i)}{\begin{array}{cc} (1941\text{–}43 \text{ average} & \times & 1941\text{–}43 \text{ average} \\ \text{market price}_i & & \text{outstanding shares}_i) \end{array}} \times 10$$

Henry recalled that a change in the denominator, or old base-market value, occurred only with a change in capitalization. The professor had given the class a formula for calculating the new base-market value:

$$\text{old base-market value} \times \frac{\begin{array}{c}\text{market value as of base date,}\\ \text{reflecting the change in}\\ \text{capitalization}\end{array}}{\begin{array}{c}\text{market value as of base date,}\\ \text{before the change in}\\ \text{capitalization}\end{array}}$$

$$= \text{new base-market value}$$

Henry decided to experiment with a new index of petroleum refining companies calculated in the same way as the S&P Industrial Index. First he expanded the number of companies in the index from 7 to 20. The names of the 20 companies, the share prices, and the number of shares outstanding are shown in Table 2.2. Henry thought that if he used December 31, 1986, as the date for the original base-market value and assigned the index a beginning value of 50 (the approximate average price of the 20 securities on that date), he would be able to produce a better measure of performance than the current index.

QUESTIONS

1. What are the major arguments against the use of the *Midland Inquirer* Oil Index as a measure of the performance of petroleum refining companies? What are some arguments in favor of the continued use of this measure?

2. Why did the index divisor decline from its beginning value of 7 to 1.4238 by December 31, 1987?

3. What are the advantages and disadvantages of Henry's new index relative to the present index?

4. Assuming no changes in capitalization between December 31, 1986, and March 30, 1987, calculate the values for the *Inquirer* Oil Index and Henry's proposed index on December 31, 1986, and March 30, 1987. Compare the percentage changes in the two performance measures between December 31, 1986, and March 30, 1987.

TABLE	The *Midland Inquirer*
2.1	Typical Oil Index Column

Oil Equities Up 2.75

Oil stocks advanced 2.75 Thursday in heavier trading with two issues advancing, two declining, and three unchanged.

The *Midland Inquirer* Oil Index closed at 206.64. Total volume for the seven stocks in the index was 994,344 shares, compared with 1,341,200 the previous session.

Mobil gained two points, closing at 39½, while Murphy Oil gained one point to 27.

Texaco traded 354,000 shares; Murphy Oil, 49,244; Standard Oil, 175,400; Exxon, 147,400; Phillips Petroleum, 132,100; Atlantic Richfield, 74,100; and Mobil, 62,100.

TABLE	The *Midland Inquirer*
2.2	Petroleum Refining Companies

Company	Share Price 12/31/86	Shares Outstanding 12/31/86 (000)	Share Price 3/30/87
Amerada Hess Corp.	23¾	83,063	31⅝
Ashland Oil Corp.	56	32,541	59¾
Atlantic Richfield[1]	60	176,473	80
British Petroleum Co., Ltd.	43½	182,857	59⅛
Chevron Co. (Calif.)[1]	45⅜	342,109	56⅛
Exxon Corp.[1]	70⅛	722,155	85¾
Kerr-McGee Corp.	28⅛	48,358	34⅝
Mobil Corp.[1]	40⅛	408,239	47⅝
Murphy Oil Corp.[1]	25	33,591	33
Pennzoil Co.	67	41,426	79¾
Phillips Petroleum Co.[1]	11¾	227,883	15⅞
Quaker State Oil Refining	25	26,335	28¼
Royal Dutch Petroleum Co.	95½	268,037	117⅞
Shell Transp./Trading	58½	276,209	80⅜
Standard Oil Co.	49⅜	234,685	70¼
Sun Co.	54¼	107,712	68¼
Tesoro Petroleum Corp.	10¾	13,731	12¼
Texaco, Inc.[1]	35⅞	241,474	37⅜
Unocal	26⅝	116,305	37⅛
Witco Chemical Corp.	38⅝	22,231	44⅞

[1] Included in the currently published *Midland Inquirer* Oil Index.

The Flaherty Brothers
(Alternative Investments)

The three Flaherty brothers live in Atlantic City, New Jersey. John, age thirty-eight, had been an accountant with one of the older Atlantic City hotels until it was sold and converted into a casino. Jim and Tim, thirty-six-year-old twins, had been fortunate enough to own considerable real estate in Atlantic City prior to the legalization of gambling. As a result of the sales of this real estate, they were both independently wealthy and were not seeking employment. The twins had always respected John's business judgment, and when he lost his job, they asked him to manage their affairs. John, having no immediate prospects for employment, agreed to become their investment counselor.

Although John was familiar with accounting techniques, he had virtually no experience as an investment counselor. This concerned him since he knew that his brothers depended completely on his investment decisions. To gain some time, John invested his brothers' money in a money market fund. He was familiar with this investment because the hotel had used a money market fund as a temporary investment for idle cash during the off-season. He realized that this was only a stopgap measure and that other investment media would have to be found to satisfy his brothers' financial needs.

During the six months that the money was invested in the money market fund, John researched the various aspects of security analysis and portfolio management. Although he did not consider himself an expert, he did begin to get a feel for the questions he should ask before he made investment decisions. He thought he knew the appropriate risk levels for his brothers and the nature of their immediate and long-term needs. However, he could not identify the appropriate investments for meeting those needs. John decided that he needed to investigate expected returns, levels of risk, and some measure of comovement of the returns of the various assets with each other.

John found many articles describing the historical returns and risks of various types of assets. One of the articles appeared to be particularly interesting.[1] Its authors examined a large number of investment media, not only for their risk-return characteristics but also for the relationships of their returns.

Although the period examined in the article, 1949–69, was dated, John found the article to be particularly relevant because it answered some of his questions about portfolio construction. However, he thought that the 21-year investment horizon used in the article was too long for his brothers and decided to divide the period into subperiods of 10 and 11 years. Table 3.1 shows the risk-return relationships among various assets for the two subperiods and for the entire period. Table 3.2 shows, as the original authors had indicated, the correlation among the returns of the various investment media over the entire 21-year period.

Satisfied with his efforts to this point, John reviewed the information he had gathered so that he could discuss it intelligently with Jim and Tim. He knew that it was only a matter of time before he would have to remove the money from the money market fund and invest it in other types of assets.

█ QUESTIONS

1. Rate each of the twelve investment alternatives in Table 3.1 according to the following characteristics:
   a. Risk exposure
   b. Current yield
   c. Capital gains potential
   d. Liquidity
   e. Protection against inflation
   f. Expense of acquisition or sale
   g. Expense of holding

For each of the characteristics, score the relative value of the investment characteristics, using the following scheme:

1 = high, 2 = average, 3 = low, and 4 = none or 0

2. What investment alternatives other than those listed in Table 3.1 could be considered for an individual's portfolio? Score the characteristics of these investments as you did in Question 1.

3. From Table 3.1, using the coefficient of variation as the measure of risk and the arithmetic mean as the measure of return, does there appear to be a significant change in the risk-return relationships for the series between the 1949–58 period and the 1959–69 period? Is it reasonable to expect the historical returns, standard deviations, and interinvestment correlation coefficients shown in Tables 3.1 and 3.2 to be valid predictors in 1988?

---

[1] Alexander A. Robichek, Richard A. Cohn, and John J. Pringle, "Returns on Alternative Investment Media and Implications for Portfolio Construction," *Journal of Business*, 45, no. 3 (July 1972): 427–43.

4. For the entire period, does any investment alternative appear to dominate any other series?

5. After examining the correlation coefficients in Table 3.2, what can you conclude about the improvement of portfolio efficiency by using multimedia diversification?

TABLE 3.1	The Flaherty Brothers Historical Risks and Returns; 1949–69

Series	Years	Arithmetic Mean Return (%)	Geometric Mean Return (%)	Arithmetic Mean Std. Deviation (%)	Coefficient of Variation***
S&P Industrials	1949–58	19.55	17.99	19.09	.98
	1959–69	7.00	6.15	13.35	1.91
	1949–69	12.97	11.63	17.50	1.35
S&P Utilities	1949–58	14.22	13.68	11.36	.80
	1959–69	4.84	4.19	11.60	2.40
	1949–69	9.31	8.61	12.41	1.33
Japanese Stocks	1949–58	27.03	18.67	53.49	1.98
	1959–69	21.38	19.19	24.29	1.14
	1949–69	24.07	18.95	40.97	1.70
Australian Stocks	1949–58	5.15	3.96	15.31	2.97
	1959–69	10.20	9.49	12.62	1.24
	1949–69	7.80	6.82	14.20	1.82
Canadian Pacific Perpetual 4% Bond	1949–58	3.27	3.18	4.28	1.31
	1959–69	.01	−.20	6.36	636.00
	1949–69	1.56	1.40	5.70	3.65
Bethlehem Steel 2¾% Bond, 1970	1949–58	1.12	1.04	4.02	3.59
	1959–69	2.91	2.88	2.41	.83
	1949–69	2.06	2.00	3.40	1.65
U.S. Government 2½% Bond, 1970–65	1949–58	1.02	.92	4.46	4.37
	1959–69	3.81	3.71	4.46	1.17
	1949–69	2.48	2.37	4.68	1.89
Treasury Bill Yields	1949–58	1.81	1.81	.69	.38
	1959–69	4.10	4.09	1.33	.32
	1949–69	3.01	3.00	1.57	.52
Farm Real Estate	1949–58*	9.84	9.67	6.32	.64
	1959–69	9.36	9.33	2.41	.26
	1949–69*	9.56	9.47	4.50	.47
Cotton Futures	1949–58	39.17	19.92	83.27	2.13
	1959–69	−2.97	−8.96	31.99	10.77
	1949–69	17.10	3.80	41.35	2.42
Wheat Futures	1949–58	12.74	−8.62	67.87	5.33
	1959–69	−12.54	−36.30	48.85	3.90
	1949–69	−.49	−22.88	60.03	122.51
Copper Futures	1949–58**	155.74	4.18	261.01	1.68
	1959–69	117.77	52.28	208.72	1.77
	1949–69**	133.76	29.79	232.93	1.74

Source: Alexander A. Robichek, Richard A. Cohn, and John J. Pringle, "Returns on Alternative Investment Media and Implications for Portfolio Construction," *Journal of Business* 45, no. 3 (July, 1972): 427–43. Copyright 1972 by the University of Chicago Press. Reprinted by permission of the University of Chicago Press.

*Rates of return information not available for 1949 and 1950.

**Copper contracts not traded in 1951 and 1952 because of the Korean War. Rates of return for these years treated as not available rather than zero rates of return.

***Coefficient of variation is defined as the absolute value of the arithmetic mean standard deviation divided by the arithmetic mean return.

**TABLE
3.2** | The Flaherty Brothers
Correlation Coefficients

	S&P Ind.	S&P Util.	Japanese Stocks	Australian Stocks	Can. Pacific
S&P Utilities	.59**				
Japanese Stocks	−.07	.11			
Australian Stocks	.22	−.17	−.15		
Canadian Pacific Perpetual 4% Bond	.23	.34	.05	.44*	
Bethlehem Steel 2¾% Bond, 1970	−.30	−.08	−.19	−.05	.10
U.S. Government 2½% Bond, 1970–65	−.54*	−.17	−.21	−.28	.02
Treasury Bill Yields	−.55**	−.66**	−.02	.14	−.40
Farm Real Estate	−.13	−.15	.48*	−.29	−.13
Cotton Futures	.29	−.04	−.31	.33	−.01
Wheat Futures	.29	.06	−.09	.04	.14
Copper Futures	.32	−.24	−.13	.13	.12

	Bethlehem Steel	U.S. Govt.	Treas. Bills	Farm Real Estate	Cotton Futures	Wheat Futures
S&P Utilities						
Japanese Stocks						
Australian Stocks						
Canadian Pacific Perpetual 4% Bond						
Bethlehem Steel 2 3/4% Bond, 1970						
U.S. Government 2½% Bond, 1970–65	.81**					
Treasury Bill Yields	.20	.26				
Farm Real Estate	−.26	−.19	.06			
Cotton Futures	−.12	−.21	−.41	−.09		
Wheat Futures	−.41	−.31	−.35	−.24	.67**	
Copper Futures	−.10	−.20	.05	−.21	.23	.38

Source: Alexander A. Robichek, Richard A. Cohn, and John J. Pringle, "Returns on Alternative Investment Media and Implications for Portfolio Construction," *Journal of Business* 45, no. 3 (July, 1972): 427–43. Copyright 1972 by the University of Chicago Press. Reprinted by permission of the University of Chicago Press.
*Significant at the .05 level.
**Significant at the .01 level.

Equity Valuation

Tri-State Airlines, Inc. (Adjustment of Accounting Data for Comparability)

Mr. Henry Ascott, President of Tri-State Airlines, Inc. (TAL), is faced with a dilemma. He is scheduled to make a presentation on TAL to the Financial Analysts Society of Chicago during December 1988, in just two months. However, some recent events could have a significant impact on his presentation. An increase in pension benefits was granted to the firm's employees during recent labor negotiations. In addition, two of the firm's ten aircraft were destroyed by a hangar that collapsed during a severe windstorm. The destroyed aircraft were old, and little reimbursement is expected from the insurance company. As a direct result of the aircraft destruction, many flights had to be cancelled for three weeks, before replacement aircraft could be rented. These cancellations resulted in lower revenues for the current quarter.

TAL is a small airline, operating in Illinois, Wisconsin, and Indiana. The firm's sales and earnings per share have grown rapidly in recent years and are expected to be $20,857,000 and $1.05, respectively, in 1988. TAL has also enjoyed a "perfect" safety record, of which the employees and management are very proud. The firm was tightly controlled by the Ascott family until about four years ago when, due to an overwhelming need for additional capital, the first public offering of common stock was made. Mr. Ascott expects TAL to go back into the equity market within a year to support continued growth.

Since early September 1987, the price of TAL's common stock has fallen from $19 to $16 1/2 a share. Mr. Ascott thinks that the price decline was a direct result of the destroyed aircraft and the increased pension liabilities. To examine alternative solutions to the problems, Mr. Ascott met with his key managers. Meeting with Mr. Ascott were Mr. Whipley, the firm's treasurer; Mr. Beatty, the comptroller; Mr. Farnsworth, the chief financial officer; and Mr. O'Patrick, the vice president in charge of operations and maintenance. The comptroller and the treasurer did most of the talking.

Whipley: From our earlier studies, we know that an aircraft leasing arrangement is more advantageous to us than the borrow-and-buy alternative. The problem we face is whether to use an operating or a capital lease. The type of lease will dictate how the lease will be accounted for on the financial statements.

Beatty: That's correct. If it is an operating lease, no asset or related liability will appear on our balance sheet. The rental payments will be charged as operating expenses as they become payable. However, the financial statements must disclose adequate information about the lease to enable the reader to determine the effect of the lease commitments on our present and future operations and financial position. This requirement can be met by disclosure in a footnote. I have prepared some pro forma statements for 1989, assuming the use of an operating lease to acquire the needed aircraft (see Tables 4.1 and 4.2).

If we go with a capital lease, the value of the aircraft will appear on the balance sheet as a "capital lease," an asset. The corresponding liability would appear on the balance sheet as an "obligation under capital lease." The dollar amount of the asset and liability would be the present value of the minimum lease payments, which for us would include only the rental payments. The discount rate to be employed in finding the present value of the lease payments should be the implicit rate in the lease if it is below the lessee's incremental borrowing rate. If it is not known or is above the incremental borrowing rate, the incremental borrowing rate should be used. In our case the rate would be 10 percent. The asset would be amortized, using our normal depreciation methods. The liability account would be reduced by the "principal" portion of the rental payment. The "interest" portion of the rental payment would be charged to the income statement.

Whipley: We did some checking and found that we can obtain the desired aircraft under a lease that, with some minor modifications, would qualify as either an operating or a capital lease. The Financial Accounting Standards Board specifies what characteristics a lease must have to qualify as a capital lease versus an operating lease. This lease arrangement woud require a $150,000 year-end annual payment for a five-year period.

Ascott: Given the need for new external equity capital in the near future, some priority should be given to maximizing the firm's earnings per share in the near term as well as improving the appearance of the firm's financial position. Mr. Whipley, I would like you to take the responsibility for determining how that can best be done with respect to the leasing alternatives.

Mr. Beatty, it appears to me that we have a problem with funding the pension plan. The new benefits will raise the normal costs (pension costs based on service after the plan's inception or recent plan modification) for 1989 to $619,000 from $553,000. This will reduce our earnings. Additionally, given our need for capital, there is a remote possibility that we will be unable to fund the pension expense.

The unfunded past-service costs (those pension costs associated with services provided before the change in the plan and that have not yet been expensed or funded) are expected to total $200,000. The amount of our pension costs that have been expensed but not yet funded, which appears on the balance sheet as "±accrued pension liability," is expected to total $303,000. What are our options for handling this on our financial statements?

Beatty: Regarding the annual cost of the plan, Accounting Principles Board Opinion No. 8 specifies a maximum and a minimum amount that can be expensed.

The minimum cost in a year is the total of normal costs plus interest equivalents on the unfunded past-service costs. The interest rate used to determine the interest equivalents is the long-term rate assumed to be earned on all pension funds. For our purposes, we can assume an annual rate of 10.5 percent.

The maximum cost in a year is the sum of normal costs, 10 percent of any past- and prior-service costs until fully amortized, and interest equivalents at 10 percent on the cumulative amount expensed but not yet funded.

The pension expense that is determined with these guidelines need not be funded in each year. Any portion not actually funded becomes a liability (generally long-term) on the balance sheet entitled "accrued pension liability."

Ascott: Mr. Beatty, I need not repeat my concern for current earnings and a strong financial position. I want you to prepare a proposal on how pension costs and funding should be handled.

QUESTIONS

1. Tables 4.1 and 4.2 reflect the pro forma financial statements of TAL for 1989, assuming an operating lease to acquire the aircraft and minimum pension expenses. Reconstruct the income statement and balance sheet, assuming a capital lease and minimum pension expenses. Assume that the aircraft are to be acquired on January 1, 1989, and amortized over a five-year period using straight-line depreciation.

2. Using Tables 4.1 and 4.2 and your reconstructed financial statements from Question 1, compare measures of liquidity, asset utilization, profitability, and leverage for TAL under the two leasing alternatives.

3. Calculate the 1989 earnings per share for TAL if the company employs the maximum method of pension costing (assume an operating lease to acquire the aircraft).

4. a. Discuss the impact on TAL if management increases the assumed 10.5 percent return that can be earned on pension fund assets.

  b. Why is it important to examine the footnotes of a firm's financial statements to determine the value of pension assets and the present value of the firm's vested and nonvested benefits?

5. Discuss the implications of pension fund accounting and of leasing for the work of the financial analyst.

TABLE 4.1	Tri-State Airlines Pro Forma Income Statement [1] Year Ending 12/31/89 (in thousands) [2]	
Operating revenues		$22,048
Operating expenses (aircraft related) [3]		17,707
General and administrative expenses [4]		1,123
Depreciation and amortization		1,722
Operating profit		$ 1,496
Other income and expenses:		
Interest expense		847
Interest income		418
Total other income and expenses		$ (429)
Net income before taxes		$ 1,067
Income tax expense		469
Net income to retained earnings [5]		$ 598
Average shares outstanding during the year		514
Earnings per share		$ 1.16

[1] Statement assumes the use of an operating lease and the minimum pension expenses.
[2] Except for earnings per share.
[3] Includes an operating lease expense of $150,000 for the new aircraft.
[4] Includes pension expense.
[5] Assumes no dividends paid on the common stock.

TABLE 4.2	Tri-State Airlines, Inc. Pro Forma Balance Sheet[1] 12/31/89 (in thousands)

Assets

Current assets:

Cash	$ 149
Marketable securities	1,441
Accounts receivable	2,874
Spare parts, materials, and supplies	863
Total current assets	$ 5,327
Operating property and equipment	18,853
Less: reserves for depreciation	7,309
Net property and equipment	$11,544
Leased property under capital leases[2]	5,324
Less: reserves for amortization	1,937
Net leased property under capital leases	$ 3,387
Other assets	224
Total assets	$20,482

Liabilities and Stockholders' Equity

Current liabilities:

Current maturities of long-term debt	$ 355
Current obligations under capital leases[2]	298
Accounts payable and accrued liabilities	3,279
Other	1,198
Total current liabilities	$ 5,130
Long-term debt	4,732
Long-term obligations under capital leases[2]	3,839
Accrued pension liability	303
Total long-term liabilities	$ 8,874

Stockholders' equity:

Capital stock—34.5 cents par value; authorized 1,100,000 shares; 514,935 shares issued	178
Other paid-in capital	3,982
Retained earnings	2,325
Less: treasury stock, 798 shares at cost	(7)
Total stockholders' equity	6,478
Total liabilities and stockholders' equity	$20,482

[1] Assumes the use of an operating lease and minimum pension expenditures.
[2] These figures are the result of capital leases previously entered into by TAL.

Ramada Inns, Inc. (Calculation of Earnings per Share)

Roger Craig has been employed by the Citizens Bank and Trust Company of Philadelphia (CB&T) for several months. Although he has improved his skills as a financial analyst while going through the training program at CB&T, he still has problems in several areas: the concept of "fully diluted" versus "primary" earnings-per-share (EPS) figures; the adjustment of past EPS figures for stock splits and stock dividends; the calculation of cash flow per share; and the handling of extraordinary items, discontinued operations, and contingency reserves.

When Roger mentioned these problems to Bill Riley, the senior analyst at CB&T, Riley outlined the following guidelines.

1. **Simple EPS versus primary and fully diluted EPS:** Whether the company reports simple EPS or the dual primary and fully diluted EPS depends on the 3 percent test. If fully diluted EPS is 3 percent or more lower than simple EPS, then dual presentation is made. If fully diluted EPS is less than 3 percent lower than the simple EPS, then a simple EPS is reported.

    The first step is to calculate the simple EPS. Next, the primary EPS is computed. In calculating the primary EPS, the numerator is net income and the denominator is the weighted average of the number of common shares outstanding during the year plus common stock equivlents. Dilution is considered only when it decreases EPS.

    Common stock equivalents include options, warrants, and those convertible securities which, at issue, provide yields of less than two-thirds of the prime rate in effect at that time. It is assumed that the options and warrants are exercised at the beginning of the period and that the proceeds are used to purchase treasury stock at the average market price for the period covered by the financial statements. It is also assumed that convertible securities are converted to common stock at the start of the year and that no interest is paid on the debt converted. In assuming conversion, the tax effect of paying less interest must also be considered.

For fully diluted EPS, *all* common stock equivalents are assumed exercised at the beginning of the period, and the proceeds used to purchase shares at the ending market price if it is higher than the average market price for the period. In addition, all convertible debentures are assumed exercised at the beginning of the period, requiring appropriate adjustments to net income to reflect the elimination of interest on the debentures.

2. **Cash flow per share:** The analyst may want to observe the cash flow per share of a firm over time as an indication of the firm's profitability trend. In using such a measure, the income statement distortions caused by depreciation and other noncash expenses may be avoided. There are several methods of calculating the cash-flow figures. One method is simply to add back depreciation to net income. A second method is to calculate the after-tax effect of depreciation $((1 - \text{tax rate}) \times \text{depreciation})$ and add this amount to net income. This method reflects the impact of depreciation on a company's income tax liability. A third alternative is to calculate pretax cash flow, which is equal to net income before depreciation and income taxes.

3. **Adjustment of per-share data for stock splits and stock dividends:** In adjusting per-share data (earnings, price, etc.) for stock splits and stock dividends, the pre-stock-split or pre-stock-dividend data are divided by 1 plus the percentage of increase (in decimal form) in stock resulting from the stock dividend or split:

$$\text{Adjusted Data} = \frac{\text{Unadjusted Data}}{1 + \% \text{ increase in stock}}$$

For example, the adjusted price of a stock that sold for $50 per share prior to a 3-for-1 stock split would be

$$\frac{\$50.00}{1+2.00} = \$16.67$$

The 2.00 figure in the denominator reflects the fact that for every share held by a stockholder prior to the 3-for-1 split, the stockholder will have 3 shares, a 200 percent increase after the split.

4. **Extraordinary items, discontinued operations, and contingency reserves:** An analyst exerts a great deal of effort in attempting to identify the normal earnings capability of a firm. These normal earnings calculations may or may not include extraordinary items (realized income or expense that is both unusual and infrequent), contingency reserves (charges to income or expense that are not yet realized but that are probable and can be reasonably estimated), and discontinued operations (realized income or expense resulting from operations which are from a part of the business that is in the process of being discontinued).

When the analyst thinks that the firm can be expected to realize any of these items on a recurring basis, he may identify them as a regular part of the firm's activities and include them in the calculation of EPS.

After discussing these guidelines, Riley handed Roger information from the 1985 Ramada Inns, Inc. Annual Report and other sources (Tables 5.1–5.4) and suggested that he use the information to test his understanding of the guidelines.

QUESTIONS

1. What are the primary and fully diluted EPS figures for Ramada Inns, Inc. in 1986? (Assume that the weighted average exercise price of stock options was $4.00.)

2. Which EPS figure, primary or fully diluted, should be used in comparing Ramada Inns' EPS to those of Ramada's competitors? Why?

3. What was the primary pretax cash flow per share for Ramada for 1986? What are the advantages and disadvantages of looking at cash-flow trends instead of EPS trends? (Assume depreciation expense of $28,350,000.)

4. If, in some year after 1986, Ramada pays a 5 percent stock dividend, what would be the adjusted primary EPS, the end-of-year stock price, and the dividend-per-share figures for 1986?

TABLE 5.1	Ramada Inns, Inc. Subordinated Debentures Outstanding 12/31/86 (in thousands of dollars)

	Par Value of Outstanding Debt
10% due 1993, not convertible	$74,270
5% due 1996, convertible at $17.05 per share (sold when prime rate was 6%)	$ 7,100

TABLE 5.2	Ramada Inns, Inc. Shares of Common Stock Reserved for Stock Options/Conversion of Debentures

	Number
Reserved for stock options	2,279,000
Reserved for conversion of debentures	416,000

TABLE 5.3	Ramada Inns, Inc. 1986 Stock Data

Stock price on 12/31/86	$ 6⅝
Average market price of stock for 1986	$ 8½
Stock price range for 1986	$ 6 to $ 11
Stock price range for 1985	$ 4¼ to $ 9½
Dividend paid during 1986	$ 0
Weighted average shares outstanding in 1986, not including common stock equivalents or potential dilution from convertibles	37,446,556

TABLE 5.4	Ramada Inns, Inc. Consolidated Statements of Income for the Fiscal Years Ending 1/1/86 and 1/1/85 (in thousands except per-share data)

	1986	1985
Revenue:		
Hotel	$238,206	$265,272
Gaming	341,814	332,861
Other	2,349	1,162
Total revenue	$582,369	$599,295
Operating expenses:		
Hotel	$219,814	$240,214
Gaming	312,867	289,601
Total operating expenses	$532,681	$529,815
Operating income:		
Hotel operations	$ 18,392	$ 25,052
Gaming	28,947	43,260
Other	2,349	1,162
Gain on hotel property sale	23,199	10,943
Total operating income	$ 72,887	$ 80,423
Corporate expenses	$ (14,607)	$ (17,361)
Reduction in (provision for) litigation settlement	650	(1,800)
Interest expense (net of capitalization)	(35,096)	(45,776)
Foreign currency loss	(111)	(579)
Others	(3,333)	(2,610)
Income before income taxes & extraordinary items	$ 20,390	$ 12,297
Provision for income taxes	(6,597)	(7,592)
Income before extraordinary items	$ 13,793	$ 4,705
Extraordinary items	3,414	4,116
Net income	$ 17,207	$ 8,821

The May Department Stores Company
(Acquisitions and Mergers)

Shortly after May Department Stores (MDS) completed a 2-for-1 stock split on June 30, 1986, Linda Mason received a letter from the president and chairman of the board of MDS (Table 6.1). The letter indicated that the managements of Associated Dry Goods Corporation (ADG) and MDS had tentatively agreed to a merger in which 1.72 shares of MDS would be exchanged for each share of ADG common stock.

As a security analyst for Central Florida Investment Advisors, Inc., an Orlando investment advisory firm, Linda followed the retail industry. In fact, she had recently advised Ted White, the firm's senior investment advisor, to consider both ADG and MDS for inclusion in high-quality, growth-oriented portfolios. Based on her recommendation, White had purchased shares of MDS for three of the firm's largest accounts. Linda discussed the proposed merger with White, and they agreed that, at least on the surface, such a business combination was promising. White asked her to keep him informed about the details of the merger.

In November 1986, Linda reported that MDS had just completed the merger with ADG and that the transaction was accounted for on a "pooling-of-interests" basis. MDS issued shares of its capital stock for all of the ADG shares outstanding, using an exchange ratio of 1.72 MDS shares for each share of ADG. Also, all outstanding ADG preferred stock was convertible into ADG common stock at the rate of 3.2 common shares per 1 preferred share. ADG's management expected all of their preferred stockholders to take advantage of this offer. At the time of the merger, MDS's outstanding stock options were estimated to be equivalent to 400,000 shares of MDS common stock. Dividends on outstanding MDS preferred shares were expected to range between $3–$5 million for the next two years. White asked what the likely impact of the merger would be on MDS's financial situation, particularly its earnings per share (EPS) for 1987. Linda asked for time to study the matter further.

Linda decided that her first task should be to adjust MDS's financial statements for periods prior to 1987, to reflect the financial records that would have existed if the firms had been merged during those earlier years. Once this adjustment was completed, she could better forecast MDS's earnings for 1987 and provide a better historical perspective for the estimate.

To adjust the earlier financial statements to reflect the merger, Linda wanted to refresh her memory about the rules for handling mergers and acquisitions. She found the following notes about accounting for mergers that she had taken while participating in a Chartered Financial Analysts training program a few years earlier.[1]

1. The two main methods of accounting for mergers are the purchase-of-assets method and the pooling-of-interests method.
2. The pooling-of-interests method is to be used when certain characteristics exist:
   a. The merging companies have been completely autonomous for the previous two years, with no intercorporate stockholding of more than 10 percent.
   b. The merger was conducted through an exchange of the acquired company's stock (at least 90 percent) for shares in the acquiring company's stock. The new shares must have the same rights as the old shares, with no contingent payments required.

3. To effect the pooling-of-interests method, the following guidelines apply:
   a. The existing book values of the assets and the liabilities of the merging companies are added together. The difference between the resulting assets and liabilities is the equity of the merged firm. If the acquiring firm gives up more value than it receives in assets, this is recognized as a reduction of the firm's equity and is never charged against income. In the equity account, retained earnings are added together, the common stock reflects the par value of shares outstanding, and capital in excess of par value absorbs the balance of the equity in the firm.
   b. The earnings of the acquired company are reflected in the combined firm's earnings for the entire year, regardless of when the merger took place.

4. The purchase-of-assets method must be used in any merger where the pooling-of-interests method cannot be used. The key characteristics of the purchase-of-assets method are:
   a. If the amount paid by the acquiring firm exceeds the book value of the net assets acquired, the excess amount can be set up as an intangible asset labeled goodwill or "cost in excess of book value" and amortized over a period not to exceed forty years, or the excess amount can be added to the plant and equipment accounts and depreciated over a period of years. Although amortization and depreciation are

---

[1] This information is from Jerome B. Cohen, Edward D. Zinbarg, and Arthur Zeikel, *Investment Analysis and Portfolio Management,* 3d ed. (Homewood, Ill.: Richard D. Irwin, 1977), pp. 213–16.

expensed against earnings, they are usually not considered tax deductible items.

b. Only that portion of the acquired firm's earnings that were realized after the date of the merger are included in the acquiring firm's financial statements in the year of the merger. Additionally, prior years' earnings are not restated for the acquiring firm as in the pooling-of-interests method.

After studying these notes, Linda reconstructed the 1986 year-end income statement and balance sheet for ADG to reflect MDS's accounting practices and fiscal year end (Tables 6.2 and 6.3).

QUESTIONS

1. Calculate the 1986 EPS figure for MDS, adjusted to reflect the merger on a pooling-of-interests basis and the stock split. (Do not change the taxes paid in 1986 by either firm). If Linda projects MDS's 1987 EPS at $1.32 (post merger), what is MDS's 1987 EPS growth rate? Why is the adjustment of 1986 EPS important to the analyst?

2. Reconstruct MDS's 1986 balance sheet, adjusting for the merger with ADG on a pooling-of-interests basis and the stock split.

3. The EPS growth rate of a firm can be increased if the book value per share rises while the return on equity (ROE) remains the same. This relationship holds true because EPS is the product of ROE and book value per share:

$$\frac{\text{Net Income}}{\text{Number of Shares}} = \frac{\text{Net Income}}{\text{Common Equity}} \times \frac{\text{Common Equity}}{\text{Number of Shares}}$$

One way to increase book value per share is through a merger where the book value of the acquired shares is greater than the book value of the shares given up in the acquisition. Using year-end 1986 data adjusted for the split, show why MDS did or did not benefit from this source of EPS growth.

4. What is the impact on MDS's 1986 debt ratios, current ratio, and return on investment after adjusting for the merger? Do these changes reflect favorably on MDS? What other benefits should the analyst look for in a merger?

TABLE	The May Department Stores Company
6.1	Letter to Stockholders[1]

September 2, 1986

Dear Fellow Shareholder:

You are cordially invited to attend the Special Meeting of Shareholders of the May Department Stores Company to be held on October 3, 1986, at 10:00 a.m., Central Daylight Time, in the ninth floor auditorium of our Famous-Barr store, Sixth and Olive Streets, St. Louis, Missouri.

At this important Special Meeting, you will be asked to consider and vote upon the approval and adoption of an Agreement and Plan of Merger between May and Associated Dry Goods Corporation pursuant to which a wholly-owned subsidiary of May will merge into Associated and Associated will become a wholly-owned subsidiary of May (the "Merger"). In the Merger each holder of Associated Common Stock will become entitled to receive 1.72 shares of May Common Stock for each share of Associated Common Stock. As part of the vote on the Merger, shareholders are also being asked to approve and adopt an amendment to May's Certificate of Incorporation to increase the authorized number of shares of May Common Stock from 200,000,000 to 350,000,000.

This combination will create one of the nation's largest retailing companies with combined sales of over $10 billion and excellent opportunities for increased growth and improved returns. Specifically, the Merger broadens and strengthens two well-respected, well-managed national retailers with attractive business operations: strong regional department stores, upscale discount stores and specialty retail stores; similar operating philosophies; and a complementary nationwide market reach. The combined strength of these two organizations, together with a strong asset base, ought to provide significant benefits to the shareholders, customers and employees of both companies.

Very truly yours,

David C. Farrell   Thomas A. Hays
Chairman of the Board   President
and Chief Executive Officer

---

[1] Reproduced in part from The May Department Stores Company merger prospectus. Reprinted with permission.

TABLE 6.2	The May Department Stores Company Associated Dry Goods Corp. and Consolidated Subsidiaries Consolidated Statement of Earnings for 52 Weeks Ending 2/1/1986 (in thousands)

Net sales, including leased departments	$4,385,019
Miscellaneous revenue—net	14,802
Total revenues	$4,399,821
Costs and expenses:	
Cost of sales	$3,318,129
Selling, general, and admin. expenses	786,382
Interest—net	71,736
Total costs and expenses	$4,176,247
Earnings before income taxes	$ 223,574
Income taxes	103,878
Net earnings	$ 119,696

TABLE 6.3	The May Department Stores Company Associated Dry Goods Corp. and Consolidated Subsidiaries Consolidated Balance Sheet as of 2/1/86 (in thousands, except par value and shares outstanding)

Assets

Current assets:

Cash and cash equivalents	$ 3,987
Accounts receivable—net	400,881
Merchandise inventories	740,457
Other current assets	25,878
Total current assets	$1,171,203
Property and equipment—net	946,391
Other assets	171,052
Total assets	$2,288,646

Liabilities and Shareholders' Equity

Current liabilities:

Notes payable	$ 69,455
Accounts payable	268,166
Other accrued liabilities	135,756
Taxes other than income taxes	13,441
Dividends payable	14,019
Income taxes	164,102
Long-term debt due within one year	19,730
Total current liabilities	$ 684,669
Long-term debt	419,540
Deferred income taxes	58,002
Deferred compensation and other liabilities	73,817
Shareholders' equity:	
Preferred stock, $50 par value per share—1,502,115 outstanding	75,106
Common stock, $.50 par value per share—34,966,516 outstanding	17,484
Additional paid-in capital	208,310
Retained earnings	752,037
Treasury stock, at cost	(319)
Total shareholders' equity	$1,052,618
Total liabilities and shareholders' equity	$2,288,646

TABLE 6.4	The May Department Stores Company The May Department Stores Company and Subsidiaries Consolidated Statement of Earnings for 52 Weeks Ending 2/1/86 (in thousands)

Net retail sales and rental revenues	$5,079,900
Cost and expenses:	
Cost of merchandise sold, including occupancy and buying costs	3,611,200
Selling, general and administrative and other expenses	983,900
Interest expense, net	50,900
Total costs and expenses	$4,646,000
Earnings before income taxes	$ 433,900
Provision for income taxes	198,500
Net earnings	$ 235,400

TABLE 6.5	The May Department Stores Company The May Department Stores Company and Subsidiaries Consolidated Balance Sheet as of 2/1/86 (in thousands)

Assets

Current assets:

Cash (including marketable securities)	$ 175,000
Accounts receivable, net	995,700
Merchandise inventories	730,900
Other current assets	20,400
Total current assets	$1,922,000

Property and equipment:

Land	194,100
Buildings and building equipment	1,127,000
Furniture, fixtures and equipment	797,500
Property under capital leases	77,300
Gross property and equipment	2,195,900
Less: accumulated depreciation	(724,300)
Net property and equipment	$1,471,600
Other assets	48,700
Total assets	$3,442,300

Liabilities and Common Shareholders' Equity

Current liabilities:

Current maturities of long-term debt	$ 30,200
Accounts payable	441,600
Accrued expenses	257,400
Income taxes	
—currently payable	79,200
—deferred	125,700
Total current liabilities	$ 934,100
Long-term debt and capitalized lease obligations	634,400
Deferred income taxes	170,400
Deferred investment tax credit	43,700
Deferred compensation	63,500
Unrealized appreciation—real estate partnership	73,800
Redeemable preferred stock	102,800

Common shareholders' equity:

Common stock[1]	71,300
Additional paid-in capital	---
Retained earnings	1,346,300
Total common shareholders' equity	$1,417,600
Total liabilities and common shareholders' equity	$3,442,300

[1]Common stock has a par value of $1.667 per share, and 100,000,000 shares are authorized. At February 1, 1986, 44,492,549 shares were issued, and 42,762,873 shares were outstanding (before 2-for-1 split effective 6/30/86).

TABLE 6.6	The May Department Stores Company Shares of Stock Outstanding[1]		
		2/1/86	**1985 Average**
Associated Dry Goods Corp.		34,966,516	31,918,000
The May Department Stores Co.		42,762,873	39,304,833

[1]Not adjusted for May's 2-for-1 split on June 30, 1986, or for the merger.

Venus Motors Corporation (Earnings per Share Growth)

As senior vice-president of the Trust Company of Detroit (Michigan), Bryan Scott presides over the trust department's weekly portfolio strategy meetings. At a recent meeting, Scott expressed concern about a stock that had been purchased for the portfolio of one of its larger clients, the United Car Workers (UCW). The union had directed the Trust Company of Detroit (TCD) to purchase 20,000 shares of Venus Motors Corporation, a major employer of its members. While UCW did not generally select the stocks to be included in its pension fund portfolio, to do so was within the scope of the existing agreement between UCW and TCD.

The union explained to TCD that the union members were very impressed with the long-range plans that Venus Motors had just made public. The plan included the replacement of all existing lines of vehicles over a sixteen-year period, beginning in 1986. A new line of vehicles would be introduced every four years. Full-sized cars would be the first line to be replaced, followed by intermediates, compacts, and trucks. Prior to introduction of the new models, the plants producing these lines were to be modernized. Such a comprehensive plan would require new investment capital of $7.5 billion, $700 million of which would come from external sources. The union thought that it would like to take part in this effort by investing in the future of Venus Motors.

In expressing his concern about the union's investment in Venus Motors, Scott stated that although his knowledge of the automobile industry was limited, he had reservations about the investment. He further reminded the other officers that TCD had a responsibility to its clients to keep them apprised of the investment outlook of their holdings, regardless of why they were acquired.

Scott asked Rexford Ennis to prepare an in-depth analysis of Venus Motors and write a special report on the company's prospects. This report would then be presented to the union. Ennis, a young analyst in the trust department, had been identified as a prospect for rapid advancement.

Ennis has begun to gather data for his task. Like most of the analysts at TCD, Ennis utilizes several valuation techniques, including a variation of the Gordon Model (present value of expected dividends) and an analysis of price/earnings (P/E) ratios. He plans to estimate the holding period return for Venus Motors, using both methods, and then to attempt to reconcile any differences in the holding period returns. At the heart of both valuation methods is the expected growth rate of the firm in terms of earnings per share (EPS) and dividends. Ennis feels that his most difficult task is to estimate the growth rate of Venus Motors' EPS over the two-year investment horizon employed by TCD in their decision-making process.

Figure 7.1 provides a model of EPS growth-rate components employed by many of the analysts at TCD. The model identifies key variables that affect the EPS growth rate. Ennis normally analyzes each major component of the EPS growth model before pulling the components together. Selected ratios for the two largest competitors of Venus Motors are shown in Table 7.4.

SALES

Realizing the importance of accurate sales forecasts, Ennis takes special care in estimating this variable. Table 7.1 provides total auto and truck sales in the United States for the three most recent years, as well as Ennis's forecast of U.S. auto and truck sales for 1985 and 1986. The forecast is for an increase in 1985, followed by a decline in 1986 due to a forecast recession and rising interest rates.

Estimates of Venus Motors' shrinking market share also appear in Table 7.1. These estimates are based on a resurgence of oil prices, which Ennis thinks will shift demand to fuel-efficient imports. He expects a continued decrease in Venus's market share for compact and full-sized autos. It is also probable that Venus Motors will lose some ground in the intermediate automobile market.

Ennis finds that Venus's foreign sales (in dollars) have been somewhat unstable in the past. However, based on Venus's competitive position and the economies of the foreign countries in which Venus sells its products, foreign sales should represent approximately 23.8 percent of the company's auto and truck sales in 1985 and 19.9 percent in 1986. He realizes that these forecasts of foreign sales are somewhat tenuous because of the fluctuations of the U.S. dollar against foreign currencies. Ennis forecasts that auto and truck sales will represent approximately 94.3 percent of Venus's total sales revenue in 1985, and 93.8 percent in 1986.

NET MARGIN ON SALES

The net margin on sales is defined as the percentage of sales dollars remaining after deducting all operating expenses, interest, and taxes. Ennis's approach is to look at each component of expense as a percentage of sales over time (see Table 7.2) to determine the past trend. Then he estimates expected net margin by combining this information with his judgment regarding the relationships between the expense items and future sales.

Because of the expected continued pressure on U.S. automakers from fuel-efficient and less-expensive imports, Ennis feels that Venus will not be able to increase prices rapidly enough to offset the rising costs of materials and labor. For this reason, Ennis expects the income statement item, "costs, other than items below," to be 92.4 percent of sales in 1985 and 96.9 percent in 1986.

Because of the modernization plans and increased capital expenditures, depreciation as a percentage of sales is expected to increase after decreasing in 1983. Ennis expects depreciation to be 1.1 percent of sales in 1985 and 1.5 percent in 1986. The amortization of special tools is expected to remain fairly low as a percentage of sales. This expense is estimated to be 1.6 percent of sales in 1985 and 1.8 percent in 1986.

Ennis anticipates a relatively large increase in selling and administrative expenses because of the expected high rate of inflation. He projects the 1985 figure to be 4.2 percent of sales and the 1986 figure to be 5 percent.

The pension plan expense as a percentage of sales is expected to decline to the 1983 level in 1985 because of decreased production. This would be followed by an increase in 1986 to the 1984 level.

Because of the forecast rise in short-term interest rates, Ennis is forecasting interest expense to increase to .9 percent of sales in 1985. He expects the 1986 debt expense to increase significantly because of continued rising interest rates and the acquisition of additional debt needed to finance Venus's modernization program. Combining the increased debt expense with an expected decrease in sales, Ennis projects interest expense to be 1.8 percent of sales in 1986.

Ennis projects that 1985 tax credits resulting from losses on domestic operations will more than offset the significant tax expense from foreign operations; he estimates 1985 net tax credits of $81.2 million. Although 1986 income taxes due to foreign governments on foreign operations will be significant, they are expected to be offset by tax credits from losses on U.S. operations.

TOTAL ASSET TURNOVER

The total asset turnover ratio (sales/total assets) provides a measure of the level of assets required to support a given level of sales. Ennis's approach is to forecast the turnover of each major asset category separately and then combine them to arrive at the total asset turnover ratio.

Because of the expected increase in capital expenditures, Venus may increase its holding of marketable securities as a temporary investment. This would reduce the turnover of 30.17 for the 1982–84 period over the next several years.

Recent changes by management are expected to result in an improvement in accounts receivable and inventory turnover. Senior management has recognized the need to streamline the firm to reduce financing needs in the face of rising interest rates. For 1985, the turnover of accounts receivable is expected to increase by 10 percent over the 1982–84 average of 15 times. An increase of 22 percent is expected in 1986 over the 1985 figure.

Tighter controls on inventories are also expected to increase the inventory turnover ratio in 1985. The trend has been good in the recent past; as shown in Table 7.3, the 1984 and 1983 inventory turnovers represent an improvement over the 1982 figure. The 1985 ratio is expected to improve to 137 percent of the 1982–84 average of 5.1. Because of the decline in sales that Ennis expects for 1985, he is projecting a decrease in inventory turnover to 6.4 in that year.

Ennis recognizes that the turnover of "other current assets" and "investments and miscellaneous assets" has been very volatile in the last few years. He is also uncertain how Venus's activities in the next few years will affect these ratios. He therefore forecasts that both turnovers for 1985 and 1986 will equal the average for the 1982–84 period.

The turnover of net land, plant, and equipment also improved in 1984 and 1983 relative to 1982. Ennis expects this trend to continue into 1985, as sales increase and the firm moves closer to capacity. The result is expected to be an increase in net land, plant, and equipment turnover to a level 24 percent higher than the 1982–84 average of 7.8. However, because of the estimated decline in 1986 sales, the turnover ratio is expected to decrease to the 1982–84 average in that year.

The turnover of special tools (less amortization) has also been on the rise in 1983 and 1984. It is forecast to decrease slightly in 1985, to a level 7 percent below the 1983–84 average of 20.8 because of a relatively large increase in special tools. Given the forecast decline in sales and expected further increase in special tools required in 1986, the special tools turnover in 1986 is forecast to be 30 percent below the 1983–84 average.

▌LEVERAGE (TOTAL ASSETS/NET WORTH)

Ennis thinks that Venus Motors will have to sell new equity shares in order to maintain viability in the eyes of its creditors. He estimates that in 1985, Venus Motors will sell $217.5 million worth of preferred stock, on which the firm will pay $14 million in dividends. Dividends on the preferred stock are estimated at $29 million in subsequent years. Additionally, Ennis estimates that the firm will sell $55 million in new common stock in 1986. This will help to offset expected operating losses in those years and help to finance the modernization program. Because of the decrease in assets expected in 1985 due to some streamlining, Ennis projects a leverage ratio equal to that in 1984. However, 1986's projected losses and modernization program are expected to increase the leverage ratio for 1986 to 161 percent of the 1982–84 average of 2.6.

DIVIDENDS

Despite the financial difficulties that Ennis expects Venus Motors to face, he thinks that the company would like to maintain the dividend on the common stock for as long as possible. He forecasts a 1985 dividend of $52.2 million and a 1986 dividend of $13 million for the first six months, with elimination of the dividend for the remainder of 1986. He calculates the earnings retention rate using the following formula:

$$\frac{\text{Net income} - \text{dividends paid}}{\text{Net income}}$$

QUESTIONS

1. Estimate the total sales revenue for Venus Motors for 1985 and 1986.

2. Based on the information provided, estimate the net margin on sales before and after preferred stock dividends in 1985 and 1986. Evaluate Venus Motors' net margin on sales in terms of trend and comparison with competitors.

3. Forecast the total asset turnover ratio for 1985 and 1986 based on the information provided. Evaluate Venus Motors' total asset turnover ratio in terms of trend and comparison with competitors.

4. Estimate the leverage ratio in 1985 and 1986. Evaluate Venus's leverage ratio in terms of trend and comparison with competitors.

5. Analyze the earnings retention rate for the past three years. Estimate the earnings retention rate for 1985 and 1986.

6. If Ennis assumes that the *average* of the estimates of the financial variables in 1985 and 1986 will be typical of Venus's performance in the future, estimate the expected growth rate of EPS. Use Figure 7.1 as a guide.

7. If the experience from 1982 to 1984 proves to be more typical of Venus Motors in the future, estimate the expected growth rate in EPS.

FIGURE | **Venus Motors Corporation**
7.1 | **EPS Growth Rate Model**

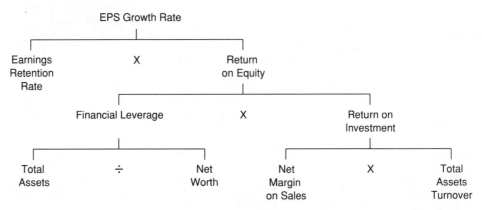

TABLE | Venus Motors Corporation
7.1 | Auto and Truck Sales in the United States

	Industry Sales (000 units)	Venus Motors Market Share (%)	Venus Motors Sales (000 units)	Venus Motors Average Nominal Sales Price per Unit[1]
1982	10,939	12.3	1,346	6,280
1983	12,313	13.6	1,675	7,353
1984	14,279	12.4	1,771	7,370
1985 (est.)	14,993	11.3	1,694	7,658
1986 (est.)	14,545	10.4	1,513	8,165

[1]Represents the average price for autos and trucks sold by Venus Motors in the United States. The 1985 and 1986 figures were estimated by Ennis based on price increases due to inflation.

TABLE 7.2 | Venus Motors Corporation
Consolidated Summary of Operations[1] (in millions, except earnings and dividends per share)

| | Year Ending 12/31 | | | | | |
	1984		1983		1982	
Net Sales	$13,051	100.0%	$12,317	100.0%	$8,453	100.0%
Costs, other than items below	$11,726	89.8	$10,742	87.2	$7,793	92.2
Depreciation, plant & equipment	130	1.0	108	.9	93	1.1
Amortization of special tools	190	1.5	229	1.9	149	1.8
Selling and admin. expenses	459	3.5	447	3.6	339	4.0
Pension plans	274	2.1	234	1.9	197	2.3
Interest expense	75	.6	76	.6	99	1.2
Total expenses	$12,854	98.5%	$11,836	96.1%	$8,670	102.6%
Earnings (loss) before taxes	197	1.5	481	3.9	(217)	(2.6)
Taxes on income (credit)	72	.5	152	1.2	(9)	(.1)
Net earnings (loss)	$ 125	1.0%	$ 329	2.7%	$ (208)	(2.5)%
Average number of shares of common stock outstanding (000)	60,278		60,205		59,942	
Earnings per share of common stock	$2.07		$5.46		$(3.47)	
Dividends per share of common stock	.90		.30		–	

[1] Figures have been adjusted to eliminate extraordinary items and the effect of accounting changes.

TABLE 7.3 | Venus Motors Corporation
Consolidated Balance Sheet (in millions)

	As of 12/31		
	1984	1983	1982
Assets			
Cash and marketable securities	$ 408.8	$ 572.0	$ 227.7
Accounts receivable	896.7	797.6	684.6
Inventories	2,622.6	2,354.0	2,068.8
Other current assets	224.7	154.7	135.6
Total current assets	$4,152.8	$3,878.3	$3,116.7
Investments and misc. assets	1,090.2	1,108.9	1,035.1
Land, plant, and equipment	4,218.3	3,867.0	3,726.9
Less: accumulated depreciation	2,463.8	2,339.8	2,239.6
Net land, plant, and equipment	1,754.5	1,527.2	1,487.3
Special tools—less amortization	670.7	560.0	627.6
Total assets	$7,668.2	$7,074.4	$6,266.7
Liabilities and Stockholders' Equity			
Accounts payable	$1,911.9	$1,762.8	$1,400.2
Accrued expenses	773.4	728.8	610.5
Short-term debt	249.9	172.4	374.3
Long-term debt due in one year	90.8	68.7	59.3
Taxes payable	63.9	93.2	18.0
Total current liabilities	$3,089.9	$2,825.9	$2,462.3
Other liabilities and deferred credits	381.4	366.6	325.9
Long-term debt	1,240.4	1,047.7	1,053.5
Obligations under capital leases	12.6	–	–
Minority interest in consolidated subsidiary	19.3	18.9	15.8
Common stock ($6.25 par)	376.8	376.5	375.6
Additional paid-in capital	648.7	648.6	647.9
Retained earnings	1,899.1	1,790.2	1,385.7
Total stockholders' equity	$2,924.6	$2,815.3	$2,409.2
Total liabilities and stockholders' equity	$7,668.2	$7,074.4	$6,266.7

TABLE **7.4**	Venus Motors Corporation Selected Ratios for Two Largest U.S. Competitors of Venus Motors					
	1984	**1983**	**1982**	**1981**	**1980**	**1979**
Net Margin on Sales						
Company A	6.4%	6.2%	3.5%	3.0%	6.7%	7.1%
Company B	4.4%	3.4%	1.3%	1.4%	3.9%	4.3%
Total Asset Turnover						
Company A	2.06×	1.93×	1.66×	1.59×	1.76×	1.67×
Company B	1.97×	1.83×	1.71×	1.67×	1.78×	1.74×
Total Assets/Net Worth						
Company A	1.72×	1.73×	1.68×	1.62×	1.65×	1.60×
Company B	2.28×	2.22×	2.20×	2.27×	2.02×	1.95×
Earnings Retention Ratio						
Company A	41.5%	45.0%	44.9%	(3.9%)	37.1%	40.8%
Company B	78.5%	73.2%	24.8%	8.9%	65.0%	68.6%

Marquette Investment Management (Market Analysis)

Marquette Investment Management, an investment advisory firm in Marquette, Michigan, provides security analysis and portfolio management services for institutional and private clients. Marquette serves investors throughout northern Michigan as well as several out-of-state clients. The company has a dual mission. It sells an investment strategy service to approximately fifty clients; this service includes economic forecasts, portfolio strategy, and security selection. In addition, Marquette manages thirty portfolios for individual investors, profit-sharing accounts, and pension plans.

Marquette's management holds a monthly economic forecasting and investment strategy "brainstorming session." The objective of this meeting is to develop for Marquette's clients appropriate investment strategies based upon management's beliefs about future economic conditions.

Prior to the January 1988 session, Scott Russell, Marquette's president, distributed copies of the 1988 economic forecasts made by several leading banks. Russell asked each member of the staff to comment on the forecasts.

At the January strategy session, David Vickers, Marquette's economist, summarized his 1988 economic forecast. The stock market crash in October 1987 led to consumer retrenchment. As a result, current automobile, furniture, and clothing sales were running significantly below their earlier peaks.

Because manufacturers did not fully anticipate such weak consumer spending, they added dramatically to their inventories during the fourth quarter of 1987. Although manufacturers probably desired some of this inventory buildup, the automobile industry clearly has too high an inventory accumulation. As automobile inventories are worked down during the first quarter, economic activity will decline slightly and construction will weaken.

During the remainder of 1988, consumer activity will grow modestly, while export activity will boost most manufacturing. As a result, the probability of a recession occurring in 1988 is only one in three. Annual growth in real GNP (gross national product after adjustment for inflation) will average 2.0 percent in 1988 and a sluggish 1.6 percent in 1989.

Inflation will gradually intensify during 1988 and 1989. Oil and grocery store prices will begin rebounding later in 1988. Such increases will cause gains in the GNP price deflator of 3.1 percent in 1988 and 4.1 percent in 1989.

Although a recession will probably be avoided, the economy must work its way through several necessary adjustments. For several quarters in 1988 and 1989, therefore, the nation will be skirting a recession. Minor shortfalls in forecast inventory accumulations or consumer spending would shift the economy into recession.

Vickers also presented his forecasts for the financial markets. The stock market has already discounted the relatively weak economic outlook; hence, the market will not show much of a price trend, up or down, during 1988 or 1989. The prime rate will soon decline to 8.25 percent and then dip to 8 percent in 1989. Long-term U.S. government bond yields will fall as low as 8.25 percent during the first half of 1988 and then rebound to more than 9 percent by the end of 1989.

Kathy Adams, the Marquette analyst who follows the auto industry, was the next speaker. (Marquette's clients are especially interested in the auto and truck industry because of its importance to the Michigan economy.) Adams predicted that domestic auto sales will decline in 1988 because of slow growth in consumers' real disposable income, consumers' relatively heavy debt burden, and the decline in consumers' wealth due to the October market crash. She projected that domestic auto sales will decrease by 5 percent, from 10.3 million units in 1987 to 9.8 million in 1988, and that domestic truck sales will decline by 4 percent, from 4.9 million units in 1987 to 4.7 million in 1988. Because of the dollar's fall relative to the yen, import shares of the domestic market in 1988 will remain at last year's levels: 31 percent of autos and 17 percent of trucks. Industry profits in 1988 will fall more than sales because price competition intensifies as volume declines, the industry has high fixed costs, and reduced costs from plant closings and consolidations cannot fully offset the declining volume and more-competitive pricing.

Christopher Dalton, the Marquette analyst who follows the housing industry, noted that housing starts (the number of housing units upon which construction is begun) declined from 1.82 million in 1986 to 1.62 million in 1987. He predicts that housing starts will further decline to 1.55 million in 1988.

Dalton based his prediction on several factors. Immediately after the stock market crash, home buyers hesitated, and sale cancellations were above average. Now, however, buyers are returning to the market, and sales are rebounding. In addition, adjustable-rate mortgages, available at rates of around 8 percent, are keeping new homes affordable. About 60 percent of new mortgages are adjustable-rate. Fixed-rate thirty-year mortgages are currently available at about 10.5 percent, up from 9 percent a year ago but well below the 12 percent (plus) before the stock market collapsed and the bond market rallied in October. This moderation in mortgage rates partially will override the drop in consumer confidence and wealth caused by the stock market decline. Furthermore, as a result of the stock market collapse, consumers may increasingly prefer houses to stocks as long-term investments.

Russell concluded the meeting by summarizing his thoughts on the 1988 economic outlook. Consumer retrenchment following the October stock market collapse led to excessive inventories of housing and consumer products. Although some consumer products are produced abroad, working off excess auto inventories will necessitate a decrease in U.S. economic activity early in 1988. Construction is also heading downward to adjust for inventory excesses.

As the economy works through the necessary adjustments, it will experience two moderate bouts of economic weakness. One will arrive early in 1988 and should leave by the second half of that year. The other will arrive in the middle quarters of 1989.

This economic sluggishness will not be sufficient to forestall increased inflationary pressures later in 1988 and 1989. These pressures will cause yields on long-term bonds to move upward, although the prime rate is expected to decline modestly. Mortgage rates will go below 10 percent during 1988.

Because the economy will not be moving vigorously upward and could edge into a recession with only minor further sluggishness in exports or consumer spending, no dramatic gains in stock prices are anticipated. Although the chances of avoiding a recession in 1988 and 1989 are two out of three, the cost of avoiding a recession is to accept an extended period of relatively sluggish growth.

▌QUESTIONS

1. Given the current economic environment, discuss some of the difficulties and risks that an economic forecaster encounters.

2. How can economic forecasts be used to develop an investment strategy?

3. Based on the economic forecasts presented by the Marquette Investment Management staff, how would you have assessed the prospects for any five of the following industries in 1988?

    a.   aerospace/defense
    b.   computer software and services
    c.   cosmetics
    d.   drug manufacturing
    e.   fast-food restaurants
    f.   forest products and lumber
    g.   home appliance manufacturers
    h.   hotel and motel chains
    i.   integrated oil producers
    j.   medical supplies
    k.   paper
    l.   railroads
    m. steel
    n.   tobacco
    o.   trucking

4. In retrospect, how well did the Marquette Investment Management staff forecast the 1988 economy?

5. Do you think that the various regions of the United States are affected differently by economic factors? Explain.

Rocky Mountains National Bank
(Industry Analysis)

The trust department of the Rocky Mountains National Bank, headquartered in Pueblo, Colorado, manages $460 million in trust assets. The largest portfolio in the trust department is its Pooled Common Stock Fund, a vehicle for pooling the common stock investments of many small trust accounts into one fund. With the Pooled Common Stock Fund, the trust department can provide more intensive investment management than it could if the common stocks in each trust account were followed individually.

The fund seeks to provide its clients with regular income, conservation of principal, and an opportunity for growth of principal and income through investment in dividend-paying, financially strong companies with sound economic backgrounds. As of February 26, 1988, the fund contains forty-one stocks valued at $107 million and has a portfolio beta of 0.95. Because of the mostly conservative clientele and the fiduciary responsibilities of the trust department, the fund usually has a portfolio beta of less than 1.10.

Primary responsibility for managing the fund rests with Michael Pratt, the trust department's senior investment officer. In late February 1988, Pratt is concerned about the outlook for the stock market during the year ahead. The economists upon whom he relies are predicting that real GNP (gross national product adjusted for inflation) will increase just 2 percent in 1988 and only 1.6 percent in 1989. Thus, minor shortfalls in predicted inventory accumulations, consumer spending, or exports could tilt the economy into recession. Moreover, with productivity gains slowing as the economy slows and with import and agricultural prices rising, inflation will probably gradually accelerate, and the prime rate will rise from its current level of 8.5 percent. With the economy apparently teetering near a recession and the prime rate heading upward, the overall stock market will probably not gain much and may decline during the year ahead. The investment climate is thus one in which a highly selective strategy will have to be followed.

Accordingly, Pratt asks John Lightfoot, an assistant investment officer in the trust department, to search out defensive stocks which might outperform the overall stock market in the coming year. By "defensive" Pratt means low-risk stocks whose price movements do not tend to follow the cyclical variations in the economy. For example, U.S. Steel and Ford Motor Company would not fall into this category because their common stocks tend to behave in a cyclical manner.

Lightfoot identifies a number of industries which appear to have recession-resistant sales and earnings patterns. After further analysis, he chooses two such industries which he thinks will probably outperform the market during the coming year: brewing and grocery stores. Pratt and Lightfoot divide the remaining work, with Pratt concentrating on brewing and Lightfoot on grocery stores.

Lightfoot contacts Martha Fulford, a securities analyst specializing in the grocery store industry at Dunn & Phillips, a leading investment advisory firm in Chicago. Fulford begins by briefly reviewing the general stock market and the grocery store industry relative to the market. Based on Dunn & Phillips's estimates, the Standard & Poor's 500 Stock Composite Index, at its current level of 262, is yielding 3.5 percent on the indicated 1988 dividend of $9.21 and selling at 11.4 times estimated 1988 earnings of $22.94. Based on these 1988 estimated earnings, the price/earnings ratio for the S&P 500 during the past twelve months has ranged between 9.8 and 14.7. Dunn & Phillips thinks that the grocery store industry will probably outperform the general stock market over the next twelve months.

Fulford then provides an overview of the industry. In 1987, for the first time in six years, grocery sales after adjustment for inflation declined by 1.5 percent. Consumers spent only 9.6 percent of their 1987 disposable income on food at home, a trend which is motivating supermarkets to widen their product lines. In 1988, operating profits will probably remain under pressure, despite a string of notable successes in cost containment, because of probable grocery price deflation and heightened competition. Thus pretax profits in 1988 will not improve much; but after-tax profits will rise because of lower federal tax rates.

Many chains are continuing major capital spending programs directed at venturing into new territories and solidifying positions in current markets. However, not all chains are aiming at the "hot" growth areas (such as northern Florida) because some regions with favorable demographic projections have become saturated with supermarkets.

Responding to perceived changes in consumer desires and trying to improve profit margins, chains are using a variety of store formats. Chains operate combination stores, super stores, warehouse stores, and super-warehouse stores, each offering a different combination of product mixes and service departments. (Operating counter to this trend, however, has been Food Lion, which has achieved remarkable earnings growth with conventional supermarkets exclusively.)

A store format beginning to appear in the United States is the "hypermarket." This format, which has been successful in Europe for several years, is sometimes called a mall without walls. A hypermarket is the ultimate in the one-stop shopping demanded by consumers facing time constraints. Hypermarkets range from 100,000 to 200,000 square feet in size. They sell up to 70,000 grocery, service, appliance, apparel, and other products at very competitive prices.

How well hypermarkets will do in the United States remains to be seen. Conventional wisdom suggests that hypermarkets will succeed primarily in the suburbs and in rural sections of economically disadvantaged areas. Moreover, many observers are skeptical about the hypermarkets' ability to control costs.

Fulford believes that the common stocks of four major grocery chains— Albertson's, Food Lion, Giant Food, and Weis Markets—may outperform the market in the coming year. She furnishes Lightfoot with the industry and company data shown in Tables 9.1 through 9.5. Fulford also provides descriptions of the four companies she was recommending.

Albertson's, headquartered in Boise, Idaho, operates a chain of 465 stores in seventeen western and southern states. The chain consists of 109 food/drug-stores averaging 56,000 square feet in size, 142 super stores averaging 42,000 square feet, 27 warehouse stores averaging 40,000 square feet, and 187 conventional supermarkets averaging 26,000 square feet. The company has achieved its rapid growth in earnings per share through impressive same-store sales gains, ambitious territorial expansion, and strict cost controls. Currently priced at $27 1/8 per share, the stock is selling at 13.6 times estimated fiscal 1988 earnings of $2.00 and yielding 1.8 percent on an indicated 1988 dividend of $0.48.

Food Lion, headquartered in Salisbury, North Carolina, operates a chain of 411 conventional supermarkets in North Carolina, South Carolina, Virginia, and other southeastern states. The company has attained its very rapid growth in earnings through impressive same-store sales gains, aggressive territorial expansion, and tight cost controls. At a current price of $11 1/4 per class B share, the stock is selling at 32.1 times estimated 1988 earnings of $0.35 and yielding 0.6 percent on an indicated 1988 dividend of 6.4 cents per share.

Giant Food, headquartered in Landover, Maryland, operates a chain of 144 supermarkets selling food and general merchandise: 103 stores are located in metropolitan Washington, D.C., 32 in metropolitan Baltimore, and 9 in other parts of Maryland and Virginia. With Weis Markets and Shoppers Food Warehouse entering suburban Washington, competition in the area is heating up. Giant Food is fighting back by matching the prices of its competitors and by giving its customers gift certificates. A modest reduction in profit margins at the few points of head-on competition should not importantly affect Giant Food's fiscal 1988 earnings. Currently priced at $35 3/4 per share, the stock sells at 12.8 times estimated fiscal 1988 earnings of $2.80 and yields 1.8 percent on the indicated dividend of $0.66.

Weis Markets, headquartered in Sunbury, Pennsylvania, operates 116 retail stores in Maryland, Pennsylvania, New York, and West Virginia. The stores feature both nationally advertised and private brands (principally, Big Top, Carnival, and Weis Quality). Weis is planning to open 3 new stores in 1988; 2 of these will be in the Baltimore-Washington corridor, where they will compete head-on with Giant Food. Giant Food, with its 45 percent share of the metropolitan Washington market, will be a formidable rival. Although Fulford believes that Weis will establish a viable presence in its new markets, such intense competition could temporarily jeopardize Weis's legendary profit margins. At a current price of $31.25 per share, the stock is selling at 17.4 times estimated 1988 earnings of $1.80 and yielding 1.4 percent on the indicated dividend of $0.44.

Lightfoot plans to study carefully the information which Fulford has furnished and then to decide which of the four stocks should be purchased for the Pooled Common Stock Fund.

▌ QUESTIONS

1. Why do grocery store chains and the brewing industry have noncyclical, stable sales and earnings patterns?

2. What factors do you believe to be most important in analyzing the grocery store industry and companies in the industry?

3. Discuss the specific economic and regional factors that you think will affect the financial performance of Albertson's, Food Lion, Giant Food, and Weis Markets.

4. Compare growth in sales, growth in earnings per share, return on shareholders' equity, and dividend payout ratios for Albertson's, Food Lion, Giant Food, and Weis Markets over the periods shown in Tables 9.1 through 9.5.

TABLE 9.1 Rocky Mountains National Bank
Selected Financial Data for the Grocery Store Industry

	1983	1984	1985	1986	1987*	1988*	1991*
Number of stores (thousands)	13.1	13.8	15.4	18.1	20.1	20.5	21.9
Sales (billions, $)	58.7	67.5	73.7	74.9	89.2	96.0	120.2
Net profit (billions, $)	.761	.859	.983	1.02	1.20	1.36	1.95
Net profit margin	1.30%	1.27%	1.33%	1.36%	1.34%	1.41%	1.62%
Return on net worth	15.7%	14.7%	15.0%	15.1%	14.0%	15.0%	15.5%
Inventory turnover	13.2×	13.1×	12.4×	13.4×	13.3×	13.5×	13.8×
Working capital (billions, $)	2.06	2.05	2.12	1.87	2.10	2.25	3.77
Long-term debt (billions, $)	2.91	3.82	4.24	4.37	5.36	5.86	6.36
Net worth (billions, $)	4.85	5.86	6.54	6.72	9.55	10.8	15.2
Dividend payout	39%	38%	37%	38%	33%	30%	28%
Dividend yield	3.1%	3.3%	2.7%	2.3%	N.A.	N.A.	2.0%
Average price/earnings ratio	12.1	11.2	13.0	15.9	N.A.	N.A.	13.0
Industry's P/E ratio relative to market's P/E	1.02	1.04	1.06	1.08	N.A.	N.A.	1.10

*Figures for 1987, 1988, and 1991 are estimates. Figures for Tables 9.1–9.5 were obtained from the *Value Line Investment Survey.* © 1988 by Value Line Inc.; used by permission of Value Line, Inc.

TABLE 9.2 Rocky Mountains National Bank
Selected Financial Data for Albertson's, Inc.*

	1983	1984	1985	1986	Est. 1987	Est. 1988
Number of stores	432	434	444	452	475	500
Sales (millions, $)	4279	4736	5060	5380	5950	6600
Net profit (millions, $)	70.3	79.7	85.1	100	120	135
Net profit margin	1.64%	1.68%	1.68%	1.86%	2.02%	2.05%
Return on net worth	17.9%	17.6%	16.4%	16.9%	18.5%	18.0%
Inventory turnover	16.9×	17.7×	16.8×	17.0×	17.0×	17.1×
Working capital (millions, $)	209	206	244	245	225	160
Long-term debt (millions, $)	200	194	188	187	210	235
Net worth (millions, $)	392	454	519	594	650	745
Earnings per share	1.09	1.21	1.28	1.50	1.80	2.00
Dividends declared per share	0.30	0.34	0.38	0.42	0.47	0.48
Stockholders' equity per share	5.97	6.87	7.80	8.90	9.80	11.25
Average price/earnings ratio	11.8	10.8	11.8	13.8	14.9	N.A.

*Fiscal year ends on the Thursday nearest to January 31 of the following calendar year. There are 66.69 million common shares currently outstanding. The shares have a beta of 0.95.

TABLE 9.3 | Rocky Mountains National Bank
Selected Financial Data for Food Lion, Inc.*

	1983	1984	1985	1986	1987	Est. 1988
Number of stores	226	251	317	388	475	575
Sales (millions, $)	1173	1470	1866	2407	2954	3600
Net profit (millions, $)	27.7	37.3	47.6	61.8	85.8	110
Net profit margin	2.36%	2.54%	2.55%	2.57%	2.90%	3.06%
Return on net worth	22.4%	22.8%	23.0%	23.3%	25.5%	25.5%
Inventory turnover	9.9×	10.8×	9.6×	9.3×	9.2×	9.2×
Working capital (millions, $)	40.3	73.3	65.9	88.5	135	160
Long-term debt (millions, $)	46.2	51.3	58.0	91.4	120	150
Net worth (millions, $)	124	163	207	265	339	430
Earnings per share	0.09	0.12	0.15	0.19	0.27	0.35
Dividends declared per share	0.01	0.01	0.01	0.02	0.05	0.07
Stockholders' equity per share	0.39	0.52	0.65	0.83	1.06	1.35
Average price/earnings ratio for the class B shares	23.9	15.4	19.7	30.9	35.3	N.A.

*The fiscal year ends on the closest Saturday to December 31. There are 162.0 million (non-voting) class A shares currently outstanding and 159.6 million class B shares. The class B shares have a beta of 1.05.

TABLE 9.4 | Rocky Mountains National Bank
Selected Financial Data for Giant Food*

	1983	1984	1985	1986	Est. 1987	Est. 1988
Number of stores	164	162	136	141	145	150
Sales (millions, $)	1957	2139	2247	2528	2700	2900
Net profit (millions, $)	40.5	45.2	57.0	46.5	72.5	82.5
Net profit margin	2.07%	2.11%	2.54%	1.84%	2.69%	2.84%
Return on net worth	21.0%	19.8%	21.0%	15.5%	20.5%	20.0%
Inventory turnover	17.8×	17.5×	16.5×	16.1×	16.4×	16.7×
Working capital (millions, $)	57.0	68.4	62.9	78.5	100	110
Long-term debt (millions, $)	113	117	126	200	230	240
Net worth (millions, $)	193	229	271	300	355	415
Earnings per share	1.39	1.53	1.90	1.55	2.45	2.75
Dividends declared per share	0.30	0.40	0.50	0.60	0.66	0.72
Stockholders' equity per share	6.61	7.68	9.05	9.98	11.80	13.80
Average price/earnings ratio	7.7	8.1	11.5	18.4	N.A.	N.A.

*Fiscal year ends on the last Saturday in February of following calendar year. There are 30.03 million common shares currently outstanding. The shares have a beta of 0.90.

TABLE | Rocky Mountains National Bank
9.5 | Selected Financial Data for Weis' Markets, Inc.*

	1983	1984	1985	1986	Est. 1987	Est. 1988
Number of stores	116	119	122	125	127	135
Sales (millions, $)	892	958	1017	1102	1128	1250
Net profit (millions, $)	50.1	55.3	60.1	65.3	76.0	80.0
Net profit margin	5.62%	5.77%	5.91%	5.92%	6.74%	6.40%
Return on net worth	17.7%	17.1%	16.4%	16.0%	16.5%	15.5%
Inventory turnover	14.3×	15.3×	14.6×	16.7×	16.1×	16.0×
Working capital (millions, $)	180	217	238	277	315	350
Long-term debt (millions, $)	Nil	Nil	Nil	Nil	Nil	Nil
Net worth (millions, $)	284	324	366	408	455	510
Earnings per share	1.08	1.19	1.30	1.42	1.66	1.75
Dividends declared per share	0.25	0.28	0.32	0.36	0.43	0.44
Stockholders' equity per share	6.12	6.99	7.93	8.60	9.95	11.20
Average price/earnings ratio	13.8	12.3	15.1	17.3	19.2	N.A.

*There are 45.66 million common shares currently outstanding. The shares have a beta of 0.90.

CASE

10

American Investment Management (Industry and Company Analysis)

American Investment Management (AIM), an investment consulting firm in Wellesley, Massachusetts, provides investor services to individual and corporate clients. AIM manages approximately $50 million and sells investment advice to 125 other clients. The ten-year-old firm's success is due to the diligence of its founders, Susan Adams and Bradford Taylor. They insist that the company originate innovative investment ideas. Their clients tend to be performance-oriented and look to AIM for investment advice that will yield above-average rates of return. Most of the firm's clients are willing and able to accept above-average risk in their portfolios.

During April 1988, several of AIM's larger clients express concern about the outlook for the economy and the stock market in 1989. During the first quarter of 1988, economic growth, fueled by a trade-related upturn in manufacturing, has been unexpectedly strong and is beginning to drive up inflation and interest rates. Economists are typically predicting that the rate of inflation (as measured by the Consumer Price Index) will accelerate from 3.7 percent in 1987 to 4.2 percent in 1988 and 5.0 percent in 1989; and that the prime rate will increase from 8.5 percent to 10 percent by the end of 1989.

Many economists also believe that the next president, no matter who is elected, will have no choice but to reduce the federal deficit by cutting defense and other federal spending and raising taxes. This deficit reduction package, although much-needed and overdue, could, if mistimed, trigger a recession.

In light of the unexpectedly strong first quarter and the need to reduce the federal deficit, many economists are now predicting that real GNP (gross national product adjusted for inflation) will increase 3 percent in 1988, but only 1.3 percent in 1989. Thus, minor shortfalls in projected exports, inventory accumulations, or consumer spending could tilt the economy into a recession in 1989.

In an economy flirting with recession next year, the overall stock market will probably not show much of an upward price trend during the year ahead. Thus, the investment climate is one in which investors in stocks will have to follow a highly selective strategy if they are to achieve above-average returns. Recognizing this, several of AIM's larger clients are becoming concerned about the stock market and looking to AIM for guidance. For various reasons, they are committed to buying stocks and thus want purchase suggestions.

Because the economy might teeter into a recession in the year ahead, Adams and Taylor decide against recommending large cyclical companies. A recession would adversely affect the operating results of the big cyclical companies like General Motors. Thus, Adams and Taylor decide to investigate stocks which would be affected less by a recession.

Adams believes that although single-family housing starts might decline by 6 percent in 1988 and by another 5 percent in 1989, companies selling products in the consumer home improvement or "do-it-yourself" market might be attractive investments. She has four reasons for considering such companies. First, because the cost of new houses has been rising faster than personal income, new houses have became less affordable, and people have more incentive to repair and remodel their existing homes. Second, the current relative strength in single-family turnovers will benefit the home improvement industry; most repairs are made the year before the planned sale of a home and two to three years after its purchase. Third, the cost of contracting for home improvements has climbed rapidly because of increases in labor costs. Fourth, a recession would result in decreased overtime and increased unemployment, hence more free time for home improvement activities.

Adams contacts Miguel de Braganca, of Independence Investment Associates in Boston, to obtain more information. De Braganca is an experienced financial analyst who closely follows the building supplies industry. Adams and de Braganca focus their discussion on four firms selling products to the do-it-yourself market: Hechinger, Home Depot, Lowe's Companies, and Payless Cashways. Hechinger's class A common shares are traded over the counter; the other companies' stocks are traded on the New York Stock Exchange. Tables 10.1–10.4 contain recent financial information and de Braganca's projections for these companies. De Braganca also provides additional information about the four companies.

Hechinger Company operates seventy retail do-it-yourself building-supply stores. Nearly half are in the Washington, D.C. area; the rest are located principally along the mid-Atlantic coast. The stores are 80,000 to 100,000 square feet in size and sell about 40,000 items. Hechinger recently purchased seven warehouse outlets. In 1988 it plans to expand by adding four new warehouse stores and seven to ten more traditional stores. De Braganca estimates that because Hechinger is lowering its prices and putting more emphasis on promotional pricing, fiscal 1988 sales will advance 40 percent, but earnings only 15 percent. He also predicts that during the next three to five years, per-share sales and earnings will likely grow 18 to 19 percent annually. At a current price of $17.50 per share, this medium-quality equity is selling at 13.0 times estimated 1988 earnings of $1.35 and yielding 0.9 percent on an indicated 1988 dividend of $0.16.

Home Depot, incorporated in 1978, operates seventy-five retail "warehouse" do-it-yourself building-supply stores located in Alabama, Arizona, California, Florida, Georgia, Louisiana, Tennessee, and Texas. Stores carry about 25,000 items and range in size from 64,000 to 140,000 square feet. Management plans to add twenty-one additional stores in 1988. Two of these will be in metropolitan New York City, a new area for Home Depot, and nineteen in existing territories where the company can benefit from marketing and advertising economies. De Braganca forecasts that because of the increasing number of stores and the chain-wide implementation of everyday low pricing, per-share earnings will increase about 28 percent in fiscal 1988 to a new high. He estimates that because of a growing reputation for quality customer service, an everyday low-pricing policy, and rapid store expansion, per-share sales over the next three to five years will increase about 29 percent annually, and per-share earnings about 39 percent annually. At a current price of $26.25 per share, this riskier-than-average equity is selling at 18.1 times estimated 1988 earnings of $1.45 and yielding 0.3 percent on an indicated 1988 dividend of $0.08.

Lowe's Companies operates 295 building-materials and hardgoods stores in twenty-one states, principally in the Southeast. About 45 percent of sales are to professional contractors; 55 percent are to retail customers. The average store has 14,800 square feet. Lowe's plans to open 6 new stores in existing territories in 1988. De Braganca expects that because of Lowe's closing of 21 unprofitable stores in the economically depressed "oil patch" last year and declining sales to contractors this year, Lowe's sales in fiscal 1988 will increase only 5 percent. However, earnings per share this year should benefit from last year's store closings and rise 20 percent over 1987 earnings. De Braganca further predicts that over the next three to five years, as a result of an expanding retail emphasis and a stronger store base, per-share sales and earnings will grow 8 to 10 percent annually. At a current price of $20.12 per share, this average-quality equity is selling at 11.8 times estimated 1988 earnings of $1.70 and yielding 2.2 percent on an indicated 1988 dividend of $0.44.

Payless Cashways operates 194 retail do-it-yourself stores in 23 midwestern, southwestern, Pacific Coast, and New England states. The average store contains 28,000 square feet. Payless plans to increase its retail space 8 percent in 1988 by adding 13 stores. Earnings last year declined by 21 percent to $0.97 a share. Attempts to establish an everyday low-pricing policy depressed gross margins; closing stores in overlapping territories and unexciting markets cost 23 cents a share. This year Payless is raising prices back to their 1986 levels and substituting promotional discounts and more advertising. De Braganca estimates that in fiscal 1988 per-share sales will grow 13 percent and that aided by the absence of last year's store-closing charge and by a 17-cents-a-share gain due to 1988's lower tax rates, earnings will rebound 44 percent to a record $1.40 per share. De Braganca predicts that during the next three to five years, per-share sales will grow by 12 percent annually, and aided by improved pricing and operating margins, per-share earnings will advance 16 percent annually. At a current price of $17.38 per share, this average-quality stock is selling at 12.4 times estimated 1988 earnings of $1.40 and yielding 0.9 percent on an indicated 1988 dividend of $0.16.

Adams plans to compare and contrast the investment fundamentals of the four stocks which she and de Braganca have discussed and then decide which, if any, she will recommend to AIM's clients.

QUESTIONS

1. What economic and other factors have a significant impact upon the do-it-yourself home improvement industry?

2. In general terms, do you believe that companies in the do-it-yourself home improvement industry are countercyclical investments? Why, or why not?

3. Compare and contrast the expected returns and risks of the four stocks which Adams and de Braganca discussed.

4. Which, if any, of the four stocks would you recommend to AIM's clients? Why?

TABLE 10.1 | American Investment Management
Selected Financial Data for the Hechinger Company*   risky

	Est. 1988	1987	1986	1985	1984
Number of stores	92	70	61	54	45
Sales (millions, $)	1015	725.1	588.4	479.4	405.1
Net profit (millions, $)	50.0	40.0	28.3	23.1	20.9
Net profit margin	4.9%	5.5%	4.8%	4.8%	5.2%
Return on net worth	13.5%	12.5%	14.2%	13.5%	17.3%
Inventory turnover	6.0×	6.0×	5.9×	5.7×	6.1×
Working capital (millions, $)	320.0	360.0	243.0	207.4	182.4
Long-term debt (millions, $)	150.0	150.0	108.1	109.1	109.5
Net worth (millions, $)	370.0	325.0	198.5	171.7	121.0
Earnings per share	1.35	1.17	0.92	0.78	0.74
Dividends declared per share	0.17	0.16	0.15	0.12	0.10
Stockholders' equity per share	10.20	8.95	6.51	5.65	4.27
Average annual price/earnings ratio	N.A.	17.9	21.2	20.0	16.0
	1983	**1982**	**1981**	**1980**	**1979**
Number of stores	41	34	31	27	26
Sales (millions, $)	309.5	241.3	210.6	170.4	146.8
Net profit (millions, $)	16.2	11.7	8.6	6.8	5.5
Net profit margin	5.3%	4.9%	4.1%	4.0%	3.7%
Return on net worth	16.2%	16.5%	14.5%	13.4%	19.9%
Inventory turnover	5.3×	6.4×	6.6×	6.6×	5.9×
Working capital (millions, $)	92.0	60.7	45.1	4.6	21.3
Long-term debt (millions, $)	28.3	22.2	18.8	19.0	19.2
Net worth (millions, $)	100.5	71.1	59.4	50.9	27.5
Earnings per share	0.58	0.44	0.32	0.28	0.24
Dividends declared per share	0.08	0.04	0.03	0.02	0.02
Stockholders' equity per share	3.56	2.65	2.23	1.92	1.25
Average annual price/earnings ratio	23.5	16.1	14.4	11.3	7.5

*Fiscal year ends on the Sunday closest to January 31 of the following year. There are 20.2 million class A shares currently outstanding and 16.0 million class B. The class A shares have a beta of 1.10. N.A. = not available. Figures for Tables 10.1–10.4 were obtained from the *Value Line Investment Survey.* © 1988 by Value Line, Inc.; used by permission of Value Line, Inc.

TABLE 10.2	American Investment Management Selected Financial Data for Home Depot, Inc.*

	Est. 1988	1987	1986	1985	1984
Number of stores	96	75	60	50	31
Sales (millions, $)	1950	1454	1011	700.7	432.8
Net profit (millions, $)	70.0	54.1	23.9	8.22	14.1
Net profit margin	3.6%	3.7%	2.4%	1.2%	3.3%
Return on net worth	18.0%	16.9%	14.6%	9.2%	17.6%
Inventory turnover	6.9×	6.9×	6.1×	4.6×	5.2×
Working capital (millions, $)	65.0	110.6	91.1	106.5	100.1
Long-term debt (millions, $)	15.0	52.3	116.9	199.9	117.9
Net worth (millions, $)	385.0	320.6	163.0	89.1	80.2
Earnings per share	1.45	1.13	0.60	0.22	0.37
Dividends declared per share	0.08	0.05	None	None	None
Stockholders' equity per share	7.60	6.40	3.83	2.36	2.13
Average annual price/earnings ratio	N.A.	18.1	19.8	48.5	31.7

	1983	1982	1981	1980	1979
Number of stores	19	10	8	4	3
Sales (millions, $)	256.2	117.7	51.5	22.3	7.0
Net profit (millions, $)	10.3	5.3	1.2	0.5	(.9)
Net profit margin	4.0%	4.5%	2.4%	2.1%	N.M.
Return on net worth	15.7%	28.9%	23.3%	28.1%	N.M.
Inventory turnover	4.4×	6.7×	4.6×	7.8×	N.A.
Working capital (millions, $)	49.3	12.9	5.5	1.4	N.A.
Long-term debt (millions, $)	4.4	0.2	3.7	1.0	N.A.
Net worth (millions, $)	65.3	18.4	5.2	1.6	N.A.
Earnings per share	0.28	0.16	0.04	0.01	N.A.
Dividends declared per share	None	None	None	None	None
Stockholders' equity per share	1.75	0.54	0.17	0.05	N.A.
Average annual price/earnings ratio	57.0	27.5	37.4	N.A.	N.A.

*Fiscal year ends on the Sunday closest to January 31 of the following year. There are 49.1 million common shares currently outstanding. The stock has a beta of 1.30. N.M. = not meaningful; N.A. = not available.

TABLE 10.3	American Investment Management Selected Financial Data for Lowe's Companies, Inc.*

	Est. 1988	1987	1986	1985	1984
Number of stores	301	295	300	282	248
Sales (millions, $)	2565	2442	2264	2073	1689
Net profit (millions, $)	65.0	56.0	55.1	59.7	61.4
Net profit margin	2.5%	2.3%	2.4%	2.9%	3.6%
Return on net worth	10.5%	9.6%	10.2%	14.7%	18.0%
Inventory turnover	6.8×	6.5×	6.2×	6.6×	6.8×
Working capital (millions, $)	290.0	320.5	289.6	283.0	243.0
Long-term debt (millions, $)	180.0	186.2	153.0	186.9	92.5
Net worth (millions, $)	620.0	582.4	540.5	407.4	341.4
Earnings per share	1.70	1.41	1.41	1.64	1.70
Dividends declared per share	0.44	0.43	0.40	0.36	0.32
Stockholders' equity per share	15.95	14.80	13.64	10.99	9.42
Average annual price/earnings ratio	N.A.	17.7	22.3	15.7	12.5
	1983	**1982**	**1981**	**1980**	**1979**
Number of stores	238	236	229	214	209
Sales (millions, $)	1431	1034	888.0	883.6	904.7
Net profit (millions, $)	50.6	25.1	17.9	18.9	25.0
Net profit margin	3.5%	2.4%	2.0%	2.1%	2.8%
Return on net worth	17.4%	12.6%	10.1%	11.1%	15.7%
Inventory turnover	7.0×	6.2×	7.8×	7.1×	7.6×
Working capital (millions, $)	208.8	136.5	115.2	130.2	126.2
Long-term debt (millions, $)	51.9	56.2	48.9	51.9	56.1
Net worth (millions, $)	291.5	198.8	177.5	170.2	159.1
Earnings per share	1.40	0.75	0.55	0.58	0.77
Dividends declared per share	0.32	0.29	0.29	0.24	0.20
Stockholders' equity per share	8.04	5.96	5.45	5.23	4.89
Average annual price/earnings ratio	17.3	16.5	16.3	13.1	9.6

*Fiscal year ends January 31 of the following calendar year. There are 39.4 million common shares currently outstanding. The stock has a beta of 1.40. N.A. = not available.

TABLE 10.4 American Investment Management
Selected Financial Data for Payless Cashways, Inc.*

	Est. 1988	1987	1986	1985	1984
Number of stores	207	194	181	169	157
Sales (millions, $)	2000	1768	1526	1388	1174
Net profit (millions, $)	45.0	33.9	42.4	38.1	37.1
Net profit margin	2.3%	1.9%	2.8%	2.7%	3.2%
Return on net worth	10.5%	8.9%	11.5%	11.4%	14.4%
Inventory turnover	5.8×	5.7×	5.5×	5.9×	4.7×
Working capital (millions, $)	130.0	122.8	131.7	125.7	139.2
Long-term debt (millions, $)	225.0	179.6	132.4	119.7	161.4
Net worth (millions, $)	420.0	379.4	369.6	332.9	257.2
Earnings per share	1.40	0.97	1.22	1.12	1.15
Dividends declared per share	0.16	0.16	0.16	0.16	0.16
Stockholders' equity per share	12.50	11.27	10.67	9.61	7.96
Average annual price/earnings ratio	N.A.	21.2	16.7	15.8	15.3
	1983	**1982**	**1981**	**1980**	**1979**
Number of stores	118	100	86	78	68
Sales (millions, $)	864.9	603.2	479.1	383.1	316.1
Net profit (millions, $)	34.6	23.1	16.6	11.0	14.5
Net profit margin	4.0%	3.8%	3.5%	2.9%	4.6%
Return on net worth	16.9%	16.1%	16.7%	13.0%	19.2%
Inventory turnover	5.2×	5.4×	5.0×	4.6×	3.6×
Working capital (millions, $)	101.0	91.1	63.4	57.6	49.5
Long-term debt (millions, $)	72.9	60.1	64.4	52.3	39.5
Net worth (millions, $)	205.2	143.7	99.6	84.4	75.5
Earnings per share	1.29	0.96	0.72	0.48	0.63
Dividends declared per share	0.12	0.10	0.08	0.08	0.06
Stockholders' equity per share	7.61	5.65	4.29	3.66	3.26
Average annual price/earnings ratio	19.8	12.2	12.8	14.7	11.5

*Fiscal year ends around November 30. There are 33.7 million common shares currently outstanding. The stock has a beta of 1.25. N.A. = not available.

MacAllister Machinery Company
(Equity Valuation Techniques)

In early December 1987, Andrew MacAllister, president of MacAllister Machinery Company, decided to start an employee stock purchase plan. However, because the company's shares are closely held and seldom traded, their market value is unknown. Therefore, Mr. MacAllister asks James Whitehead, investment research director at the company's principal bank, to evaluate the stock.

Whitehead has obtained the information he needs for his evaluation from the company's management, the bank's economist, and the investment research department's library. Whitehead plans to analyze the data, determine the stock's market value as of December 18, and write an evaluation in preparation for a meeting with MacAllister.

ECONOMIC CONDITIONS

The stock market has been volatile during 1987. From January to August, the market (as measured by the Standard & Poor's Composite Index) soared by 39 percent, from 242 to a new high of 337. Then, as investors became increasingly concerned about the federal deficit, the trade deficit, and the plunge of the dollar against other major currencies, the index began falling. On October 19, "Black Monday," the index plummeted by an astonishing 20.5 percent to 225, and one trillion dollars of consumer, corporate, and pension fund wealth were wiped out. By December 18, the index has seesawed back up to 249. At 249 the index yields 3.6 percent on estimated 1987 dividends of $9.08, and it sells at 17.2 times 1986 earnings of $14.48, 14.1 times estimated 1987 earnings of $17.65, and 13.7 times estimated 1988 earnings of $18.16.

Sarah Fernhoff, the bank's economist, believes that the stock market crash on Black Monday will dampen customer spending, business investment, and demand for foreign goods (with attendant beneficial effects on the trade deficit). Thus she is forecasting that real growth in the gross national product will slow from 2.7 percent in 1987 to 2.0 percent in 1988, while the rise in the consumer price index will lessen from 3.6 percent in 1987 to 3.2 percent in 1988. Dr. Fernhoff also forecasts that during 1988, the long-term AAA corporate bond yield will stay, on average, around its current level of 9.6 percent, and that purchases of capital goods such as those produced by MacAllister Machinery will increase about 5.7 percent.

MACALLISTER MACHINERY COMPANY

MacAllister Machinery maintains its headquarters and manufacturing facilities in Pittsburgh, Pennsylvania. The company manufactures centrifugal and reciprocating pumping machinery for the food, distilling, chemical, petroleum, and other processing industries. The firm markets its products through manufacturers' representatives, specialized industrial distributors, and company sales people operating out of sales offices in Pittsburgh, Chicago, and New York City.

The firm has been family-owned and -managed since its founding in 1869. But as its profitability declined from 1978 to 1984, the family became divided into two warring camps. Finally, in October 1984, a family group headed by Andrew MacAllister took control of management from his grandfather. The new group bought out the former management and other dissenting stockholders in October 1985.

MacAllister has provided company balance sheets for the five fiscal years ending September 30, 1987, as shown in Table 11.1. He believes that because the firm has been so conservatively capitalized and was highly liquid at the start of fiscal 1986, the recapitalization has not impaired the company's financial strength and liquidity. He points out that cash constituted 15.2% of total assets in 1986, and 10.4% in 1987; the quick ratio was 2.5 in 1986, and 1.7 in 1987; the current ratio was 4.2 in 1986, and 3.3 in 1987.

MacAllister has also provided income statements for the past ten years, as shown in Tables 11.2 and 11.3. The recent earnings improvement, he explains, has stemmed from the completion of a ten-year $900,000 asset write-down program begun in 1977, increased customer spending for capital goods, improved budgetary and cost controls, and introduction of new products that cost less to make and command higher prices. Moreover, MacAllister believes that the earnings level achieved in fiscal 1987 constitutes a base from which the company will grow, at about the same rate as its major competitors.

MacAllister has supplied the following information about the company's shares for the last five fiscal years ending September 30, 1987. He also notes that the board of directors split the shares ten-for-one on October 1, 1986, and has paid out, on average, about 40 percent of earnings as cash dividends.

MacAllister Machinery Company

	1987	1986	1985	1984	1983
Earnings per share:	$ 3.77	$ 25.25	$ 6.19	$ 1.86	$ 4.30
Dividends per share:	$ 1.50	$ 10.00	$ 2.50	$ 1.00	$ 1.00
Payout percentage:	39.8%	39.6%	40.4%	53.8%	23.3%
Equity per share:	$19.84	$177.66	$151.80	$148.01	$147.22
Return on equity:	19.0%	14.2%	4.1%	1.3%	2.9%
Shares outstanding:	118,110	11,811	22,593	22,593	22,593

COMPARABLE COMPANIES

Mr. Whitehead believes that a good way to value the common stock of a profitable, closely held firm like MacAllister Machinery is to analyze the relationships between the market values and the investment characteristics of companies having comparable product lines and actively traded common stocks. After studying in detail firms which make pumps and have publicly traded shares, he determines that there are three companies that are reasonably comparable to MacAllister Machinery. In descending order of comparability, the three companies are Hydrodynamics, which manufactures centrifugal, reciprocating, and rotary pumps and domestic water systems; Neptune Pump Company, which produces corrosion-resistant equipment and castings such as pumps, valves, and fittings; and Welbilt Pumps, which manufactures rotary pumps (sometimes used in conjunction with MacAllister's pumps). Two important competitors, Ingersoll-Rand and Studebaker-Worthington, cannot be used because pumps constitute only a small fraction of their sales and profits. Financial data for the comparable companies for the last five years are presented in Tables 11.4, 11.5, and 11.6.

EVALUATION PROCEDURE

To evaluate MacAllister Machinery's shares, Whitehead will first determine their normalized earnings. That is, he will estimate the level of earnings that will currently prevail if the company experiences normal operations, unaffected by strikes, natural disasters, and other nonrecurring events, and if the general economy is at neither a cyclical peak nor a trough. In thinking about MacAllister Machinery's normalized earnings, Whitehead is impressed by how much the firm has changed under Andrew MacAllister's management; he wonders how relevant the operations and financial statements of the prior management are to assessing the company's future.

After estimating normalized earnings per share for fiscal 1988, Whitehead will then determine an appropriate price/earnings (P/E) ratio for the stock. He is well acquainted with studies relating P/E ratios to investment characteristics such as growth, dividend payout, and risk. He hopes that an analysis of the three comparable companies will reveal a relationship between their P/E ratios and their growth, dividend payout, and risk. To assess their risk, he knows that he cannot use their betas; while the comparable companies have return histories from which their betas can be calculated, MacAllister Machinery stock, being seldom traded, does not. Instead, he will consider other dimensions of risk such as financial leverage, size, and marketability.

If Whitehead finds economically meaningful relationships between the P/E's and the investment characteristics of the comparable companies, then he will analyze the investment features of the MacAllister Machinery shares, relate them to those of the comparison companies, and thereby arrive at a judgment of an appropriate P/E ratio for MacAllister Machinery. If he finds no meaningful relationships, he will try to relate the investment characteristics of the company to those of industrial firms in general and adjust the current P/E ratio for the S&P Composite Index accordingly to arrive at an appropriate P/E ratio for MacAllister Machinery.

Whitehead will then determine the current market value of the stock by multiplying its current normalized earnings per share by its appropriate P/E ratio. Finally, after checking his figures for consistency and reasonableness, he will write his evaluation.

QUESTIONS

1. What factors are important in evaluating the common stock of a closely held corporation?

2. Outline briefly the evaluation process Whitehead uses to determine the current market value of MacAllister Machinery's stock. What justifications can you think of for using Whitehead's approach rather than the present value of expected cash flow model?

3. What are the current normalized earnings per share of MacAllister Machinery? Why?

4. What is an appropriate P/E ratio for MacAllister Machinery? Why?

5. What is an appropriate price for the stock? Based on your estimated price, what dividend yield and growth in price is this stock likely to provide? Does this estimated annual return from dividends and capital appreciation seem reasonable in view of the returns on alternative investments?

TABLE | MacAllister Machinery Company
11.1 | Balance Sheets as of 9/30 (in thousands)

	1987	1986	1985	1984	1983
Assets					
Cash & equivalent	$ 381.7	$ 481.3	$1226.4	$ 652.8	$ 414.0
Accounts receivable	1150.5	950.1	843.0	1062.6	1157.7
Inventories	1310.4	926.7	882.3	1019.7	1199.1
Prepaid expenses	49.2	58.2	39.3	49.5	27.3
Current assets	$2891.8	$2416.3	$2991.0	$2784.6	$2798.1
Net plant & equipment	778.5	733.8	796.8	786.9	810.3
Patterns & drawings	3.9	18.3	60.3	91.8	133.8
Total assets	$3674.2	$3168.4	$3848.1	$3663.3	$3742.2
Liabilities & Equity					
Current liabilities	$ 880.7	$ 570.0	$ 418.5	$ 319.2	$ 416.1
Long-term debt	450.0	500.0	None	None	None
Stockholders' equity	2343.5	2098.4	3429.6	3344.1	3326.1
Total liabilities & equity	$3674.2	$3168.4	$3848.1	$3663.3	$3742.2

**Balance Sheets as of 9/30
Common-Size Ratios***

	1987	1986	1985	1984	1983
Assets					
Cash & equivalent	10.4%	15.2%	31.9%	17.8%	11.1%
Accounts receivable	31.3	30.0	21.9	29.0	30.9
Inventories	35.7	29.3	22.9	27.8	32.0
Prepaid expenses	1.3	1.8	1.0	1.4	.7
Current assets	78.7%	76.3%	77.7%	76.0%	74.8%
Net plant & equipment	21.2	23.2	20.7	21.5	21.7
Patterns & drawings	.1	.6	1.6	2.5	3.6
Total assets	100.0%	100.0%	100.0%	100.0%	100.0%
Liabilities & Equity					
Current liabilities	24.0%	18.0%	10.9%	8.7%	11.1%
Long-term debt	12.2	15.8	.0	.0	.0
Stockholders' equity	63.8	66.2	89.1	91.3	88.9
Total liabilities & equity	100.0%	100.0%	100.0%	100.0%	100.0%

*Figures may not sum because of rounding.

TABLE 11.2	MacAllister Machinery Company Income Statements for Years Ending 9/30 (in thousands)

	1987	**1986**	**1985**	**1984**	**1983**
Net sales	$8258.8	$7127.6	$5175.3	$6499.5	$7547.7
Cost of goods sold	4898.4	4223.7	3231.9	4868.1	5458.5
Gross margin	3360.4	2903.9	1943.4	1631.4	2089.2
Selling & admin. expenses	2644.2	2389.2	1722.3	1617.6	1978.8
Operating profit	716.2	514.7	221.1	13.8	110.4
Other income	20.3	16.3	43.8	45.9	56.1
Income before federal taxes	736.5	531.0	264.9	59.7	166.5
Federal income taxes	291.2	232.8	125.1	17.7	69.3
Net Income	$ 445.3	$ 298.2	$ 139.8	$ 42.0	$ 97.2

	1982	**1981**	**1980**	**1979**	**1978**
Net sales	$7188.0	$6213.9	$6529.5	$6533.1	$6266.9
Cost of goods sold	5509.8	4790.1	4713.6	4438.2	4326.8
Gross margin	1678.2	1423.8	1815.9	2094.9	1940.1
Selling & admin. expenses	1764.9	1737.0	1683.0	1915.5	1569.3
Operating profit	(86.7)	(313.2)	132.9	179.4	370.8
Other income	15.0	98.4	37.8	38.7	33.3
Income before federal taxes	(71.7)	(214.8)	170.7	218.1	404.1
Federal income taxes	(37.2)	(109.5)	72.0	101.1	187.2
Net Income	$ (34.5)	$ (105.3)	$ 98.7	$ 117.0	$ 216.9

TABLE	MacAllister Machinery Company
11.3	Income Statements for Years Ending 9/30
	Common-Size Ratios*

	1987	**1986**	**1985**	**1984**	**1983**
Net sales	100.0%	100.0%	100.0%	100.0%	100.0%
Cost of goods sold	59.3	59.3	62.4	74.9	72.3
Gross margin	40.7	40.7	37.6	25.1	27.7
Selling & admin. expenses	32.0	33.5	33.3	24.9	26.2
Operating profit	8.7	7.2	4.3	.2	1.5
Other income	.2	.2	.8	.7	.7
Income before federal taxes	8.9	7.4	5.1	.9	2.2
Federal income taxes	3.5	3.3	2.4	.3	.9
Net Income	5.4%	4.2%	2.7%	.6%	1.3%

	1982	**1981**	**1980**	**1979**	**1978**
Net sales	100.0%	100.0%	100.0%	100.0%	100.0%
Cost of goods sold	76.7	77.1	72.2	67.9	69.0
Gross margin	23.3	22.9	27.8	32.1	31.0
Selling & admin. expenses	24.5	28.0	25.8	29.3	25.0
Operating profit	(1.2)	(5.0)	2.0	2.7	5.9
Other income	.2	1.6	.6	.6	.5
Income before federal taxes	(1.0)	(3.5)	2.6	3.3	6.4
Federal income taxes	.5	1.8	1.1	1.5	3.0
Net Income	(.5)%	(1.7)%	1.5%	1.8%	3.5%

*Figures may not sum because of rounding.

TABLE 11.4 | MacAllister Machinery Company
Selected Financial Data for Welbilt Pumps, Inc.*

	Years Ending September 30				
	1987	1986	1985	1984	1983
Operating Data:					
Net sales (000's)	$48,008	$42,630	$37,468	$32,532	$31,896
Net income (000's)	2,866	2,324	1,950	1,620	1,546
Net income as % of net sales	6.0%	5.5%	5.2%	5.0%	4.8%
Balance Sheet Data:					
Current ratio	3.8×	3.6×	3.4×	3.3×	3.5×
Long-term debt as % of total assets	None	None	None	None	None
Owners' equity as % of total assets	78.0%	76.5%	75.2%	75.0%	77.0%
Per-Share Data:					
Earnings	$ 6.53	$ 5.28	$ 4.40	$ 3.61	$ 3.62
Cash dividends	2.90	2.40	2.00	1.60	1.60
Net tangible book value	25.68	23.17	21.20	19.63	18.88
Mean market price**	64.50	49.50	37.25	37.25	30.50
Valuation Factors:					
Price/earnings ratio	9.9×	9.4×	8.5×	10.3×	8.4×
Mean yield	4.5%	4.8%	5.4%	4.3%	5.2%
Payout %	44.4	45.5	45.5	44.3	44.2
Earnings as % of book value	25.4	22.8	20.8	18.3	19.2
Market price as % of book value	251.2	213.6	175.7	189.8	161.5

*Listed on the New York Stock Exchange.

**Mean market prices are for calendar years, except for 1987 which is through December 18. All other data are for fiscal years ending September 30.

TABLE | MacAllister Machinery Company
11.5 | Selected Financial Data for the Neptune Pump Company*

	Years Ending September 30				
	1987	1986	1985	1984	1983
Operating Data:					
Net sales (000's)	$41,440	$36,120	$31,226	$31,254	$33,412
Net income (000's)	2,898	2,244	1,738	1,848	2,336
Net income as % of net sales	7.0%	6.2%	5.6%	5.9%	7.0%
Balance Sheet Data:					
Current ratio	4.1×	4.4×	5.2×	4.2×	3.6×
Long-term debt as % of total assets	12.2%	14.3%	16.8%	11.2%	11.4%
Owners' equity as % of total assets	69.4	68.9	70.2	74.0	70.0
Per-Share Data:					
Earnings	$ 3.29	$ 2.56	$ 2.00	$ 2.15	$ 2.74
Cash dividends	1.40	1.00	1.00	1.00	1.00
Net tangible book value	15.69	13.80	12.24	11.24	10.09
Mean market price**	27.00	22.00	21.75	26.50	22.44
Valuation Factors:					
Price/earnings ratio	8.2×	8.6×	10.9×	12.3×	8.2×
Mean yield	5.2%	4.5%	4.6%	3.8%	4.5%
Payout %	42.6	39.1	50.0	46.5	36.5
Earnings as % of book value	21.0	18.6	16.3	19.1	27.2
Market price as % of book value	172.1	159.4	177.7	235.8	222.4

*Listed on the American Stock Exchange.

**Mean market prices are for calendar years, except for 1987 which is through December 18. All other data are for fiscal years ending September 30.

TABLE 11.6 | MacAllister Machinery Company
Selected Financial Data for Hydrodynamics, Inc.*

	Years Ending September 30				
	1987	1986	1985	1984	1983
Operating Data:					
Net sales (000's)	$15,812	N.A.	N.A.	N.A.	N.A.
Net income (000's)	1,652	$ 954	$ 980	$ 538	$ 688
Net income as % of net sales	10.4%	N.A.	N.A.	N.A.	N.A.
Balance Sheet Data:					
Current ratio	3.3×	3.8×	3.1×	3.8×	3.7×
Long-term debt as % of total assets	12.0%	12.2%	None	None	None
Owners' equity as % of total assets	66.0	69.1	77.8%	82.6%	82.7%
Per-Share Data:					
Earnings	$ 4.34	$ 2.51	$ 2.58	$ 1.41	$ 1.81
Cash dividends	1.70	1.55	1.55	1.40	1.40
Net tangible book value	15.92	13.28	12.25	12.24	11.83
Mean market price**	31.75	27.50	24.75	26.75	28.50
Valuation Factors:					
Price/earnings ratio	7.3×	11.0×	9.6×	19.0×	15.7×
Mean yield	5.4%	5.6%	6.3%	5.2%	4.9%
Payout %	39.2	61.8	60.1	99.3	77.3
Earnings as % of book value	27.3	18.9	21.1	11.5	15.3
Market price as % of book value	199.4	207.1	202.0	218.5	240.9

*Traded over the counter.

**Mean market prices are for calendar years, except for 1987 which is through December 18. All other data are for fiscal years ending September 30. N.A. = not available.

Reliable Truck Leasing, Inc.
(Equity Valuation Techniques)

In mid-November 1982, Julie Martin, a financial analyst with the investment advisory firm of Agnor & Hanson, is working on an assessment of the fair market value, as of November 3, 1982, of a minority interest in a closely held firm, Reliable Truck Leasing, Inc. Martin is making the assessment for three of the firm's former employees who are seeking relief in court from actions taken by the firm's majority stockholder. He had promised to give stock in the firm to the three plaintiffs if they would continue to work for it during a difficult period. The three employees stayed, and the firm prospered. But when the time came to deliver the stock, the majority stockholder reneged on his promise. The disappointed potential minority stockholders subsequently sued him for breach of contract. They retained Martin to help them ascertain how much they should seek to recover in damages.

ECONOMIC CONDITIONS

In July 1981, the U.S. economy entered a recession from which it has not recovered by the fall of 1982. In October, the nation's factories operated at only 68.4 percent of capacity, the lowest level recorded since the Federal Reserve began keeping records in 1948; in addition, unemployment exceeded 10 percent, the highest level in forty-five years. As slack in the economy has increased, the annual rate of inflation (as measured by the GNP deflator) has decreased from 9.4 percent during 1981 to 4.7 percent in the third quarter of 1982. Yet, even with the halving of inflation, the prime rate has only declined from an average of 18.9 percent during 1981 to an average of 14.7 percent in the third quarter of 1982. Similarly, the rate on new AA utility bonds has merely dipped from an average of 16.2 percent in 1981 to an average of 15.0 percent in the third quarter of 1982.

The only real signs of life in the economy are in those sectors which are highly sensitive to changes in interest rates. Housing starts have risen 7 percent in September and 1 percent in October. Sales of domestic cars during the first ten days of November have run at an annual rate of nearly 7 million units, a 30 percent gain over October's 5.4 million rate.

Despite the improvement in auto sales, however, total consumer spending remains weak. Personal consumption in October has risen only 0.1 percent over September's level. The main problem is not consumer income but consumer unwillingness to spend in the face of an uncertain economic future.

The economy is also weak because real interest rates (interest rates after adjustment for inflation) are still unusually high. Although Agnor & Hanson's economist, Stephen Smith, expects that inflation (as measured by the GNP deflator) will average 6.0 percent in 1982 and 5.0 percent in 1983, the prime rate is still quite high by historical standards. Smith believes that the Federal Reserve has room to reduce interest rates further without stimulating inflation; the domestic economy has considerable slack, and potential external sources of inflation such as oil prices are not a problem. Smith expects the Federal Reserve, in order to trigger stronger business conditions, to cut its discount rate by the end of the year.

If interest rates do decline, Smith believes that the economy will begin to recover. Housing starts will continue to rise, and led by the auto industry, industrial production will pick up. The unemployment rate will then begin to fall, and consumer spending will start expanding—probably at a faster rate than the overall economy.

Smith thinks that further progress on the inflation front lies ahead. Wage pressures have moderated as unemployment has climbed, and productivity in the third quarter has increased at a vigorous 4 percent annual rate. Thus, unit labor costs will expand at a modest pace for some time. Moreover, while industrial commodity prices will firm as business picks up, major commodities like oil and grain will probably remain in surplus.

Smith is forecasting that although real GNP (gross national product after adjustment for inflation) will decline 1.7 percent in 1982, it will advance 2.6 percent in 1983. Inflation (as measured by the GNP deflator) will moderate from 9.4 percent in 1981 to 6.0 percent in 1982, then to 5.0 percent in 1983. As a result, the prime rate, currently 12 percent, will decline to 11 percent during the first quarter of 1983 and to 10 percent for the rest of the year. The rate on newly issued AA corporate bonds will also decline from an average of 12.5 percent in the fourth quarter of 1982 to 11 percent during the first quarter of 1983, then to 10.75 percent for the remainder of the year. In addition, corporate profits will respond quickly to firming demand. Although after-tax corporate profits will decline from $151 billion in 1981 to around $116 billion in 1982, they will rebound to $145 billion in 1983.

Smith believes that the recovery during 1983 will be weaker than usual for this stage of an economic cycle. He thinks that the high level of real interest rates will continue to discourage business investment. In addition, the powerful surge in the dollar will continue to damage America's trade balance.

As a result of the declines in inflation and interest rates, the stock market, as measured by the S&P 500 stock index has risen from mid-August to November 3 by 39 percent, to an all-time high of 143. At that level, the index is providing a dividend yield of 4.79 percent and selling at 10.8 times estimated 1982 earnings of $13.19.

Smith thinks that for several reasons, the stock market will advance still further. The current level of stock prices does not fully reflect the substantial expansion of earnings, asset values, and dividends over the past decade. Although the S&P 500 is now 77 percent above its level at the beginning of 1967, its value in 1967 dollars has declined 40 percent. Simply to have kept pace with inflation over the past fifteen years, the Index should now be at 240, not 143. Moreover, if interest rates continue to decline as he is predicting, stocks will be even more attractive than they are now. Consequently, Smith is bullish on the stock market.

THE TRUCK LEASING INDUSTRY

Many truck lessors have faced rough going the past two years. Companies that leased intermodal equipment (trailers, containers, and chassis) depended on world trade, which had not yet picked up. Container utilization has thus been declining as units have come off long-term leases, although chassis and trailers have been leasing a bit better. When the U.S. and world economies pick up, however, most lessors will register hefty profit gains because of their high operating and financial leverage.

Martin also thinks that the Motor Carrier Act of 1980 will increase the efficiency of the private truck carriers, the primary source of customers in the truck leasing industry. Full-service leasing will be enhanced particularly because the intercorporate-hauling provision helps to eliminate empty backhauls. Leasing will also be enhanced by the high real interest rates, which encourage private carriers to lease rather than buy, because of the minimal up-front financial commitment.

RELIABLE TRUCK LEASING, INC

Reliable Truck Leasing is a full-service truck lessor. Originally it was a subsidiary of Standard Transportation Services (STS). Although the subsidiary was profitable, the parent was not, and ultimately STS became the biggest bankruptcy in the history of Oregon. On January 1, 1976, the secured creditors sold Reliable Truck Leasing for $5,000 to Bud Gavial, who had been president of Reliable when it was a subsidiary of STS. When sold, Reliable was carrying substantial accumulated losses and a deficit net worth of over $1.5 million. Since then, Reliable has made substantial progress; presently, it is operating at a profit and has a net worth of over $2.4 million.

Balance sheets and income statements for the company for the past six years appear in Tables 12.1–12.5. An analysis by Martin of the company's financial condition, operations, and investment characteristics is presented in Table 12.6.

THE EVALUATION PROCEDURE

Martin plans to determine the market value of a share of Reliable by multiplying its earnings times an appropriate multiplier. She can determine Reliable's earnings directly by examining its financial statements in light of conditions prevailing in the company, the truck industry, and the economy. However, she must determine Reliable's earnings multiplier indirectly through market comparisons because Reliable is not a publicly traded company.

The earnings she will use in assessing Reliable's market value will be normalized. Thus, she will have to estimate the level of earnings which will currently prevail if the firm is experiencing normal operations unaffected by strikes, natural disasters, and other nonrecurring events, and if the general economy is experiencing neither boom or bust conditions.

However, Martin knows that the general economy for the past three years has not been normal. One recession occurred in the first and second quarters of 1980, and a second recession began in the third quarter of 1981 and is still not over.

Poor business conditions have, of course, meant reduced leasing volume, excess capacity, and stiff price competition. As a result, Reliable's earnings have been depressed for the past three years.

Consequently, Martin believes that Reliable's normalized earnings will best be reflected by averaging actual earnings over a period in excess of three years. She will decide the exact number of years after she has analyzed all the facts at hand.

She will determine an appropriate earnings multiplier for Reliable by examining truck lessors with publicly traded stocks. She will calculate the multipliers which investors place on the comparison companies by dividing market prices by earnings. Then she will obtain an average multiplier for the comparison companies. She will next adjust the average multiplier (up or down) if the risk, growth, and dividend payout of Reliable differ materially from the investment characteristics of the typical comparison company.

She knows that research suggests that investors place above-average multipliers on stocks with above-average dividend payout and growth potential, and below-average risk. Conversely, investors accord below-average multiplies to stocks with below-average dividend payout and growth prospects and above-average risk. Hence, Reliable's multiplier will equal the average multiplier of the comparison companies, plus or minus any adjustments for differences between the investment characteristics of Reliable and those of the average comparison company.

Martin has obtained the comparison companies by screening the more than 300 transportation and leasing corporations listed in Moody's OTC Industrial and Transportation manuals. She has eliminated companies which have dissimilar lines of business, are too large, are near bankruptcy, or have their common stocks listed on the New York Stock Exchange.

She has found four publicly traded corporations similar to Reliable: Trans-National Leasing, a car and truck lessor; Sandgate, a car and truck lessor; Southwest Leasing, a car and truck lessor; and Saunders Leasing System, a full-service truck lessor.

Data concerning the operating results, financial condition, and investment characteristics of the comparison companies for the past six years appear in Tables 12.7–12.10. Recent stock market and share data for the comparison companies are presented in Table 12.11.

After determining Reliable's market value per share, Martin will calculate the value of each plaintiff's claimed shares. She knows that Reliable has 76,118 shares currently outstanding and that each plaintiff claims 3,425 additional shares. Hence, if the three plaintiffs' claims are honored, the total number of shares outstanding will be 86,393. Accordingly, the percentage ownership claimed by each plaintiff is 3,425/86,393, or 3.96 percent. The market value of the ownership claimed by each plaintiff is thus 3.96 percent of the total market value of the company. Martin also reasons that in calculating Reliable's total market value, she should not add a premium for the value of corporate control because the plaintiffs' claims are for only minority interests in the company. Thus, she can calculate Reliable's total market value simply by multiplying its market value per share by its 76,118 currently outstanding shares. The value of each plaintiff's claim is therefore 3.96 percent of that total market value.

QUESTIONS

1. What is the fair market value of a share of Reliable Truck Leasing? Why?

2. What is the market value of each plaintiff's claim?

3. What justifications can you think of for using Martin's approach rather than the present value of future cash flows approach?

TABLE 12.1	Reliable Truck Leasing, Inc. Unaudited Consolidated Balance Sheet as of September 30, 1982 (in thousands of dollars)*

Assets

Cash	$ 700
Accounts receivable, net	4,266
Inventories	549
Prepaid expenses	580
Total current assets	$ 6,095
Property and equipment, net	$36,023
Notes receivable from stockholders, organization costs, and other assets	209
Total assets	$42,327

Liabilities and equity

Note payable to bank	$ 150
Current portion of long-term debt	281
Accounts payable	1,191
Taxes payable	410
Other accrued liabilities	140
Total current liabilities	$ 2,173
Equipment obligations	$37,720
Long-term obligations	—
Deferred income taxes	(13)
Stockholders' equity	2,448
Total liabilities and equity	$42,327

*Figures may not sum because of rounding.

TABLE | Reliable Truck Leasing, Inc.
12.2 | Audited Consolidated Balance Sheets
      | (in thousands of dollars)*

	As of December 31				
	1981	1980	1979	1978	1977
Assets					
Cash	$ 1,455	$ 99	$ 13	$ 5	$ 215
Accounts receivable, net	3,943	3,982	3,826	3,269	2,617
Inventories	805	640	611	363	280
Prepaid expenses	478	378	462	414	287
Total current assets	$ 6,682	$ 5,099	$ 4,913	$ 4,051	$ 3,399
Property and equipment, net	$37,777	$34,585	$33,797	$28,429	$22,781
Notes·receivable from stockholders, organization costs, and other assets	230	150	157	277	284
Total assets	$44,688	$39,834	$38,867	$32,758	$26,464
Liabilities and equity					
Note payable to bank	$ 100	$ –	$ –	$ –	$ –
Current portion of long-term debt	339	296	209	319	450
Accounts payable	1,512	1,515	819	293	219
Taxes payable	334	214	289	342	246
Other accrued liabilities	429	208	166	118	144
Total current liabilities	$ 2,714	$ 2,234	$ 1,482	$ 1,072	$ 1,059
Equipment obligations	$10,448	$11,878	$ 9,785	$ 7,653	$ 5,740
Long-term obligations	29,338	24,130	25,673	23,025	19,708
Deferred income taxes	25	–	–	–	–
Stockholders' equity	2,163	1,593	1,927	1,008	(42)
Total liabilities and equity	$44,688	$39,835	$38,867	$32,758	$26,464

*Figures may not sum because of rounding.

TABLE 12.3	Reliable Truck Leasing, Inc. Unaudited Consolidated Income Statement For Nine Months Ending September 30, 1982

	In Thousands of Dollars	Common-Size Ratios*
Total revenues	$23,714	100.0%
Operating expenses	8,598	36.3
General and admin. expenses	3,102	13.1
Depreciation	6,856	28.9
Interest	4,944	20.8
Total costs and expenses	$23,500	99.1
Earnings (loss) before income taxes	$ 214	.9
Income taxes	N.A.	N.A.
Earnings (loss) before extraord. credit	N.A.	N.A.
Tax benefit from carry forward of prior years' operating losses	N.A.	N.A.
Net earnings (loss)	N.A.	N.A.

*Figures may not sum because of rounding. N.A. = not available.

RELIABLE TRUCK LEASING, INC. **81**

TABLE 12.4 | Reliable Truck Leasing, Inc.
Audited Consolidated Income Statements
(in thousands of dollars)*

	For Years Ending December 31				
	1981	1980	1979	1978	1977
Total revenues	$30,420	$27,687	$27,772	$24,581	$21,602
Operating expenses	$11,482	$11,683	$12,440	$11,960	$10,849
General and admin. expenses	4,438	3,509	3,285	3,248	2,710
Depreciation	8,449	7,977	7,031	5,382	4,972
Interest	5,435	4,854	4,065	2,900	2,328
Total costs and expenses	$29,805	$28,022	$26,820	$23,491	$20,858
Earnings (loss) before income taxes	$ 615	$ (334)	$ 952	$ 1,091	$ 743
Income taxes	162	–	460	550	370
Earnings (loss) before extraord. credit	$ 453	$ (334)	$ 492	$ 541	$ 373
Tax benefit from carry forward of prior years' operating losses	117	–	427	510	360
Net earnings (loss)	$ 570	$ (334)	$ 919	$ 1,051	$ 733

*Figures may not sum because of rounding.

TABLE 12.5 | Reliable Truck Leasing, Inc.
Audited Consolidated Income Statements
Common-size Ratios*

	For Years Ending December 31				
	1981	1980	1979	1978	1977
Total revenues	100.0%	100.0%	100.0%	100.0%	100.0%
Operating expenses	37.7	42.2	44.8	48.7	50.2
General and admin. expenses	14.6	12.7	11.8	13.2	12.5
Depreciation	27.8	28.8	25.3	21.9	23.0
Interest	17.9	17.5	14.6	11.8	10.8
Total costs and expenses	98.0%	101.2%	96.6%	95.6%	96.6%
Earnings (loss) before income taxes	2.0	(1.2)	3.4	4.4	3.4
Income taxes	.5	–	1.7	2.2	1.7
Earnings (loss) before extraord. credit	1.5%	(1.2)%	1.8%	2.2%	1.7%
Tax benefit from carry forward of prior years' operating losses	.4	–	1.5	2.1	1.7
Net earnings (loss)	1.9%	(1.2)%	3.3%	4.3%	3.4%

*Figures may not sum because of rounding.

TABLE 12.6	Reliable Truck Leasing, Inc.* Selected Financial Data

	1982	1981	1980	1979	1978	1977	1977–82 Average
Earnings per share	3.59[c,d]	7.49	(4.39)	12.07	13.81	14.38	7.83
Dividends per share	0[a]	0	0	0	0	0	0
Dividend payout	0[a]	0	0	0	0	0	0
Book value per share	32.16[b]	28.42	20.93	25.32	13.25	(.56)	19.92
Net revenues (in millions)	32[d]	30	28	28	25	22	28
Total assets (in millions)	42[b]	45	40	39	33	26	38
Current ratio	2.8[b]	2.5	2.3	3.3	3.8	3.2	3.0
Long-term debt/ capital	93.9%[b]	89.0%	90.4%	91.2%	93.7%	96.2%	92.4%
Common equity/ total assets	5.8%[b]	4.8%	4.0%	5.0%	3.1%	(0.0)	3.8%
Times interest earned	1.0[a]	1.1	0.9	1.2	1.4	1.3	1.2
Effective tax rate	N.A.	7.3%	N.M.	3.5%	3.8%	1.3%	4.2%[e]
Earnings after taxes/ revenues	.9%[a,c]	1.9%	(1.2)%	3.3%	4.3%	3.4%	2.1%
Return on equity	11.2%[c,d]	26.4%	(21.0)%	47.7%	104.2%	N.M.	43.2%

*Company fiscal year ends December 31. N.A. = not available. N.M. = not meaningful. [a]For 9 months ending September 30, 1982. [b]As of September 30, 1982. [c]Earnings after taxes for 9 months ending September 30, 1982, estimated to be $214,094 times (1 minus 1977–81 average effective tax rate). [d]Figure for 9 months ending September 30, 1982, annualized. [e]Average for 5 years.

TABLE 12.7	Reliable Truck Leasing, Inc. Selected Financial Data for Trans-National Leasing, Inc.*

	1982	1981	1980	1979	1978	1977	1977–82 Average
Earnings per share[b]	.70[c]	.64	.39	.27	.20	.19[d]	.40
Dividends per share	0[c]	0	0	0	0	0	0
Dividend payout	0[c]	0	0	0	0	0	0
Prices[a,b]—high	3.00	2.62	1.81	.97	.87	1.08	1.73
—low	2.50	1.50	.79	.65	.68	.39	.92
P/E ratio range	4–4	4–2	5–2	4–2	4–3	6–2	4–2
Average dividend yield	0	0	0	0	0	0	0
Book value per share[b]	4.11[e]	3.57	2.94	2.55	2.27	2.07	2.92
Ratio of average market price to book value	.67	.58	.44	.32	.34	.36	.45
Net revenues (in millions)	8[c]	7	5	4	3	3	5
Total assets (in millions)	N.A.	37	31	27	24	21	28[f]
Current ratio	N.A.	N.A.	N.A.	N.A.	N.A.	N.A.	N.A.
Long-term debt/ capital	N.A.	N.A.	N.A.	N.A.	N.A.	N.A.	N.A.
Common equity/ total assets	N.A.	8.6%	8.2%	8.3%	8.3%	8.9%	8.5%[f]
Times interest earned	N.A.	1.1	1.1	1.1	1.1	1.2	1.1[f]
Effective tax rate	N.A.	7.7%	10.3%	18.4%	18.0%	13.1%	13.5%[f]
Earnings after taxes/ revenues	7.4%[c]	8.3%	6.8%	6.3%	5.9%	6.6%	6.9%
Return on equity	17.0%[c]	17.9%	13.3%	10.6%	8.8%	9.2%	12.8%

*Company fiscal year ends June 30. N.A. = not available.

[a]For calendar year. [b]Adjusted for December 1981 5% stock dividend. [c]For 12 months ending March 31, 1982. [d]Before extraordinary items. [e]As of March 31, 1982. [f]Average for 5 years.

TABLE 12.8	Reliable Truck Leasing, Inc. Selected Financial Data for Sandgate Corporation*

	1982	1981	1980	1979	1978	1977	1977–82 Average
Earnings per share[b,c]	1.61	.59	.51	.49	.22	1.20	.77
Dividends per share[b]	.80	.40	.36	.28	.20	.20	.37
Dividend payout	.50	.68	.71	.57	.91	.17	.48
Prices[a,b]—high	18.25	9.40	6.70	11.80	6.60	6.10	9.81
—low	5.70	4.90	3.90	4.70	4.00	3.40	4.43
P/E ratio range	11–4	16–8	13–8	24–10	30–18	5–3	13–7
Average dividend yield	6.7%	5.6%	6.8%	3.4%	3.8%	3.8%	5.2%
Book value per share[b]	11.57	10.68	9.97	9.74	8.58	7.44	9.66
Ratio of average market price to book value	1.04	.67	.54	.85	.62	.64	.74
Net revenues (in millions)	50	50	40	31	29	33	39
Total assets (in millions)	82	60	59	53	57	48	60
Current ratio	1.4	1.5	1.5	2.0	1.5	1.6	1.6
Long-term debt/ capital	73.6%	64.2%	64.8%	62.5%	68.2%	66.8%	66.7%
Common equity/ total assets	15.0%	19.1%	18.4%	20.6%	16.1%	17.5%	17.8%
Times interest earned	1.4	1.4	1.2	1.3	1.2	2.0	1.4
Effective tax rate	31.4%	54.0%	41.3%	47.8%	44.5%	46.3%	44.2%
Earnings after taxes/ revenues	3.3%	1.2%	1.4%	1.7%	.8%	3.4%	2.0%
Return on equity	13.9%	5.5%	5.2%	5.0%	2.6%	16.1%	8.0%

*Company fiscal year ends June 30.
[a]For calendar year. [b]Adjusted for October 1982 5-for-4 split. [c]Before results of discontinued operations.

TABLE | Reliable Truck Leasing, Inc.
12.9 | Selected Financial Data for Southwest Leasing, Corp.*

	1982	1981	1980	1979	1978	1977	1977–82 Average
Earnings per share	.85[b]	.86	.74	(.58)	.22	.56[d]	.44
Dividends per share	0[b]	0	0	0	.12	.11	.04
Dividend payout	0	0	0	0	.54	.20	.09
Prices[a]—high	7.50	7.50	2.50	7.25	6.25	5.00	6.00
—low	4.50	1.50	1.00	1.50	2.50	3.00	2.33
P/E ratio range	9–5	9–2	3–1	N.M.	28–11	9–5	14–5
Average dividend yield	0	0	0	0	2.7%	2.7%	2.1%
Book value per share	5.37[c]	5.28	4.42	3.68	4.28	4.58	4.60
Ratio of average market price to book value	1.12	.85	.40	1.19	1.02	.87	.91
Net revenues (in millions)	43[b]	43	44	64	67	59	53
Total assets (in millions)	N.A.	79	89	100	110	91	94[e]
Current ratio	N.A.	1.8	1.2	N.A.	N.A.	N.A.	N.A.
Long-term debt/ capital	N.A.	81.1%	85.0%	N.A.	N.A.	N.A.	N.A.
Common equity/ total assets	N.A.	11.3%	8.4%	6.0%	6.6%	7.6%	8.0%[e]
Times interest earned	N.A.	1.2	1.1	1.0	1.1	1.5	1.2[e]
Effective tax rate	1.2%[b]	4.0%	18.6%	N.M.	25.9%	47.8%	17.7%
Earnings after taxes/ revenues	3.4%[b]	3.3%	2.9%	(1.5)%	.6%	1.6%	1.7%
Return on equity	15.8%[b]	16.3%	16.7%	(15.8)%	5.1%	12.2%	8.4%

*Company fiscal year ends on March 31 following the year indicated; for example, 1981 company data are those for the fiscal year ending March 31, 1982. N.A. = not available. N.M. = not meaningful.

[a]For calendar year. [b]For 12 months ending June 30, 1982. [c]As of June 30, 1982. [d]Excluding gain on sale of corporate property. [e]Average for 5 years.

TABLE 12.10 | Reliable Truck Leasing, Inc.
Selected Financial Data for Saunders Leasing System*

	1982	1981	1980	1979	1978	1977	1977–82 Average
Earnings per share[b,c]	.47[d]	.77	.58	.86	.51	.78	.66
Dividends per share[b]	.15[e]	.15	.15	.13	.10	.08	.13
Dividend payout	.32	.20	.26	.15	.20	.10	.20
Prices[a,b]—high	4.50	6.12	5.50	4.62	3.88	3.38	4.67
—low	2.38	3.75	4.12	3.38	2.50	2.00	3.02
P/E ratio range	10–5	8–5	9–7	5–4	8–5	4–3	7–5
Average dividend yield	4.4%	3.0%	3.1%	3.3%	3.1%	3.0%	3.4%
Book value per share[b]	5.92[f]	5.92	5.39	5.09	4.34	3.94	5.10
Ratio of average market price to book value	.58	.83	.89	.79	.74	.68	.76
Net revenues (in millions)	274[d]	261	221	159	133	118	194
Total assets (in millions)	N.A.	204	213	158	145	131	170[g]
Current ratio	N.A.	2.3	2.0	3.3	2.8	2.9	2.7[g]
Long-term debt/ capital	N.A.	74.2%	77.1%	70.7%	71.4%	75.6%	73.8%[g]
Common equity/ total assets	N.A.	18.6%	15.8%	19.5%	18.1%	18.2%	18.0%[g]
Times interest earned	N.A.	1.3	1.2	1.6	1.4	1.8	1.5[g]
Effective tax rate	N.A.	N.M.	N.M.	11.2%	25.1%	23.5%	6.8%[g]
Earnings after taxes/ revenues	1.2%[d]	2.0%	1.8%	3.6%	2.3%	4.0%	2.5%
Return on equity	7.9%[d]	13.0%	10.8%	16.9%	11.8%	19.8%	13.4%

*Company fiscal year ends December 31. N.A. = not available. N.M. = not meaningful.
[a]For calendar year. [b]Adjusted for January 1982 100% stock dividend. [c]Before special items. [d]For 12 months ending June 30, 1982. [e]Class B shares. [f]As of June 30, 1982. [g]Average for 5 years.

TABLE 12.11 | Reliable Truck Leasing, Inc.
Recent Stock Market and Share Data
for Comparison Companies*

	Trans-National Leasing	Sandgate Corp.	Southwest Leasing Corp.	Saunders Leasing System
Price—November 3, 1982	$2.75	$18.25	$5.00	$4.50
Price/earnings ratio—November 3, 1982	3.9	11.3	5.9	9.6
Dividend Yield—November 3, 1982	0	4.4%	0	3.3%
Shares outstanding (in thousands)	883[a,c]	1,004[b,d]	1,684[b,e]	6,059[b,f]
Shares traded in October 1982 (in hundreds)	4	812	N.A.	47
Shares traded/shares outstanding	.05%	8.1%	N.A.	.1%
Market traded	O.T.C.	A.S.E.	O.T.C.	A.S.E.

*N.A. = not available. O.T.C. = over the counter. A.S.E. = American Stock Exchange.
[a]As of March 31, 1982. [b]As of June 30, 1982. [c]L. J. and T. H. Maher own 62.4%. [d]Harold L. and Claire Oshry own over 40%. [e]W. D., J. M., and Louis Axelrod own about 62%, and I. B. Harris, 7%. [f]The Saunders family owns or controls about 53%, and the Societé Holding Gray d'Albion about 21%.

Calvert College Endowment Fund
(Comparative P/E Ratios)

On the morning of January 5, 1988, Margaret Peterson began to prepare for a luncheon meeting of the investment committee of the Calvert College Endowment Fund. The endowment fund had originated from private grants and alumni donations, usually in the form of securities, real estate, cash, or the proceeds from life insurance.

The assets of the fund were managed by a five-member committee appointed by the Calvert College Board of Trustees. Peterson, the vice-president in charge of investments at the American Surety Life Insurance Company, and the other four trustees were each knowledgeable about some aspect of investment management.

The major restriction in formulating investment objectives and strategy for the fund was the legal requirement that the members act in a "prudent" manner. Thus, the committee had to consider safety of principal and asset diversification. Otherwise, the committee was not circumscribed. Because the college preferred unrestricted gifts, donors had been persuaded not to impose covenants that specified how the gifts were to be managed, how the income was to be spent, or who the recipients were to be.

Federal and state taxes on income and capital gains were not a problem because the fund was tax exempt. As the fund was to be used for the future needs of the college, there was little immediate need for liquidity. With these factors in mind, the committee had decided that the main investment objective should be to seek the maximum total return obtainable at the risk level appropriate for this type of fund.

To aid Peterson in getting ready for the meeting, her administrative assistant, Jack Foster, had prepared a folder of background information. The first item in the folder was the minutes of the committee's last meeting. At that time the market value of the fund was $8.2 million; 52 percent of the assets were invested in twenty-two common stocks, 8 percent in real estate and mortgages, and 40 percent in bonds, cash, and preferred stocks. During the meeting, each investment had been reviewed, but no changes were made. The committee then discussed asset mix and decided that the percentage of the fund invested in common stocks should gradually be increased to around 55 percent. This increase was to be accomplished by investing new money received by the fund in common stocks rather than by selling other assets.

The second item in the folder was a letter from Calvert's alumni relations officer, informing the committee of the receipt of a check for $210,000 from the estate of a distinguished alumna. Peterson first considered whether to invest the $210,000 in one or more of the common stocks already owned by the fund, but she decided that there were no changes in the market prices or corporate outlooks of any of these stocks to warrant changes in the fund's present holdings. Consequently, she decided that the $210,000 should be invested in one or two stocks which were attractively priced and not currently a part of the fund's portfolio.

The next item was a report sent to the committee by a major brokerage house, Moore & Stewart. The firm recommended the purchase of eight Japanese common stocks, which offered both high quality and superior prospects for price appreciation: Canon, Fuji Photo, Hitachi, Kyocera, Matsuschita, NEC, Sony, and TDK. Because the endowment fund owned no Japanese stocks, Peterson studied the report carefully.

Moore & Stewart believed that each of these companies was likely to maintain superior growth for four reasons: (1) strong management in all functional areas, (2) product and service lines with above-average growth potential, (3) well-planned business objectives and strategies, and (4) the financial strength necessary to carry out these plans.

Moore & Stewart was also bullish on these stocks because the firm was bullish on the Japanese economy. Its real growth was continuing to outpace that of the American economy. Japan was becoming less dependent on exports because of the strong yen and trade friction. Industrial production and capital spending were rising, inventories were low, and consumer attitudes were changing. Young people in Japan were more willing to spend than their parents, and the high Japanese savings rate was declining.

Moore & Stewart also presented an analysis of the price performances of Japanese versus American stocks. This analysis led the firm to conclude that over the long term, Japanese stocks had outperformed American stocks. The firm cautioned, however, that potential investors in Japanese stocks should always analyze not only their growth prospects but also their price/earnings (P/E) ratios to determine whether the stocks would provide adequate returns for the risks involved. There had been periods in which investors had received inadequate returns over the intermediate term because Japanese stocks had sold at such high prices.

Next in the folder was a letter from David Hammond to the other members of the committee. Hammond had read Moore & Stewart's report and took strong exception to it: The average P/E ratio of the eight Japanese stocks recommended was 2 1/2 times the average multiple of U.S. stocks; hence, the P/E's of the Japanese stocks were too high to offer adequate returns over the next few years in relation to the risks involved. In addition, the eight companies recommended had already grown to significant size; thus, even if the growth envisioned by Moore & Stewart did materialize, most of these companies would be giants. Because it would become increasingly difficult for giant companies to continue to grow rapidly, only a few such companies would continue to command high P/E ratios in a "normal" stock market environment. However, the market seemed to be expecting that these companies would still sell for very high multiples a few years hence; if these stocks did not, investors would look back at another example of paying too much for a good thing.

Hammond believed that it was even more important to question the prices of these Japanese stocks when certain out-of-favor, and therefore relatively cheap, U.S. stocks were available as alternative investments. In a different market climate a few years hence, some of these "dull" domestic stock groups could turn in surprisingly good price performances, especially in relation to many overpriced Japanese stocks. Thus, Hammond concluded, the committee should question the potential profit-versus-risk relationship of the Japanese stocks recommended.

Peterson then turned to a letter from Peter Antinozzi, the treasurer of the Suffolk Power Company. Antinozzi, a new member of the endowment fund committee, had seen a recent summary of the fund's investments and noted that it contained no electric utility stocks. Based on recommendations made by a leading investment advisor, Midas Money Management, Antinozzi urged the committee to consider ten electric utility common stocks: Atlanta Energy, Commonwealth Energy, Dominion Resources, General Public Utilities, Kentucky Utilities, MDU Resources, Minnesota Power, Potomac Electric, Texas Utilities, and Utilicorp United. Midas Money Management pointed out that the ten electric utilities recommended were stronger financially than they had been a year ago. Most had either completed or were in the final stages of their construction programs. Because most would have sufficient capacity to meet the demand for power through the early 1990s, the construction of expensive facilities would continue to decrease. Therefore, the need for external financing would decline, and cash flow would increase. Balance sheets would get stronger, the median fixed charge coverage for the group would continue to rise, and earnings quality would improve.

The remaining items in the folder were descriptions and statistical analyses of the recommended stocks prepared by Foster (shown in Tables 13.1–13.5). As he explained in a note to Peterson, he had obtained much of this information from recent copies of the *Value Line Investment Survey* rather than American Surety's investment analysts. The reason was that like most life insurance companies, American Surety invested chiefly in bonds, mortgages, and privately placed loans; thus, its analysts were much more familiar with fixed-income securities than with common stocks.

For this reason, the analysts were not able to judge reasonable prices to pay for each of the recommended stocks. In spite of this lack of specific price information, Foster thought that the evaluation problem should not be ignored.

After considerable thought, he decided that the information he had could best be focused on the evaluation problem through use of the following model:

$$\frac{P_o(1 + k - d)^n}{E_n} = M_n$$

where P_o = the price of the stock at the start of the n-year horizon period;
k = the annual rate of return required by the investor;
d = the dividend yield expected during the first year;
E_n = the estimated normalized earnings at the end of n years; and
M_n = the ending price/earnings multiple necessary to provide the required rate of return.

With this model an investor can compute the terminal P/E ratio at which a stock would have to sell to provide the desired rate of return. Then, by analyzing the past P/E's of the stock and its prospective earnings, growth, dividend yield, and risk, the investor can decide whether the terminal P/E is probable—and thus whether the stock should be bought.

As an estimate of each stock's 1988 dividend yield (the d term in the model), Foster divided Value Line's forecast of the 1988 dividend by the stock's closing price on December 31, 1987. As an estimate of each stock's earnings at the end of the horizon (E_n) Foster used Value Line's forecast of average normalized earnings during the period 1990–92. Since 1991 was the mid-point in this ending forecast period, Foster used 1988–91 as the horizon period (and set n equal to four years).

As a framework for estimating the return that investors required for each stock as of December 31, 1987, Foster used the Sharpe-Lintner capital asset pricing model:

$$k_i = R_f + \beta_i(R_m - R_f)$$

where
k_i = the required annual return from stock i;
R_f = the annual return from a risk-free asset;
β_i = an index of the stock's systematic risk, "beta"; and
R_m = the expected annual return from the market.

To estimate the required return for each stock, Foster needed its systematic risk, the risk-free rate, and the market risk premium. To estimate the risk-free rate (R_f) during the four year investment horizon, he used 8.2 percent, the current yield on four year U.S. government notes. As a proxy for the market risk premium ($R_m - R_f$), he used 6.2 percent, the risk premium calculated for the period 1926–1985 by Ibbotson Associates.[1] He obtained an estimate of each stock's beta from Value Line. He then used the equation $k_i = 8.2\% + \beta_i(6.2\%)$ to calculate the required return for each recommended stock. For example, he calculated the required return for Canon's common stock to be $8.2\% + .85$ (6.2%), or 13.47 percent. (The required returns for the recommended stocks are shown in the right-hand column of Table 13.3.)

Having estimated d, E_n, and k for each stock, Foster next calculated the ending multiple at which each stock would have to sell in order to provide the required return. Then, by analyzing each stock's past P/E ratios and prospective earnings growth, dividend yield, and risk, one could decide whether the terminal P/E was likely and thus whether the stock should be purchased. Foster

[1] *Stocks, Bonds, Bills, and Inflation: 1986 Yearbook* (Chicago: Ibbotson Associates, 1986), p. 44.

noted that many investors might have avoided very large losses in the October 1987 market crash if, prior to purchase, they had examined the prices of stocks for their underlying assumptions concerning future growth rates and price/earnings multiples.

Peterson planned to study the tables carefully and then decide which if any of the recommended stocks were currently attractive for purchase.

■ QUESTIONS

1. Compare Foster's stock evaluation technique to other stock evaluation approaches. What are the advantages and disadvantages of each?

2. At the end of horizon period, what factors will determine the P/E ratio at which a given stock will then be selling?

3. In Table 13.5 verify that the required P/E ratios are 38.5 and 8.8 for Canon and Atlantic Energy, respectively.

4. Which if any of the recommended stocks appear relatively attractive for purchase? Why?

Japanese Companies

Canon is the world's largest manufacturer of copiers and a major producer of 35mm single lens reflex cameras. Copiers constitute 41% of sales; typewriters, printers, personal computers, and calculators, 33%; cameras, camcorders, and lenses, 26%. Foreign sales are 69% of total sales; research and development (R&D) expenses, 6.2%.

Fuji Photo is Japan's largest manufacturer of photographic film and paper. Fuji also makes cameras, lenses, photo processing equipment, electronic imaging systems, video and audio cassettes, and floppy disks. Foreign sales are 36% of revenues; R&D, 5.6%.

Hitachi is Japan's largest electronic and electrical producer. Computers, communication systems, and semiconductors constitute 31% of sales; TV, video, audio, and home appliances, 18%; power plant systems, 17%; industrial machinery, 17%; other products, 17%. Foreign sales are 26% of revenues; R&D, 6.3%.

Kyocera is the world's largest producer of ceramic packages for integrated circuits. Kyocera also makes industrial ceramics, electronic components, personal computers, disk drives, printers, 35mm cameras, and camcorders. Foreign sales constitute 31% of total sales; R&D, 2.9%.

Matsushita is Japan's largest manufacturer of consumer electronic and electrical products. Its trade names include Panasonic, Technics, Quasar, and National. Foreign sales are 44% of revenues; R&D, 6.2%.

NEC is Japan's largest maker of telecommunications systems and semiconductors. Computers are 40% of sales; telecommunications, 28%; semiconductors, 17%; TV and other consumer electronics, 15%. Foreign sales constitute 28% of total sales; R&D, 7.8%.

Sony is a major producer of consumer and industrial electronic equipment. Video products contribute 37% of sales; audio, 24%; TV sets, 24%; business equipment and semiconductors, 15%. International sales are 70% of revenues; R&D, 9.2%.

TDK is the world's largest producer of ferrite (magnetic ceramic) materials, related electronic components, and video and audio recording tapes. Foreign sales are 47% of total sales; R&D, 3.9%

Electric Utility Companies

Atlantic Energy supplies electricity to the southern third of New Jersey.

Commonwealth Energy provides electricity (61% of revenues), gas (37%), and steam (2%) to Cambridge, Plymouth, and 74 other towns in Massachusetts.

Dominion Resources supplies electricity and gas to Virginia, West Virginia, and North Carolina.

General Public Utilities sells electricity to customers in New Jersey and Pennsylvania.

Kentucky Utilities distributes electricity in central and western Kentucky and southwestern Virginia.

MDU Resources supplies electricity and gas to Montana, North Dakota, South Dakota, and Wyoming.

Minnesota Power provides electricity (91% of revenues) and gas (9% of revenues) in northeastern Minnesota and northwestern Wisconsin.

Potomac Electric sells electricity to customers in Washington, D.C. (44% of revenues) and in adjoining areas of Maryland (56%).

Texas Utilities distributes electricity in north central, eastern, and western Texas.

Utilicorp United sells electricity and gas to customers in Kansas City and western Missouri.

*These descriptions have been obtained primarily from the *Value Line Investment Survey.*
© 1988 by Value Line Inc.; used by permission of Value Line, Inc.

TABLE 13.2	Calvert College Endowment Fund Company Revenues

	Estimated Total Revenues** (in millions)		Annual Compound Growth*		
Recommended companies	1988	1991	During Past 10 Years	During Past 5 Years	1985 to 1991
Japanese					
Canon	$ 7,150	$ 8,900	16.5%	10.5%	8.5%
Fuji Photo	6,200	7,600	16.0	10.5	12.0
Hitachi	36,700	46,000	14.0	11.5	7.0
Kyocera	2,500	3,400	25.0	17.0	12.5
Matsushita	35,500	46,000	14.5	11.5	8.5
NEC	21,500	29,000	17.0	19.0	13.0
Sony	11,100	15,000	16.0	10.5	12.0
TDK	3,150	3,900	23.0	15.5	11.0
Utility					
Atlantic Energy	$ 680	$ 750	4.5%	2.5%	2.0%
Commonwealth Energy	700	780	5.5	3.0	.5
Dominion Resources	3,375	3,850	3.5	.5	4.0
General Public Utilities	2,810	3,280	9.5	8.5	2.5
Kentucky Utilities	550	590	1.5	−2.5	1.5
MDU Resources	375	470	11.5	11.0	.5
Minnesota Power	465	575	2.0	.5	5.0
Potomac Electric Power	1,400	1,520	7.0	6.5	2.5
Texas Utilities	4,200	4,600	7.5	5.0	−3.0
Utilicorp United	680	800	12.0	13.0	7.5

*Past growth rates reflect the trend of the compound annual rate of change in sales per share for ten- and five-year periods ending in 1986. Growth rates for 1985–91 are calculated from two figures, average actual sales during the three-year period 1984–86 and average estimated sales during the period 1990–92 under "normal" conditions for both the company and the general economy.

**These revenue data have been obtained from the *Value Line Investment Survey.* © 1988 by Value Line, Inc.; used by permission of Value Line, Inc.

TABLE | Calvert College Endowment Fund
13.3 | Share Prices, Dividends, and Market Risk

Recommended companies	Closing Price 12/31/87	Est. 1988 Div.	Est. 1988 Yield*	Market Risk (Beta)**	Required Return***
Japanese					
Canon	$ 36.12	$ .37	1.02%	.85	13.47%
Fuji Photo	63.50	.21	.33	.95	14.09
Hitachi	90.75	.67	.74	.85	13.47
Kyocera	84.75	.65	.77	.70	12.54
Matsushita	168.38	.74	.44	1.05	14.71
NEC	73.50	.33	.45	.80	13.16
Sony	37.75	.33	.87	.85	13.47
TDK	76.25	.59	.77	.80	13.16
Utility					
Atlantic Energy	$ 30.62	$2.68	8.75%	.60	11.92%
Commonwealth Energy	28.25	2.80	9.91	.70	12.54
Dominion Resources	41.38	3.08	7.44	.70	12.54
General Public Utilities	28.38	1.00	3.52	.75	12.85
Kentucky Utilities	17.88	1.33	7.43	.60	11.92
MDU Resources	17.50	1.48	8.46	.70	12.54
Minnesota Power	21.00	1.76	8.38	.70	12.54
Potomac Electric	21.88	1.43	6.54	.60	11.92
Texas Utilities	27.00	2.58	10.67	.70	12.54
Utilicorp United	15.00	1.10	7.33	.70	12.54
S&P 500 Index	$247.86	$9.08	3.66%	1.00	14.40%

*Estimated 1988 yield is the estimated 1988 dividend divided by the 12/31/87 closing price.
**Market risk (or beta) is a measure of the sensitivity of an individual stock's price to fluctuations in the entire market. For example, if a stock has a market risk of 1.5, then the stock's price is likely to increase (or decrease) 1.5% with a 1% increase (or decrease) in the overall market. Market risk data were obtained from Value Line. Each stock's market risk was calculated from a least-squares regression analysis between weekly percentage changes in the stock's price and weekly percentage changes in the overall market during a five-year period.
***Required return = .082 + .062 (Beta).

| TABLE | Calvert College Endowment Fund |
| 13.4 | Company Earnings* |

| | Estimated Earnings per share | | Annual Compound Growth | | |
Recommended companies	1988	1991	During Past 10 Years	During Past 5 Years	1985 to 1991
Japanese					
Canon	$ .70	$ 1.50	18.0%	1.5%	6.0%
Fuji Photo	2.75	3.50	22.0	12.5	13.0
Hitachi	3.55	4.75	15.0	4.5	10.0
Kyocera	2.25	3.25	15.5	10.5	12.0
Matsushita	6.25	9.00	17.5	11.0	7.5
NEC	1.00	2.00	21.5	8.5	21.5
Sony	.75	1.75	13.0	4.5	5.5
TDK	2.50	3.15	23.0	4.0	7.0
Utility					
Atlantic Energy	$ 3.75	$ 3.95	2.5%	4.0%	3.5%
Commonwealth Energy	3.60	4.90	8.0	10.0	3.0
Dominion Resources	4.50	5.00	3.0	6.5	5.5
General Public Utilities	4.00	5.00	0.5	25.0	14.0
Kentucky Utilities	1.95	2.10	1.5	8.0	6.0
MDU Resources	1.90	2.60	8.5	10.5	7.0
Minnesota Power	2.65	3.10	7.0	11.0	5.5
Potomac Electric Power	2.30	2.85	9.5	13.0	8.0
Texas Utilities	4.75	5.00	7.0	7.0	2.5
Utilicorp United	2.10	2.70	9.5	13.5	6.5
S&P 500 Index	$18.05	$24.79	5.0%	1.8%	6.9%

*Earnings estimates and growth rates for the recommended companies have been obtained from Value Line. © 1988 by Value Line, Inc.; used by permission of Value Line, Inc. The investment research staff of American Surety Life Insurance Company developed the earnings estimates and growth rates for the S&P 500 Stock Index.

TABLE 13.5 | Calvert College Endowment Fund Price/Earnings Ratios

Recommended companies	P/E Ratio as of 12/31/87	Required P/E Ratio in 1991	Average of the High and Low P/E Ratios during the Year				
			1987	1986	1985	1984	1983
Japanese							
Canon	51.6	38.5	60.1	53.6	17.0	21.6	21.8
Fuji Photo	23.1	30.4	19.3	12.6	8.9	12.7	12.1
Hitachi	25.6	30.9	29.3	26.2	11.9	12.4	13.5
Kyocera	37.7	40.7	36.7	31.8	28.7	26.7	23.1
Matsushita	26.9	31.9	25.4	15.6	8.7	11.1	12.8
NEC	73.5	59.3	N.M.*	N.M.*	47.7	26.0	33.1
Sony	50.3	34.7	53.2	18.0	5.4	12.6	26.9
TDK	30.5	38.6	25.4	28.4	15.2	19.7	19.7
Median	34.1	36.6	27.4	27.3	13.6	16.2	20.8
Utility							
Atlantic Energy	8.2	8.8	8.9	10.7	9.0	6.9	6.4
Commonwealth Energy	7.8	6.4	9.3	10.7	5.9	4.7	4.4
Dominion Resources	9.2	10.1	9.8	10.8	8.5	7.0	7.0
General Public Utilities	7.1	8.1	6.5	6.5	8.9	4.5	7.5
Kentucky Utilities	9.2	10.2	10.2	13.7	9.6	7.5	7.4
MDU Resources	9.2	7.9	13.6	12.0	8.0	7.6	7.0
Minnesota Power	7.9	8.0	10.9	9.9	7.5	6.6	6.6
Potomac Electric Power	9.5	9.5	10.6	11.0	8.3	6.8	7.1
Texas Utilities	5.7	5.8	6.9	7.4	6.5	5.8	6.3
Utilicorp United	7.1	6.8	11.1	11.1	7.0	5.3	4.9
S&P 500 Index	13.7	15.0	15.9	15.8	12.8	9.9	11.1

*These P/E ratios were not meaningful because earnings were depressed.

The Golden Gate Growth Fund
(Company Analysis)

In March 1988, Stuart Wilson, manager of the Growth Fund at Golden Gate Advisors in San Francisco, is investigating whether to buy shares in Albertson's and Food Lion. Louis Murphy, an institutional broker with Wall Street West, a large San Francisco–based brokerage firm, has informed Wilson that Wall Street West's food analyst is finishing a report on grocery stores in which he will be recommending Albertson's and Food Lion as stocks likely to outperform the market in the next twelve months.

The Golden Gate Growth Fund has $16 million in assets under management. The fund strives primarily for capital appreciation by investing in the common stocks of well-managed, undervalued companies. The fund chooses its stocks on the basis of four criteria: strong management, sound financial condition, above-average growth potential, and the likelihood of the stocks' outperforming the market during the next twelve months. The fund has outperformed the S&P 500 in each of the three years since the fund was established.

Wilson's analysis of Albertson's and Food Lion takes a two-pronged approach. First, he obtains the companies' latest annual reports and some supplemental financial data (portions of which are reproduced in Tables 14.1–14.3). Second, he telephones James Henderson, the analyst who is preparing the grocery store report at Wall Street West.

Henderson observes that Albertson's sales for fiscal 1987 increased 9.1 percent over those for fiscal 1986. This increase stemmed from inflation, new store expansion, and gains at existing stores. Sales at existing stores grew 3.9 percent in 1987 over 1986, 2.4 percent in 1986 over 1985, and 2.6 percent in 1985 over 1984. New stores provided sales increases of 3.5 percent in 1987, 2.8 percent in 1986, and 3.9 percent in 1985.

He expects Albertson's management to continue following its successful strategy of careful cost control, upgrading existing stores, and territorial expansion. In 1988 the company is planning to remodel thirty stores and to open thirty-five stores, including a combination food-and-drug unit to enter the Austin, Texas, market. In addition, the company is planning to expand into Phoenix, Arizona, by opening six combination stores in late 1989 and additional ones in 1990 and 1991. Thus, he foresees Albertson's sales and per-share earnings growing to $6.4 billion and $2.20 in 1988 and to $9.0 billion and $3.50 in 1991.

Henderson estimates Albertson's beta to be 0.95. Currently priced at $28.25 per share, the stock is selling at 12.8 times estimated 1988 earnings and yielding 2.0 percent on the recently increased dividend of $0.56. With the S&P 500 presently at 267, he considers Albertson's underpriced relative to the overall market.

He expects Food Lion's management to continue following a successful strategy of territorial expansion, upgrading existing stores, and strict cost control. While operating expenses are 21 percent of sales at the typical grocery chain, they are only 13 percent at Food Lion. Its management had achieved this cost advantage by maintaining a traditional "no frills" supermarket format, uniform store layout, lean corporate staff, tightly managed distribution system, and high worker productivity. Food Lion had then passed on its lower costs through aggressive pricing which attracted customers and forestalled competition.

While Food Lion was continuing its penetration of North Carolina and Virginia, its major thrust was currently into northern Florida. Despite tough competition, the Florida outlets are outperforming the company's typical new unit. Thus, expansion throughout Florida is likely to be a major driving force behind an 18 to 20 percent annual increase in Food Lion's stores over the foreseeable future. Henderson foresees Food Lion's sales and per share earnings increasing to $3.74 billion and $0.35 in 1988 and to $7.0 billion and $0.70 in 1991.

Henderson estimates Food Lion's beta at 1.05. At a current price of $11.75 per class B share, the stock is selling at 33.6 times estimated 1988 earnings and yielding 0.5 percent on the current $0.056 dividend. He ranks Food Lion favorably for relative market performance in the year ahead.

Wilson plans to study carefully the annual reports, the supplemental data, and the information Henderson has provided; then he will decide whether to buy shares in Albertson's and/or Food Lion.

QUESTIONS

1. How would you judge Albertson's and Food Lion's management, financial condition, and growth potential?

2. Given the March 1988 prices and current dividends noted above, estimate the one-year holding-period returns which an investor will receive from Albertson's and Food Lion's shares during the twelve months ending March 1989. Do you think the stocks are likely to outperform the S&P 500 during that period? Why?

3. Should Wilson buy shares in Albertson's and/or Food Lion? Why?

TABLE 14.1	The Golden Gate Growth Fund
	Excerpts from the Albertson's, Inc. 1987 Annual Report

Message to Stockholders

We are extremely pleased to report that 1987 was our 18th consecutive year of record sales and earnings. The credit for this accomplishment goes to our employees and I thank each and every one of them for their support and hard work. Also, I thank our loyal customers, suppliers and stockholders.

The following summarizes the year financially:

- Sales increased 9.1% to $5.87 billion from $5.38 billion last year. Identical store sales increased 3.9%.
- Gross margin decreased to 22.4% from 22.5% last year.
- Operating and administrative expenses as a percent to sales decreased to 18.7% from 19.0% in 1986.
- Net earnings increased 25.2% to $125.4 million.
- Net earnings as a percent to sales increased to 2.14% from 1.86% in 1986.
- Earnings per share was $1.88 compared to $1.50 in 1986.
- Return on assets was 9.4%, up from 7.6% five years ago.
- Return on stockholders' equity was 19.8%.

These results reflect our commitment to upgrading our asset base to bigger stores and expanding our distribution system. We have been replacing and upgrading our stores for the past 10 years and our average store size is now 39,400 square feet, up from 27,800 square feet in 1977. Nearly 74% of our square footage is now in stores over 35,000 square feet. Big stores allow us to operate much more efficiently, to keep our costs under control and to offer our customers the service departments that we feel are essential in today's stores. Our distribution system adds stability to our earnings base by keeping costs low and allowing our retail people to concentrate on operating stores.

During the year we continued to convert additional markets to our Everyday Low Price Program and at year end 50% of our volume came from stores on this program. Las Vegas and Portland were two major market areas that were converted in 1987. We will continue to fine-tune this program and expand it into other markets as needed in order to offer the lowest possible prices to our customers.

Our operating philosophy in the retail food and drug business is to make each store successful. Each store must give our customers the services and products they want and, at the same time, run at maximum volume with minimum expense. We do not believe in overlapping stores. This philosophy maximizes the use of our assets and delivers the maximum return to our stockholders.

Capital expenditures for 1987 were $194 million, an increase of 39% over the $139 million invested in 1986. These capital expenditures were principally funded by internally generated funds and we continued to own new stores wherever possible.

This year we opened 7 combination units, 26 superstores and 1 grocery warehouse store for a total of 34 stores or 1.6 million square feet of retail space. We remodeled 18 stores, three of which were expanded from conventional supermarkets to superstores. We started construction of a full-line distribution center in Gresham, Oregon which will open in October 1988. also, we completed a 57,000 square foot addition to our Sundries Center in Boise, Idaho.

At the December 1987 Board Meeting, the Directors adopted the most aggressive Five Year Plan in our history which calls for us to spend approximately $1.5 billion over the next five years.

continued

TABLE	
14.1	continued

These funds will be allocated as follows: approximately 65% for new stores, 16% for remodels, 12% for distribution and 7% for store automation and equipment replacement. These capital expenditures will be funded from internally generated funds, shopping center leases where we cannot purchase the property and approximately $100 million in new borrowings which will be repaid by the end of the five-year period. The Plan calls for:

- Opening 175 new stores. These stores will be primarily combination units or superstores built in our current operating areas. Our goal is to be the leading operator in states such as Idaho, Nevada and Utah while expanding rapidly to gain market share in the growth states of California, Florida and Texas. New market emphasis during the next 18 months will be Austin, Texas and Phoenix, Arizona.
- Remodeling 150 existing stores in order to have approximately 90% of our square footage new or remodeled within the past 10 years.
- Developing programs using in-store computers to further reduce our operating costs. Some of the system enhancements will be in the pharmacy, direct store delivery and time and attendance reporting.
- Adding extensive new additions to our current distribution system. We will spend approximately $180 million to:

  — Complete the Gresham, Oregon Distribution Center.
  — Expand the perishable section of our Salt Lake City, Utah Distribution Center.
  — Remodel and expand the dry grocery and meat-deli sections of our Brea, California Distribution Center.
  — Construct a new satellite distribution center in Roseville, California.
  — Construct a new full-line distribution center in Fort Worth, Texas.

We are increasing our capital expenditures in 1988 to $325 million, an increase of 68% over 1987. This will include 35 new stores, 30 store remodels, the completion of the Gresham Distribution Center and the beginning of the major expansion of our distribution system.

In May 1987 the Board of Directors authorized Management to repurchase up to three million shares of the Company's common stock. At year end we had repurchased and retired 1.2 million shares.

During 1987 our stockholders received $32 million in cash dividends. On February 29, 1988 the Board of Directors increased the annual dividend rate 16.7% from $.48 to $.56. This is the 17th consecutive year of dividend increases.

Our future looks bright; however, we must continue to work on the challenges. We will strive to increase our sales base, to keep our physical structures up-to-date, to develop better systems and to train people for the future. Our stockholders, employees, customers and suppliers have created a great tradition of success at Albertson's. I would like to again thank each of them for their individual contribution and to challenge them to help make us even more successful in the future.

Warren E. McCain
Chairman of the Board
and Chief Executive Officer

continued

TABLE 14.1 continued

Albertson's, Inc. Consolidated Earnings (in thousands except share and per share data)

	52 Weeks January 28, 1988	52 Weeks January 29, 1987	52 Weeks January 30, 1986
Sales	$5,869,423	$5,379,643	$5,060,265
Cost of sales	4,554,297	4,168,578	3,948,698
Gross profit	1,315,126	1,211,065	1,111,567
Operating and administrative expenses	1,098,306	1,022,420	953,432
Operating profit	216,820	188,645	158,135
Interest expense, net	(10,267)	(9,961)	(9,936)
Other income, net	5,301	6,097	6,575
Earnings before income taxes	211,854	184,781	154,774
Income taxes	86,469	84,629	69,664
Net earnings	$ 125,385	$ 100,152	$ 85,110
Earnings per share	$1.88	$1.50	$1.28
Average number of shares outstanding	66,870,408	66,666,846	66,340,986

Albertson's Inc. Consolidated Balance Sheets (in thousands)

	January 28, 1988	January 29, 1987	January 30, 1986
Assets			
Current assets:			
Cash and marketable securities	$ 201,381	$ 245,762	$ 196,850
Accounts and notes receivable	43,830	40,492	34,526
Inventories	361,579	316,473	301,985
Prepaid expenses	9,190	7,553	5,315
Deferred income tax benefits	18,981	15,004	11,030
Total current assets	634,961	625,284	549,706
Other Assets	36,793	25,853	23,053
Land, buildings and equipment:			
Land	136,073	105,570	76,442
Buildings	307,399	240,549	201,600
Fixtures and equipment	489,432	427,945	389,576
Leasehold improvements	98,338	84,204	75,077
Assets under capital leases	144,150	139,658	135,270
	1,175,392	997,926	877,965
Less accumulated depreciation and amortization	449,932	388,785	338,221
	725,460	609,141	539,744
Deferred income tax benefits	4,861	4,378	5,365
	$1,402,075	$1,264,656	$1,117,868

continued

TABLE 14.1 | continued

	January 28, 1988	January 29, 1987	January 30, 1986
Liabilities and stockholders' equity			
Current liabilities:			
Accounts payable	$ 328,307	$ 278,781	$ 237,326
Salaries and related liabilities	54,613	52,000	45,078
Taxes other than income taxes	20,775	15,307	14,482
Income taxes	14,085	13,504	8,088
Other current liabilities	11,976	10,785	11,153
Current maturities of long-term debt	5,554	5,461	5,329
Current obligations under capital leases	4,693	4,201	4,057
Total current liabilities	440,003	380,039	325,513
Long-term debt	69,696	75,003	78,491
Obligations under capital leases	113,455	112,220	109,943
Deferred credits and other long-term liabilities:			
Deferred investment tax credits	11,149	14,381	17,123
Deferred compensation	15,147	14,051	11,318
Deferred rents payable	46,558	40,081	31,722
Other long-term liabilities	40,859	34,502	25,049
	113,713	103,015	85,212
Stockholders' equity:			
Common stock	66,361	33,408	33,249
Capital in excess of par value	26,800	82,266	78,883
Retained earnings	572,047	478,705	406,577
	665,208	594,379	518,709
	$1,402,075	$1,264,656	$1,117,868

continued

TABLE 14.1 | continued

Albertson's, Inc. Five Year Summary of Selected Financial Data
(Dollars in thousands except per share data)

	52 Weeks January 28, 1988	52 Weeks January 29, 1987	52 Weeks January 30, 1986	52 Weeks January 31, 1985	52 Weeks February 2, 1984
Operating results					
Sales	$5,869,423	$5,379,643	$5,060,265	$4,735,724	$4,279,331
Gross profit	1,315,126	1,211,065	1,111,567	1,043,203	952,532
Interest expense:					
Debt	5,838	7,223	8,049	7,249	7,996
Capital leases	12,398	11,784	11,735	12,035	12,258
Earnings before income taxes	211,854	184,781	154,774	147,462	127,362
Income taxes	86,469	84,629	69,664	67,716	57,081
Net earnings	125,385	100,152	85,110	79,746	70,281
Net earnings as a percent to sales	2.14%	1.86%	1.68%	1.68%	1.64%
Common stock data:					
Earnings per share	$ 1.88	$1.50	$1.28	$1.21	$1.07
Dividends per share	.48	.42	.38	.34	.30
Book value per share	10.02	8.90	7.80	6.87	5.96
Financial position:					
Total assets	$1,402,075	$1,264,656	$1,117,868	$1,031,100	$ 935,660
Working capital	194,958	245,245	224,193	105,760	209,188
Long-term debt	69,696	75,003	78,491	82,185	83,025
Obligations under capital leases	113,455	112,220	109,943	112,050	116,644
Stockholders' equity	665,208	594,379	518,709	454,419	391,847
Other statistics:					
Number of stores at year end	465	452	444	434	432
Number of employees	43,000	40,000	37,000	35,000	34,000
Full-time equivalents	33,200	29,400	27,000	25,800	25,000

Common stock data is adjusted for the two-for-one stock split paid October 5, 1987. Reprinted by permission of Albertson's, Inc.

TABLE 14.2	Supplementary Financial Data Golden Gate Growth Fund Albertson's, Inc.*				
Fiscal Year	**1982**	**1981**	**1980**	**1979**	**1978**
Sales (millions of dollars)	3,940	3,481	3,039	2,674	2,269
Net earnings (millions of dollars)	58.4	48.5	41.6	38.3	36.4
Net earnings as a % of sales	1.48%	1.39%	1.37%	1.43%	1.61%
Earnings per share	0.95	0.79	0.68	0.62	0.60
Dividends per share	0.25	0.22	0.20	0.15	0.12
Book value per share	5.22	4.01	3.52	3.02	2.52
Working capital (millions of dollars)	193	123	112	99.3	79.3
Long-term debt (millions of dollars)	201	206	205	212	207
Stockholders' equity (millions of dollars)	340	239	209	178	149
Number of stores	416	412	396	384	365

*Fiscal years end on the Thursday nearest to January 31 of the following calendar year. For example, the company's 1982 fiscal year ends on the Thursday nearest to January 31, 1983. Reprinted by permission of Albertson's, Inc.

| **TABLE 14.3** | The Golden Gate Growth Fund
Excerpts from the 1987 Annual Report of Food Lion, Inc. |

Letter to shareholders

Food Lion's growth continues. Your Company had the finest year of its 30-year history in 1987. Sales reached $2.95 billion, up 22.7% over the 53-week fiscal 1986 (up 25.4% over the comparable 52 weeks in 1986). Earnings set yet another record at $85.8 million, up 38.8% over the 53-week fiscal 1986 (up 41.8% over the comparable 52 weeks in 1986). These outstanding results yielded a net income to sales ratio of 2.9%, which is over twice the average in the supermarket industry.

Your Company opened 95 new stores, closed eight older stores and dramatically expanded its distribution center capacity in 1987, enhancing its continued reputation as the fastest growing supermarket chain in the country.

The new stores added to our existing market coverage of present states of operation and allowed us to push out "at the edges" into Florida (six stores) and Delaware (one store). Our plans for 1988 are equally aggressive, calling for 100 new stores to be opened, with the majority of these being in North Carolina, Virginia and Florida. We intend to sign 140 leases during 1988 for store openings in 1989 and beyond. Our plans call for a total of over 800 stores by the end of 1990. We are extremely excited with this growth which we believe can be accomplished at our historically strong profit ratios.

During 1987, we completed the third and final phase of our Virginia Distribution Center, bringing it to over one million square feet. In addition, at year-end, we completed the first phase of our Dunn, North Carolina, Distribution Center, to allow our continued strong growth in the Carolinas and Virginia. We will have the first phase of our northern Florida Distribution Center operating by the end of the first quarter in 1989. It will serve our planned expansion into Florida. Subject to satisfactory soil and other tests, we will break ground for our sixth distribution center in eastern Tennessee this year, providing additional warehouse space. This strong growth in support space will allow us to continue our rapid growth.

Our growth in both stores and distribution centers necessitates a huge growth in fleet and equipment, enhancing our purchasing power of capital equipment, thereby keeping support costs to a minimum.

High-paced store growth also means a heavy demand for people. We ended the year with 27,033 employees. We have in place the necessary structure to recruit and train new employees to bring them to the high level of ability that our customers expect. We have developed and continue to develop comprehensive training programs for all facets of your Company, from training inside the store at the operational level to a detailed training program for store management and numerous programs at our headquarters for the growth of our support team there. This is a key area of focus for Food Lion and one in which we plan to continue to excel.

Many people are amazed at our high growth rate—a 20-year annual compound growth rate of over 20% in store numbers. We plan to continue this pace into the foreseeable future through our focus on standardized stores.

Most of our stores are built from scratch, rather than through acquisition. We have an attractive, 25,000-square-foot format which places a heavy emphasis on our fruit and vegetable department. In those areas where we add a Bakery/Delicatessen, the store size is 29,000 square feet. This standardized operation allows us to provide our customers with a wide selection of products and, at the same time, permits us to densely saturate a market area providing customers with the lowest prices in a store not very far from their home.

continued

TABLE	
14.3	continued

Expansion follows an "ink blot" formula. We keep adding stores in our existing market area and, at the same time, expanding the size of the ink blot. The hub of our expansion is our distribution network. As store numbers grow, we add new distribution centers whose radiuses overlap the existing distribution territory. This minimizes warehouse and transportation costs.

We are proud of the return we have earned for our shareholders during our 30-year history. One hundred shares purchased when your Company was formed in 1957 is now, due to splits, 648,000 shares of Class A and 648,000 shares of Class B stock, a total of 1,296,000 shares. That initial investment of 100 shares cost $1,000. At December 31, 1987, the value of those shares was $16,119,000. In just the past 10 years alone, the share value of Food Lion stock has compounded at an annual growth rate of 48.6%.

Growth is financed from internally generated funds and external debt. Including the original capital raised in 1957 and our initial public offering in 1970, we have raised only $8 million in equity capital from the public in our total history. We have no plans to seek additional equity capital in the foreseeable future. To allow us to continue our high rate of growth, the majority of profits will be reinvested in the Company and moderate external debt will be added as needed.

We are optimistic about the future for your Company. Our marketing concept has been favorably accepted in small country towns of less than 10,000 as well as large urban areas in excess of 1,000,000 people; in mountain areas and beach resorts; and in low, medium, and upper income neighborhoods. We believe that with our strong, loyal team of employees, combined with being the lowest cost supermarket operator in the country, we can compete successfully in any economic environment. We look forward to the challenges of the next 20 years which will take us to our 50th birthday!!

Sincerely,
EXTRA LOW PRICES

Ralph W. Ketner   Tom E. Smith
Chairman of the   President and Chief
Board of Directors   Executive Officer

continued

TABLE 14.3 | continued

Food Lion, Inc.
Ten Year Summary of Operations

(Dollars in thousands except per share amounts)		**1987**	1986 (53 Weeks)	1985
1. Net sales	$	**2,953,807**	2,406,582	1,865,632
2. Income before taxes	$	**150,702**	122,923	89,185
3. Net income	$	**85,802**	61,823	47,585
4. Current assets	$	**443,918**	311,403	220,827
5. Long-term assets	$	**361,895**	293,484	218,870
6. Total assets	$	**805,813**	604,887	439,697
7. Current liabilities	$	**315,827**	222,941	154,923
8. Long-term debt	$	**69,301**	40,533	21,401
9. Capital lease obligations, deferred taxes and other	$	**81,461**	76,549	55,994
10. Shareholders' equity	$	**339,224**	264,864	207,379
11. Cash dividends	$	**12,351**	5,700	4,523
12. Depreciation and amortization	$	**37,433**	29,585	21,381
13. Funds from operations	$	**127,580**	98,438	77,591
14. Number of stores opened (net)	#	**87**	71	66
15. Number of stores open	#	**475**	388	317
16. Number of employees	#	**27,033**	20,871	17,089
17. Weighted average shares outstanding (000)	#	**321,435**	320,234	318,771
18. Earnings per share (a)	$	**.27**	.19	.15
19. Dividends per share (a)	$	**.038**	.018	.014
20. Book value per share (a)	$	**1.06**	.83	.65
21. Asset turnover	×	**4.88**	5.47	5.63
22. Return on sales	%	**2.90**	2.57	2.55
23. Return on assets	%	**14.2**	14.1	14.4
24. Return on equity	%	**32.4**	29.8	29.1
25. Equity ratio	%	**42.1**	43.8	47.2
26. Current ratio	×	**1.41**	1.40	1.43
27. Funds from operations: Sales	%	**4.32**	4.09	4.16
28. Funds from operations: Total assets	%	**21.1**	22.4	23.4
29. Recapitalization and stock splits		**2 for 1**	3 for 1	

Notes to Ten Year Summary of Operations
(a) Amounts are based upon the weighted average number of the Class A common and Class B common shares outstanding.
Definitions
Line
13. Funds from operations—Earnings (after taxes), excluding extraordinary gains, plus depreciation, change in deferred income taxes and other non-cash items.

continued

TABLE 14.3 | continued

1984	1983	1982	1981	1980 (53 Weeks)	1979	1978
1,469,564	1,172,459	947,074	666,848	543,883	415,974	299,267
71,405	50,467	39,222	35,587	27,087	23,634	17,572
37,305	27,718	21,855	19,317	15,287	13,171	9,481
178,031	135,914	105,337	65,842	44,206	37,556	28,354
153,146	138,289	107,572	73,529	62,226	48,919	37,477
331,177	274,203	212,909	139,371	106,432	86,475	65,831
104,656	94,812	85,533	44,461	31,310	26,873	20,013
18,875	18,449	7,180	814	223	335	182
44,226	37,308	22,393	16,260	15,109	13,500	11,864
163,420	123,634	97,803	77,836	59,790	45,767	33,772
3,033	2,490	2,087	1,731	1,375	1,201	625
16,702	14,075	11,630	7,720	6,044	4,584	3,327
57,301	44,589	34,967	28,627	22,492	18,676	13,394
25	44	41	35	21	16	14
251	226	182	141	106	85	69
12,784	10,069	8,674	6,471	4,849	4,107	3,382
315,462	314,221	312,946	311,083	309,255	308,737	305,400
.12	.09	.07	.06	.05	.04	.03
.010	.008	.007	.006	.004	.004	.002
.52	.39	.31	.25	.19	.15	.11
5.36	5.51	6.80	6.27	6.29	6.32	6.14
2.54	2.36	2.31	2.90	2.81	3.17	3.17
13.6	13.0	15.7	18.1	17.7	20.0	19.5
30.2	28.3	28.1	32.3	33.4	39.0	38.3
49.3	45.1	45.9	55.8	56.2	52.9	51.3
1.70	1.43	1.23	1.48	1.41	1.40	1.42
3.90	3.80	3.69	4.29	4.14	4.49	4.48
20.9	20.9	25.1	26.9	26.0	28.4	27.5
	2 for 1	3 for 1			3 for 1	

14. Number of stores opened (net)—Number of stores opened less stores closed during year.

15. Number of stores open—Number of stores operating at year-end.

16. Number of employees—Number of full-time and part-time employees at year-end.

17. Weighted average shares outstanding—Weighted average shares outstanding have been restated to reflect the effects of the stock recapitalization in 1983 and stock splits in 1987, 1986, 1982 and 1979.

continued

TABLE | continued
14.3

Definitions (continued)
Line

18. Earnings per share—Earnings (after taxes) per common share (line 3 ÷ 17).

19. Dividends per share—Cash dividends per common share (line 11 ÷ 17).

20. Book value per share—Book value of shareholders' equity per common share (line 10 ÷ 17).

21. Asset turnover—The ratio of sales per dollar of assets employed during the year. It is one indication of how efficiently a company uses its assets. It is calculated by dividing sales by the beginning total assets (line 1 ÷ 6).

22. Return on sales—The percentage of profit earned on each dollar of sales (line 3 ÷ 1).

23. Return on assets—The percentage of profit earned on beginning total assets (line 3 ÷ 6). It is an indication of how profitably our assets are utilized.

24. Return on equity—The percentage of profit earned during the year on the beginning shareholders' equity (line 3 ÷ 10). It shows how effectively funds are invested and managed.

25. Equity ratio—Shows the share of the total assets of the business owned by the shareholders as opposed to outside sources. It is calculated by dividing year-end shareholders' equity by year-end total assets (line 10 ÷ 6).

26. Current ratio—The ratio of current assets to current liabilities (line 4 ÷ 7). It indicates the immediate availability of resources to cover short-term debt.

27. Funds from operations: Sales—The percentage of funds to sales (line 13 ÷ 1). It indicates the amount of funds generated from each dollar of sales.

28. Funds from operations: Total assets—The percentage of funds to total assets at the beginning of the year (line 13 ÷ 6). It indicates the funds generated from the assets employed.

continued

TABLE 14.3 continued

Food Lion, Inc.
Consolidated Statements of Income

(Dollars in thousands except per share amounts)	Years Ended		
	January 2, 1988	January 3, 1987	December 28, 1985
Net sales	$2,953,807	$2,406,582	1,865,632
Cost of goods sold	2,385,329	1,948,775	1,521,275
Gross profit	568,478	457,807	344,357
Selling and administrative expense	366,583	296,077	226,550
Interest expense	13,760	9,222	7,241
Depreciation and amortization	37,433	29,585	21,381
	417,776	334,884	255,172
Income before income taxes	150,702	122,923	89,185
Provisions for income taxes	64,900	61,100	41,600
Net income	$ 85,802	$ 61,823	$ 47,585
Earnings per share	$.27	$.19	$.15
(Results as a percentage of sales)			
Net sales	100.00 %	100.00%	100.00%
Cost of goods sold	80.75	80.98	81.54
Gross profit	19.25	19.02	18.46
Selling and administrative expense	12.41	12.30	12.14
Interest expense	0.47	0.38	0.39
Depreciation and amortization	1.27	1.23	1.15
	14.15	13.91	13.68
Income before income taxes	5.10	5.11	4.78
Provisions for income taxes	2.20	2.54	2.23
Net income	2.90 %	2.57 %	2.55 %

continued

**TABLE
14.3** | continued

Consolidated Balance Sheets

(Dollars in thousands except per share amounts)	January 2, 1988	January 3, 1987
Assets		
Current assets:		
Cash and temporary investments	$ 15,534	$ 22,024
Receivables	39,797	27,176
Inventories	385,276	258,860
Prepaid expenses	3,311	3,343
Total current assets	443,918	311,403
Property, at cost, less accumulated depreciation and amortization	361,895	293,484
Total assets	$805,813	$604,887
Liabilities and Shareholders' Equity		
Current liabilities:		
Notes payable	$ 92,741	$ 51,164
Accounts payable, trade	144,271	106,394
Accrued expenses	60,735	48,628
Current maturities of long-term debt	1,466	1,586
Current obligations under capital leases	1,879	1,693
Income taxes payable	14,735	13,476
Total current liabilities	315,827	222,941
Long-term debt	69,301	40,533
Obligations under capital leases	51,695	50,857
Deferred income taxes	28,333	24,533
Deferred compensation	1,433	1,159
Total liabilities	466,589	340,023
Shareholders' equity:		
Class A non-voting common stock, $.50 par value; authorized 300,000,000 shares	81,023	40,421
Class B voting common stock, $.50 par value; authorized 300,000,000 shares	79,829	39,834
Additional capital	96	466
Retained earnings	178,276	184,143
Total shareholders' equity	339,224	264,864
Total liabilities and shareholders' equity	$805,813	$604,887

SOURCE: Reprinted by permission of Food Lion, Inc.

The Lone Star Fund
(Company Analysis)

The Lone Star Fund, a mutual fund with $80 million in assets, is based in Austin, Texas. The fund is managed by Rodriguez and Associates, an investment firm. The fund's primary objective is capital appreciation from short- or long-term investment in the common stocks of selected growth companies with capable management, sound financial and accounting policies, and efficient service. A secondary objective is current income. Investments are in a variety of industries and must be highly marketable. The fund has outperformed the market in the past one-, five-, and ten-year periods.

In April, 1988, Rafael Rodriguez and his partner, Nancy Daniels, were searching for stocks to add to the fund's portfolio. Concerned about a possible recession in 1989, they wanted to find companies whose sales and earnings growth would not be heavily affected by a downturn in the business cycle.

One industry sector which they believed to have investment potential in the anticipated economic environment was the do-it-yourself sector of the building supplies industry. This conclusion rested on three factors. First, inflation was eroding consumers' buying power. Many homeowners would be forced to repair their existing dwellings rather than buy new homes as rising inflation and interest rates forced up new-home prices and carrying costs faster than consumers' incomes. Second, more consumers could not afford the high cost of contractors' home improvement work and would opt to improve their homes themselves. Third, a recession would probably throw millions of people out of work. These consumers would have idle time which could be occupied by home improvement projects.

To learn more about the industry, Rodriguez contacted Lawrence Arnold, a security analyst at Peachtree Capital Management in Atlanta. Arnold, who had specialized in following the building industry for several years, began by noting that sales of do-it-yourself building supplies had set new records every year for over twenty years; hence, the sector was very recession resistant. He thought sector sales would grow 16 percent in 1988, and 12 to 15 percent in 1989 and during the 1990s. He also furnished financial data about the sector (shown in Table 15.1).

Arnold regarded Home Depot highly among do-it-yourself building supply stocks. He had followed the company closely for years because it is headquartered in Atlanta. He believed that over the next several years, Home Depot would outperform its competitors because of five key factors: knowledgeable sales people, innovative merchandising, expert buying, efficient inventory control systems, and capable management.

Arnold provided Rodriguez with Home Depot's latest annual report and some supplementary historical data (key portions of which are shown in Tables 15.2 and 15.3). He expected Home Depot to achieve another record year in fiscal 1988 as a result of the anticipated addition of twenty-one new stores to the company's existing seventy-five, increased sales per existing store from a chain-wide implementation of everyday low pricing, the rebound of the stores in the sluggish "oil patch" (Texas), lower interest charges due to a lower debt burden, and a 4.5 percentage point drop in the company's tax rate. He was projecting Home Depot's fiscal 1988 sales at $1,950 million, up 34 percent from fiscal 1987 sales of $1,454 million. He estimated Home Depot's fiscal 1988 earnings at $1.45 per share, up 28 percent from 1987 earnings of $1.13.

Arnold observed that the stock, at its current price of $26.00 per share, was selling at 17.9 times estimated fiscal 1988 earnings and yielding 0.3 percent on an indicated 1988 dividend of $0.08. In addition, based on the last five years of weekly returns, the stock's beta was 1.30, and the coefficient of determination (R^2) of the regression equation for the returns from Home Depot's stock and the S&P 500 was 0.25. Arnold expected that during the next three to five years, Home Depot's sales per share would grow 29 percent annually; earnings per share, 39 percent.

Rodriguez planned to analyze the data Arnold had furnished and then decide whether to purchase Home Depot for the Lone Star Fund.

QUESTIONS

1. What do you think of Rodriguez's rationale for investing in the do-it-yourself building supplies sector of the building industry?

2. How would you interpret the beta and the coefficient of determination (R^2) for Home Depot shares?

3. Analyze the investment suitability of Home Depot shares. Given that the stock's closing price on April 26, 1988, was $26.00 per share, and expected cash dividends during the year ending April 26, 1989, were $0.08 per share, project a one-year holding period return for Home Depot shares. Should Rodriguez purchase Home Depot shares for the Lone Star Fund? Why, or why not?

TABLE 15.1 | The Lone Star Fund
Selected Financial Data*
Do-It-Yourself Home Improvement Industry

	1983	1984	1985	1986	1987	1988	1991
Operating margin	8.7%	8.5%	7.4%	7.7%	7.4%	7.0%	7.5%
Net profit margin	3.7%	3.6%	2.8%	2.7%	2.8%	3.0%	3.4%
Return on net worth	15.4%	15.7%	12.3%	11.2%	11.0%	12.5%	14.0%
Dividend payout	16%	18%	19%	19%	17%	15%	13%
Average dividend yield	0.8%	1.2%	1.1%	1.0%	1.0%	1.0%	0.8%
Average price/earnings ratio	21.9	15.1	17.5	19.7	N.A.	N.A.	17.0
Industry's P/E ratio, relative to market's P/E	1.85	1.41	1.42	1.34	N.A.	N.A.	1.40

*Figures for 1987, 1988, and 1991 are estimates. These figures have been obtained from the *Value Line Investment Survey*. N.A. = not available. © 1988 by Value Line, Inc.; used by permission of Value Line, Inc.

TABLE 15.2 | The Lone Star Fund
Excerpts from the 1987 Annual Report of The Home Depot

To Our Shareholders:

For The Home Depot, fiscal 1987 was another year of record performance. Our sales, earnings and customer transactions achieved record levels as we continued our plan of controlled, profitable growth in the fastest growing segment of the home improvement industry, the do-it-yourself market.

Sales for 1987 rose 44 percent to $1.454 billion, compared to last year's milestone revenues of just over $1 billion. Net earnings increased 127 percent; earnings per share improved 88 percent; and, stockholders' equity increased by 97 percent to $320.6 million.

Comparable store sales also rose a dramatic 18 percent as we successfully implemented policies and systems aimed at improving the productivity of our stores. As a result, our inventory turnover climbed to 5.4 turns in 1987 from 4.6 in 1986.

We also strengthened our financial position by redeeming $100,250,000 of our outstanding convertible debentures, thereby reducing the Company's debt. The Home Depot entered fiscal 1988 with a strong balance sheet and with bank lines of credit amounting to $200 million. These funds may be used to finance our expansion program or for other appropriate corporate purposes.

Prompted by The Home Depot's financial success, the Board of Directors declared the Company's first quarterly dividend in acknowledgement of our shareholders' loyalty as we continue to grow in the do-it-yourself business.

Total Store Space Increases to 6,161,000 Square Feet. During 1987, we opened 15 new stores, bringing our total to 75. Most new stores were opened in existing markets, but we also expanded into the new markets of Chattanooga and Knoxville, Tennessee. We now operate in 19 metropolitan areas across 8 states, including Florida, Georgia, Alabama, Tennessee, Louisiana, Texas, Arizona and California.

TABLE 15.2 | continued

Additionally, we continued following our plan for keeping all stores up-to-date on new merchandising techniques and remodeled 8 of our older stores. We increased the square footage where possible while completely refixturing and modernizing each facility. The result was that during the year, total store space increased to 6,161,000 square feet, including all remodeled stores.

The cost of expansion and remodeling was borne primarily by internally generated funds. Consequently, we did not dilute our financial position in order to expand and grow.

Currently, we are planning to open approximately 21 stores in existing and new markets during fiscal 1988. These new store openings will include locations in New Jersey and Connecticut, our first northeastern markets.

Do-It-Yourself Market Growing and Stable. Research analysts predict that the do-it-yourself market should reach approximately $100 billion by 1990. Since 1982, the do-it-yourself business has posted an impressive annual growth rate of 11.6 percent, while general retail growth has increased at only 7.1 percent annually.

Demographic figures also provide optimism about the do-it-yourself market. As baby boomers reach adulthood throughout the 1980s, this do-it-yourself population segment will grow much more rapidly through the current decade than the total population.

The do-it-yourself market continues to demonstrate its non-cyclical nature. The 2 percent drop in housing starts for 1987 did not affect The Home Depot's business.

Continuing to Create Dedicated Do-It-Yourselfers. The Home Depot's success has been built on our commitment to develop new do-it-yourselfers while serving the expanding needs of our present customers. Our trained sales people continue to create a new customer base for The Home Depot by encouraging and advising novice do-it-yourselfers. We believe that with proper guidance and instruction, home owners can learn to do their own home improvement projects and repairs, ultimately becoming dedicated do-it-yourselfers.

Our objective is to continue to pursue this commitment to growing the market and to continue as the leading retailer in those markets where we operate. We are pleased with the year's outstanding 18 percent increase in sales from existing stores.

The success of The Home Depot is the result of many—our customers, our suppliers, our shareholders and most importantly, our employees. We appreciate this support and thank each of you for your contribution to our past and your confidence in our future.

Sincerely,

Bernard Marcus   Arthur M. Blank
Chairman and   President and
Chief Executive Officer Chief Operating Officer

continued

TABLE
15.2 | continued

The Home Depot
Selected Financial Data

	Fiscal Year Ended				
Amounts in thousands except per share data	**January 31, 1988**[1]	February 1, 1987	February 2, 1986	February 3, 1985[2]	January 29, 1984
Selected consolidated statement of earnings data:					
Net sales	**$1,453,657**	$1,011,462	$700,729	$432,779	$256,184
Gross profit	**403,739**	278,160	181,457	114,319	70,014
Earnings before income taxes	**95,586**	47,073	11,619	26,252	18,986
Net earnings	**$ 54,086**	$ 23,873	$ 8,219	$ 14,122	$ 10,261
Earnings per common and common equivalent share:[3]					
Net earnings	**$ 1.13**	$ .60	$ .22	$ .37	$ .28
Weighted average number of common and common equivalent shares	**47,994**	39,870	37,871	37,953	37,251
Selected consolidated balance sheet data:					
Working capital	**$ 110,621**	$ 91,076	$106,451	$100,110	$ 49,318
Total assets	**528,270**	394,741	380,193	249,364	105,230
Long-term debt	**52,298**	116,907	199,943	117,942	4,384
Stockholders' equity	**$ 320,559**	$ 163,042	$ 89,092	$ 80,214	$ 65,278

[1] The company's fiscal year ends on the Sunday closest to January 31 of the following year. For example, fiscal year 1987 begins February 2, 1987 and ends January 31, 1988.
[2] 53-week fiscal year; all others were 52-week fiscal years.
[3] All periods have been adjusted for the three-for-two stock split-up declared in August, 1987, and effected in the form of a dividend.

---

continued

**TABLE
15.2** | continued

The Home Depot
Consolidated Statements of Earnings

	Fiscal Year Ended		
Amounts in thousands except per share data	**January 31, 1988**	February 1, 1987	February 2, 1986
Net sales	**$1,453,657**	$1,011,462	$700,729
Cost of merchandise sold	**1,049,918**	733,302	519,272
Gross profit	**403,739**	278,160	181,457
Operating expenses:			
Selling and store operating expenses	**263,212**	189,290	134,354
Pre-opening expenses	**4,608**	3,198	7,521
General and administrative expenses	**37,678**	27,376	20,555
Total operating expenses	**305,498**	219,864	162,430
Operating income	**98,241**	58,296	19,027
Other income (expense):			
Net gain on disposition of property and equipment	–	–	1,317
Interest income	**761**	1,026	1,481
Interest expense	**(3,416)**	(12,249)	(10,206)
Earnings before income taxes	**95,586**	47,073	11,619
Income taxes	**41,500**	23,200	3,400
Net earnings	**$ 54,086**	$ 23,873	$ 8,219
Earnings per common and common equivalent share	**$ 1.13**	$ .60	$ .22
Weighted average number of common and common equivalent shares	**47,994**	39,870	37,871

continued

**TABLE
15.2** | continued

The Home Depot
Consolidated Balance Sheets
Dollar amounts in thousands

Assets	January 31, 1988	February 1, 1987
Current assets:		
Cash and cash equivalents	$ 25,595	$ 17,124
Accounts receivable, net	15,228	9,937
Merchandise inventories	211,421	167,115
Prepaid expenses	5,043	3,713
Total current assets	257,287	197,889
Property and equipment, at cost:		
Land	65,841	42,990
Buildings	85,842	48,190
Furniture, fixtures, and equipment	59,563	45,233
Leasehold improvements	43,520	34,670
Construction in progress	12,427	12,799
	267,193	183,882
Less accumulated depreciation and amortization	22,690	14,901
Net property and equipment	244,503	168,981
Cost in excess of the fair value of net assets acquired, net of accumulated amortization of $1,995 at January 31, 1988 and $1,363 at February 1, 1987	23,296	23,928
Other	3,184	3,943
	$528,270	$394,741

continued

TABLE
15.2	continued

Liabilities and stockholders' equity	**January 31, 1988**	February 1, 1987
Current liabilities:		
Accounts payable	**$ 93,859**	$ 67,800
Accrued salaries and related expenses	**22,021**	11,039
Other accrued expenses	**27,322**	21,985
Income taxes payable	**3,229**	5,751
Current installments of long-term debt	**235**	238
Total current liabilities	**146,666**	106,813
Long-term debt, excluding current installments	**52,298**	116,907
Other long-term liabilities	**762**	991
Deferred income taxes	**7,985**	6,988
Stockholders' equity:		
Common stock, par value $.05. Authorized: 100,000,000 shares; issued and outstanding—49,407,000 shares at January 31, 1988 and 42,571,000 shares at February 1, 1987	**2,470**	2,129
Paid-in capital	**203,755**	98,106
Retained earnings	**114,334**	62,807
Total stockholders' equity	**320,559**	163,042
Commitments and contingencies		
	$528,270	$394,741

continued

**TABLE
15.2** | continued

The Home Depot Quarterly Financial Data (Unaudited)

The following is a summary of the unaudited quarterly results of operations for fiscal years ended January 31, 1988 and February 1, 1987 (in thousands, except per share amounts):

	Net sales	Percent increase (decrease) in comparable store sales	Gross profit	Net earnings	Net earnings per common and common equivalent share
Fiscal year ended January 31, 1988:					
First quarter	$ 333,969	22%	$ 94,116	$12,807	$ .29
Second quarter	381,443	21%	104,063	15,579	.33
Third quarter	364,245	20%	96,228	9,737	.19
Fourth quarter	374,000	12%	109,332	15,963	.32
	$1,453,657	18%	$403,739	$54,086	$1.13
Fiscal year ended February 1, 1987:					
First quarter	$ 222,619	2%	$ 62,672	$ 5,138	$ .13
Second quarter	263,433	5%	71,749	7,130	.19
Third quarter	251,537	10%	67,631	3,921	.10
Fourth quarter	273,873	8%	76,108	7,684	.18
	$1,011,462	7%	$278,160	$23,873	$ .60

SOURCE: Reprinted by permission of The Home Depot, Inc.

TABLE 15.3	The Home Depot, Inc. Selected Financial Data*			
Fiscal Year	**1980**	**1981**	**1982**	**1983**
Sales (in millions of dollars)	22.3	51.5	117.7	256.2
Net profit (in millions of dollars)	0.5	1.2	5.3	10.3
Net profit margin	2.1%	2.4%	4.5%	4.0%
Return on net worth	28.1%	23.3%	28.9%	15.7%
Inventory turnover	7.8	4.6	6.7	4.4
Working capital (in millions of dollars)	1.4	5.5	12.9	49.3
Long-term debt (in millions of dollars)	1.0	3.7	0.2	4.4
Net worth (in millions of dollars)	1.6	5.2	18.4	65.3
Earnings per share	0.01	0.04	0.16	0.28
Dividends declared per share	Nil	Nil	Nil	Nil
Book value per share	0.05	0.17	0.54	1.75
Average price/earnings ratio	N.A.	37.4	27.5	57.0
P/E ratio relative to market P/E	N.A.	4.54	3.03	4.82

*These data have been obtained from the *Value Line Investment Survey.* N.A. = not available.

Bond Valuation

CASE
16

Janet Blakely
(Bond Characteristics)

Janet Blakely has been an active investor in the stock market for a number of years. Since she majored in English in college, Janet has depended heavily on her broker for investment advice. As a consequence, her portfolio has been limited to investments in common stocks.

Janet has lately been reading such financial publications as the *Wall Street Journal*, *Business Week*, and *Fortune* rather than the literature she usually enjoys. Recently, these journals published interesting articles dealing with the bond market and the rates of return that bonds have been providing. Janet's portfolio of common stocks has not provided a satisfactory return over the past few years, so she is contemplating switching some of her funds into bonds. Janet reasons that the expansion of her stock portfolio to include bonds may reduce the risk and improve the return on the total portfolio.

Janet mentioned her idea to her broker, who did not feel that the switch was advisable. With Janet's insistence, however, he did provide some information about three corporate bonds that he thought might be appropriate for her portfolio. (Table 16.1 includes the summaries of the indenture contracts that the broker obtained from Moody's *Industrial Manual*.)

Despite the meager information and discouraging words provided by her broker, Janet was determined to pursue her idea. She was beginning to realize the importance of a basic knowledge of different types of securities and decided to begin by analyzing the indenture information the broker had provided. She checked for the current quotation on each bond from the New York Stock exchange bond listings given in the *Wall Street Journal*. In examining this information, Janet discovered that the *Wall Street Journal* provides the current yield but not the yield-to-maturity. She knew that the current yield reflects only re-

turns from interest and does not include potential returns in the form of capital gains or losses. Since two of the bonds were selling below face value and one
was selling above, Janet decided to consider the yield-to-maturity for each
bond. She found all the relevant information for the bonds under consideration
in Standard and Poor's *Bond Guide* (Tables 16.2 and 16.3).

QUESTIONS

1. Briefly compare each of the bonds in terms of denomination, registration,
callability, convertibility, sinking fund, security, additional debt, rights on default, and indenture modification. Indicate whether each of these characteristics will have a favorable or unfavorable influence on the price of the bond.

2. Interpret the information given in the quote for the Gulf & Western bond
shown in Table 16.2

3. Explain why the yield-to-maturity of the Caterpillar Tractor bond in Table
16.3 is substantially below that of the other two bonds.

4. Using your answer to question 1 and other information given in Tables 16.1
through 16.3, explain the difference in yield-to-maturity between the American Can and Gulf & Western bonds.

**TABLE | Janet Blakely
16.1 | Bond Indenture Summaries**

Gulf + Western Inc. (Gulf & Western Industries, Inc.) subordinated debenture 6s, due 1988:

Rating–A3

Outstanding–Oct. 31, 1986, $12,098,000.

Dated–July 1, 1968. **Due**–July 1, 1988.

Interest–J&J1 at office of trustee to holders registered on J&D 15 prior to interest date.

Trustee–Chemical Bank, New York.

Denominations–Fully registered, $100 and authorized multiples thereof and $1,000 and authorized multiples thereof.

Callable–As a whole or in part on at least 30 days' notice at 100 plus accrued interest to redemption date. Also callable for sinking fund (which see) at par.

Sinking Fund–Annually, on each July 1, 1973–87, to retire debs., cash (or debs.) equal to 5% debs. outstg. on June 30, 1972, plus similar optional payments.

Security–Not secured; subordinated to all senior debt.

Dividend Restriction–Co. may not pay cash divs. on or acquire capital stock in excess of consolidated net income after Aug. 1, 1967 plus $7,500,000 plus net proceeds from sale of stock.

Rights on Default–Same as Subord. Deb. 6s, 1987

Indenture Modification–Same as Subord. Deb. 6s, 1987.

Listed–On New York Stock Exchange.

Purpose–Issued in 1968 for stock of Allis-Chalmers Manufacturing Co. and Brown Co. under terms of exchange.

American Can Co. debenture 6s, due 1997:

Rating–BBB

Auth.–$75,000,000; outstg., Dec. 31, 1986, $28,852,000.

Dated–July 15, 1967. **Due**–July 15, 1997.

Interest–J&J15 by mail to registered holders.

Trustee–REGISTRAR & PAYING AGENT– Bankers Trust Co., NYC.

Denomination–Fully registered. $1,000 and authorized multiples thereof. Debs. are transferable without charge.

Callable–As a whole or in part on at least 30 days' notice to each July 14, incl., as follows:

1987 101.25	1988 101.00	1989 100.80
1990 100.60	1991 100.40	1992 100.20
1997 100.00		

Also callable for sinking fund (which see) at par.

Sinking Fund–Annually, to retire debs. at par each Jan. 15, 1979–97, cash (or debs.) equal to $3,750,000 debs. outstg. plus similar non-cumulative optional payments.

Security–Not secured; see also deb. 7¾s, due 2001, below.

Other Provisions–See deb. 7¾s, due 2001, below.

Listed–On New York Stock Exchange.

Purpose–Proceeds for general purposes.

Offered–($75,000,000) at 100 (proceeds to Co., 99⅛) on July 6, 1967 thru Morgan Stanley & Co., and associates.

American Can Co. debenture 7¾s, due 2001:

Rating–BBB

Auth.–$75,000,000; outstg. Dec. 31, 1986, $33,562,000.

Dated–Mar. 15, 1971. **Due**–Mar. 15, 2001.

Interest–M&S15 at office of trustee to holders registered on 15th day prior to interest date.

Trustee–Morgan Guaranty Trust Co., NYC.

Denomination–Fully registered, $1,000 and authorized multiples thereof. Transferable without service charge.

Callable–As a whole or in part, on at least 30 days' notice, to each Mar. 14, incl., as follows:

1987 102.90	1988 102.61	1989 102.32
1990 102.03	1991 101.74	1992 101.45
1993 101.16	1994 100.87	1995 100.58
1996 100.29	2001 100.00	

Also callable for sinking fund (which see) at par.

continued

TABLE
16.1 continued

Sinking Fund–Annually, before each Mar. 15, 1982–91 to retire debs., cash (or debs.) equal to $2,500,000 and annually, before each Mar. 15, 1992–2000, to retire debs., cash (or debs.) equal to $5,000,000; plus similar non-cumulative optional payments.

Security–Not secured. Co. or restricted subsidiary may not create any mtge. upon principal property without securing debs. equally and ratably except for (a) mtges. on any property acquired after indenture date to secure payment of cost thereof incurred after indenture date; (b) mtges. existing at time of acquisition; (c) mtges. to secure debt of a restricted subsidiary to Co. or another restricted subsidiary; (d) mtges. in favor of governmental bodies; (e) mtges. for extension, renewal or replacement thereof; (f) certain statutory liens arising in ordinary course of business or liens arising out of governmental contracts; (g) certain pledges or deposits arising under applicable legislation; (h) certain liens and deposits in connection with legal proceedings, or (i) liens for certain taxes or assessments.

Not withstanding restrictions above, Co. or restricted subsidiary may create mtges. without equally and ratably securing debs. provided that at time of creation, aggregate amount of outstg. Co. debt secured by mtges. so created plus aggregate amount of outstg. debt issued by restricted subsidiaries which could not have been so issued except for certain provisions on subsidiary debt limitation plus the attributable debt in respect of sale and lease-back transactions existing at such time which could not have been entered into by Co. except for certain provisions, does not at such time exceed 5% of book net worth of Co. and consolidated subsidiaries.

Sale & Leaseback–Co. and restricted subsidiaries may not sell and lease back principal property unless net proceeds equal lesser of cost or fair value and (a) Co. would be entitled, without equally and ratably securing debs., (1) to create mtge. on such property pursuant to provisions outlined in clauses (a) thru (e) above or (ii) to create mtge. on such property securing debt in an amount equal to attributable debt in respect of such sale and leaseback provisions described

above, or (b) an amount equal to net proceeds received from sale of property is applied to retirement of long term Co. debt.

Indenture Modification–Indenture may be modified, except as provided, with consent of 66⅔% of debs. outstg.

Listed–On New York Stock Exchange.

Purpose–Proceeds for general purposes.

Offered–($75,000,000) at 99½ (proceeds to Co., 98⅝) on Mar. 10, 1971 thru Morgan Stanley & Co., Inc. and associates.

Caterpillar Tractor Co. convertible subordinated debenture 5½s, due 2000:

Rating–Baa1

Auth.–$200,000,000; outstg., Dec. 31, 1986, $101,000,000.

Dated–May 1, 1975. **Due**–June 30, 2000.

Interest–J30 & D31 to holders registered M&N 15, payable at office of trustee, or at Co.'s option, by mail.

Trustee–Chase Manhattan Bank (N.A.), NYC.

Denomination–Fully registered, $1,000 or any multiple thereof.

Callable–As a whole or in part at any time on at least 30 but not more than 60 days' notice to each June 29, as follows:

1988 102.200   1989 101.925   1990 101.650
1991 101.375   1992 101.100   1993 100.825
1994 100.550   1995 100.275
thereafter at 100.

Also callable for sinking fund (which see) at 100.

Sinking Fund–Annually, on June 30, 1986–99, cash (or debs.) to retire $7,150,000 principal amount of debs.; plus similar optional payments.

Security–Not secured; subordinated to all senior debt.

Convertible–Into com. at any time up to and including June 30, 2000 (unless previously redeemed, such right shall terminate on the 15th day prior to redemption date) at $50.50 per sh.

continued

TABLE	
16.1	continued

(adj. for 3-for-2 split in 1976). No adjustment for interest or divs. Cash paid in lieu of fractional shs. Conversion privilege protected against dilution.

Rights on Default–Trustee, or 25% of debs. outstg., may declare principal due and payable (60 day's grace for payment of interest).

Indenture Modification–Indenture may be modified, except as provided, with consent of 66⅔% of debs. outstg.

Listed–On New York Stock Exchange.

Purpose–Proceeds to repay a portion of Co.'s short-term debt incurred for construction and working capital requirements.

Offered–($200,000,000) at 100 (proceeds to Co., 98.875) on May 6, 1975 thru Lehman Brothers, Inc., and Merrill Lynch, Pierce, Fenner & Smith, Inc. and associates.

Other Long-Term Debt–Outstg., Dec. 31, 1985, $69,000,000 other debt.

SOURCE: *Moody's Industrial Manual,* vol. 1, 1986. Reprinted by permission.

TABLE	Janet Blakely
16.2	Quotations from Standard & Poor's *Bond Guide*

Bond	Current Yield	1986 High	1986 Low	Jan. 30, 1987 Close	Net Change
1. Acan 6s 97	7.26%	86⅜	84½	82⅝	+ ¾
2. CatTR 5½ 00	5.19	107	100	106	+ 7
3. GlfWn 6s 88	6.09	98½	98⅛	98½	+ ⅜

SOURCE: Reprinted by permission of Standard & Poor's *Bond Guide.*

TABLE	Janet Blakely
16.3	Yield-to-Maturity from Standard & Poor's *Bond Guide* February 1987

Bond	Yield-to-Maturity
1. Acan 6s 97	8.44%
2. CatTR 5½ 00	4.90
3. GlfWn 6s 88	7.13

SOURCE: Reprinted by permission of Standard & Poor's *Bond Guide.*

Williams & Associates
(Bond Quality Analysis)

Having recently earned his M.B.A., Chuck Moore has accepted a position with Williams & Associates (W&A) of New York City. W&A, established in 1905, is one of the oldest and most respected investment counseling firms in the United States. The firm serves as counsel for approximately six hundred individual and institutional accounts, ranging in size from $500,000 to over $20 million.

In addition to taking several finance electives in graduate school, Chuck has an undergraduate degree in finance. Since he has always been interested in the area of investments, his position with W&A fits him perfectly. His major job responsibilities include serving as a junior analyst on the Fixed-Income Security Advisory Committee and assisting in the management of a number of accounts primarily invested in fixed-income securities.

The Fixed-Income Security Advisory Committee consists of a number of the firm's senior analysts. This committee is responsible for developing the appropriate policies and strategies to be followed by the account executives in forming and revising the fixed-income portion of their clients' portfolios. Typically, the committee primarily assesses current economic activity and its impact on interest rates. Its recommendation to the account executives usually contains a general statement concerning the appropriateness of investing in bonds at the time of the recommendation. Thus, the information it supplies is primarily used by the account executives for "timing" decisions and deciding on the proportion of portfolio funds that should be invested in fixed-income securities.

Although Chuck has been with the firm for only a few months, his impression of the committee's operation has not been entirely favorable. After reviewing the past recommendations of the committee and talking with several of its members, Chuck has concluded that the scope of the information provided by the committee should be broadened. In particular, he thinks that more educational material should be made available to the account executives. They could then apply this information to their portfolio management strategies.

Chuck's graduate investments class had an important influence on his ideas about bond portfolio management. In the class it was pointed out that the prevailing view on bond portfolio management had changed dramatically over the past several years. Historically, most bonds were purchased with the idea that they would be held to maturity. Bond maturities were matched with the anticipated future need for funds; thus, it was rarely necessary to sell bonds before maturity. In recent years this "passive" strategy had been replaced by a more "active" strategy, primarily because of the very high interest rates that had prevailed during the early 1980s and the volatility of those rates. Both of these developments provided very attractive opportunities for bond investors to profit from a strategy of more active trading in the bond markets.

Chuck thinks that he should develop his ideas thoroughly before making a recommendation to the committee. He decides that a pilot study exploring the influence of bond quality ratings on their yields-to-maturity will be a good place to start.

To assist in his analysis, Chuck collects some information that he thinks will be helpful. In addition to reviewing the definition of each bond rating of Moody's Investors Service (Table 17.1), Chuck examines a graph of the historical yields-to-maturity for four bond indexes (Figure 17.1). Each index is composed of a sample of long-term corporate bonds in each rating category from Baa to Aaa. He also collects the monthly yields from January 1983 to November 1986 for rating categories Baa to Aaa and the yields-to-maturity on long-term U.S. Treasury securities (Table 17.2). Chuck examines the yields on long-term government bonds from 1945 to 1985 (Table 17.3), the troughs and peaks of business cycles from 1927 to the present (Table 17.4) and the yields-to-maturity by rating class for peaks and troughs of the business cycle (Table 17.5).

QUESTIONS

1. From Figure 17.1, what appears to be the relationship between bond ratings and yields-to-maturity? What type of risk do ratings measure?

2. Using Table 17.2, calculate the default risk premium for each rating category, as of November 1986. How are these risk premiums related to the ratings?

3. Is the yield-to-maturity on corporate bonds the return an investor expects to receive, even if the bond is held to maturity? Explain.

4. Is default risk diversifiable? Why, or why not?

5. Given the information in Tables 17.3 through 17.5, for the 1945–85 period, does it appear that default risk premiums vary with the business cycle? What are some factors that may explain this relationship?

6. Assume that the economy is beginning to slow down and that a recession will probably occur, with a resulting decline in interest rates. What bond strategy would you pursue in terms of the ratings of bonds? Explain.

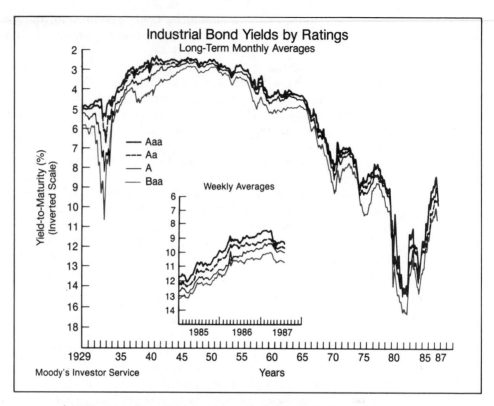

Williams & Associates: Corporate bond yields by ratings

Source: Moody's *Bond Record*, August 1987, p. 344. Reprinted by permission.

TABLE **17.1**	Williams & Associates Moody's Bond Ratings

Purpose: The system of rating securities was originated by John Moody in 1909.

The purpose of Moody's Ratings is to provide investors with a simple system of gradation by which the relative investment qualities of bonds may be noted.

Rating Symbols: Gradations of investment quality are indicated by rating symbols, each symbol representing a group in which the quality characteristics are broadly the same. There are nine symbols as shown below, from that used to designate least investment risk (i.e., highest investment quality) to that denoting greatest investment risk (i.e., lowest investment quality):

Aaa	Baa	Caa
Aa	Ba	Ca
A	B	C

continued

TABLE 17.1 | continued

The definition of each rating symbol is given in detail under "Key to Moody's Bond Ratings."

Absence of Rating: Where no rating has been assigned or where a rating has been suspended or withdrawn, it may be for reasons unrelated to the quality of the issue.

Should no rating be assigned, the reason may be one of the following:

1. An application for rating was not received or accepted.
2. The issue or issuer belongs to a group of securities or companies that are not rated as a matter of policy.
3. There is a lack of essential data pertaining to the issue or issuer.
4. The issue was privately placed, in which case the rating is not published in Moody's publications.

Suspension or withdrawal may occur if new and material circumstances arise, the effects of which preclude satisfactory analysis; if there is no longer available reasonable up-to-date data to permit a judgment to be formed; if a bond is called for redemption; or for other reasons.

Changes in Rating: The quality of most bonds is not fixed and steady over a period of time, but tends to undergo change. For this reason changes in ratings occur as to reflect these variations in the intrinsic position of individual bonds.

A change in rating may thus occur at any time in the case of an individual issue. Such rating change should serve notice that Moody's observes some alteration in the investment risks of the bond or that the previous rating did not fully reflect the quality of the bond as now seen. While because of their very nature, changes are to be expected more frequently among bonds of lower ratings than among bonds of higher ratings, nevertheless the user of bond ratings should keep close and constant check on all ratings—both high and low ratings—thereby to be able to note promptly any signs of change in investment status which may occur.

Limitations to Uses of Ratings: Bonds carrying the same rating are not claimed to be of absolutely equal quality. In a broad sense they are alike in position, but since there are a limited number of rating classes used in grading thousands of bonds, the symbols cannot reflect the fine shadings of risks which actually exist. Therefore, it should be evident to the user of ratings that two bonds identically rated are unlikely to be precisely the same in investment quality.

As ratings are designed exclusively for the purpose of grading bonds according to their investment qualities, they should not be used alone as a basis for investment operations. For example, they have no value in forecasting the direction of future trends of market price. Market price movements in bonds are influenced not only by the quality of individual issues but also by changes in money rates and general economic trends, as well as by the length of maturity, etc. During its life even the best quality bond may have wide price movements, while its high investment status remains unchanged.

The matter of market price has no bearing whatsoever on the determination of ratings which are not to be construed as recommendations with respect to "attractiveness." The attractiveness of a given bond may depend on its yield, its maturity date or other factors for which the investor may search, as well as on its investment quality, the only characteristic to which the rating refers.

continued

TABLE 17.1 | continued

Since ratings involve judgments about the future, on the one hand, and since they are used by investors as a means of protection, on the other, the effort is made when assigning ratings to look at "worst" potentialities in the "visible" future, rather than solely at the past record and the status of the present. Therefore, investors using the rating should not expect to find in them a reflection of statistical factors alone, since they are an appraisal of long-term risks including the recognition of many non-statistical factors.

Though ratings may be used by the banking authorities to classify bonds in their bank examination procedure, Moody's Ratings are not made with these bank regulations in view. Moody's Investors Service's own judgment as to desirability or non-desirability of a bond for bank investment purposes is not indicated by Moody's Ratings.

Moody's Ratings represent the mature opinion of Moody's Investors Service, Inc., as to the relative investment classification of bonds. As such, they should be used in conjunction with the description and statistics appearing in Moody's Manuals. Reference should be made to these statements for information regarding the issuer. Moody's Ratings are not commercial credit ratings. In no case is default or receivership to be inputed unless expressly so stated in the Manual.

Aaa

Bonds which are rated Aaa are judged to be of the best quality. They carry the smallest degree of investment risk and are generally referred to as "gilt edge." Interest payments are protected by a large or by an exceptionally stable margin and principal is secure. While the various protective elements are likely to change, such changes as can be visualized are most unlikely to impair the fundamentally strong position of such issues.

Aa

Bonds which are rated Aa are judged to be of high quality by all standards. Together with the Aaa group they comprise what are generally known as high grade bonds. They are rated lower than the best bonds because margins of protection may not be as large as in Aaa securities or fluctuation of protective elements may be of greater amplitude or there may be other elements present which make the long-term risks appear somewhat larger than in Aaa securities.

A

Bonds which are rated A possess many favorable investment attributes and are to be considered as upper medium grade obligations. Factors giving security to principal and interest are considered adequate but elements may be present which suggest a susceptibility to impairment sometime in the future.

Baa

Bonds which are rated Baa are considered as medium grade obligations, i.e., they are neither highly protected nor poorly secured. Interest payments and principal security appear adequate for the present but certain protective elements may be lacking or may be characteristically unreliable over any great length of time. Such bonds lack outstanding investment characteristics and in fact have speculative characteristics as well.

continued

TABLE 17.1 | continued

Ba

Bonds which are rated Ba are judged to have speculative elements; their future cannot be considered as well assured. Often the protection of interest and principal payments may be very moderate and thereby not well safeguarded during other good and bad times over the future. Uncertainty of position characterizes bonds in this class.

B

Bonds which are rated B generally lack characteristics of the desirable investment. Assurance of interest and principal payments or of maintenance of other terms of the contract over any long period of time may be small.

Caa

Bonds which are rated Caa are of poor standing. Such issues may be in default or there may be present elements of danger with respect to principal or interest.

Ca

Bonds which are rated Ca represent obligations which are speculative in a high degree. Such issues are often in default or have other marked shortcomings.

C

Bonds which are rated C are the lowest rated class of bonds and issues so rated can be regarded as having extremely poor prospects of ever attaining any real investment standing.

Note: Moody's applies numerical modifiers, 1, 2 and 3 in each generic rating classification from Aa through B in its corporate bond rating system. The modifier 1 indicates that the security ranks in the higher end of its generic rating category; the modifier 2 indicates a mid-range ranking; and the modifier 3 indicates that the issue ranks in the lower end of its generic rating category.

SOURCE: Moody's *Bond Record*, August, 1987. Reprinted by permission.

	TABLE	Williams & Associates
	17.2	Corporate & Long-Term U.S. Treasury Bonds Yield Averages by Rating Class (percent)

	Aaa	Aa	A	Baa	U.S. Treasury
1983					
Jan.	11.79	12.35	13.53	13.94	10.58
Feb.	12.01	12.58	13.52	13.95	10.88
Mar.	11.73	12.32	13.15	13.61	10.56
Apr.	11.51	12.06	12.86	13.29	10.42
May	11.46	11.95	12.68	13.09	10.41
June	11.74	12.15	12.88	13.37	10.90
July	12.15	12.39	12.99	13.39	11.33
Aug.	12.51	12.72	13.17	13.64	11.69
Sept.	12.37	12.62	13.11	13.55	11.51
Oct.	12.25	12.49	12.97	13.46	11.44
Nov.	12.41	12.61	13.09	13.61	11.59
Dec.	12.57	12.76	13.21	13.75	11.78
1984					
Jan.	12.20	12.71	13.13	13.65	11.61
Feb.	12.08	12.70	13.11	13.59	11.76
Mar.	12.57	13.22	13.54	13.99	12.28
Apr.	12.81	13.48	13.77	14.31	12.59
May	13.28	14.10	14.37	14.74	13.31
June	13.55	14.33	14.66	15.05	13.46
July	13.44	14.12	14.57	15.15	13.22
Aug.	12.87	13.47	14.13	14.63	12.60
Sept.	12.66	13.27	13.94	14.35	12.33
Oct.	12.63	13.11	13.61	13.94	11.96
Nov.	12.29	12.66	13.09	13.48	11.52
Dec.	12.13	12.50	12.92	13.40	11.40
1985					
Jan.	12.08	12.43	12.80	13.26	11.36
Feb.	12.13	12.49	12.80	13.23	11.46
Mar.	12.56	12.91	13.36	13.69	11.62
Apr.	12.23	12.69	13.14	13.51	11.46
May	11.72	12.30	12.70	13.15	11.00
June	10.94	11.46	11.98	12.40	10.31
July	10.97	11.42	11.92	12.43	10.48

continued

TABLE 17.2	continued				
	Aaa	**Aa**	**A**	**Baa**	**U.S. Treasury**
1985					
Aug.	11.05	11.47	12.00	12.50	10.54
Sept.	11.07	11.46	11.99	12.48	10.57
Oct.	11.02	11.45	11.94	12.36	10.44
Nov.	10.55	11.07	11.54	11.99	10.50
Dec.	10.16	10.63	11.19	11.58	9.43
1986					
Jan.	10.05	10.46	11.04	11.44	9.41
Feb.	9.67	10.13	10.67	11.11	8.94
Mar.	9.00	9.49	10.15	10.49	8.16
Apr.	8.79	9.21	9.83	10.19	7.58
May	9.09	9.43	9.94	10.29	8.05
June	9.13	9.49	9.96	10.34	8.29
July	8.88	9.28	9.76	10.16	7.89
Aug.	8.72	9.22	9.64	10.18	7.75
Sept.	8.89	9.36	9.73	10.20	7.99
Oct.	8.86	9.33	9.72	10.24	8.11
Nov.	8.68	9.20	9.51	10.07	7.85

SOURCE: Moody's *Bond Record*, August, 1987, p. 2. Reprinted by permission.

TABLE 17.3 | Williams & Associates
Yield-to-Maturity on Long-term Government Bonds[1]
1941–1985 (percent)

Year	Annual	Jan.	Feb.	Mar.	Apr.	May	June	July	Aug.	Sept.	Oct.	Nov.	Dec.
1941	2.05	2.12	2.22	2.12	2.07	2.04	2.01	1.98	2.01	2.02	1.98	2.34	2.47
1942	2.46	2.48	2.48	2.46	2.44	2.45	2.43	2.46	2.47	2.46	2.45	2.47	2.49
1943	2.47	2.46	2.46	2.46	2.46	2.46	2.45	2.49	2.46	2.48	2.48	2.48	2.49
1944	2.48	2.49	2.49	2.48	2.48	2.49	2.49	2.49	2.48	2.47	2.48	2.48	2.48
1945	2.37	2.44	2.38	2.40	2.39	2.39	2.35	2.34	2.36	2.37	2.35	2.33	2.33
1946	2.19	2.21	2.12	2.09	2.08	2.19	2.16	2.18	2.23	2.28	2.26	2.25	2.24
1947	2.25	2.21	2.21	2.19	2.19	2.19	2.22	2.25	2.24	2.24	2.27	2.36	2.39
1948	2.44	2.45	2.45	2.44	2.44	2.42	2.41	2.41	2.45	2.45	2.45	2.44	2.44
1949	2.31	2.42	2.39	2.38	2.38	2.38	2.38	2.27	2.24	2.22	2.22	2.20	2.19
1950	2.32	2.20	2.24	2.27	2.30	2.31	2.33	2.34	2.33	2.36	2.38	2.38	2.39
1951	2.57	2.39	2.40	2.47	2.56	2.63	2.65	2.63	2.57	2.56	2.61	2.66	2.70
1952	2.68	2.74	2.71	2.70	2.64	2.57	2.61	2.61	2.70	2.71	2.74	2.71	2.75
1953	2.94	2.80	2.83	2.89	2.97	3.12	3.13	3.04	3.05	3.01	2.87	2.86	2.79
1954	2.55	2.69	2.62	2.53	2.48	2.54	2.55	2.47	2.48	2.52	2.54	2.57	2.59
1955	2.84	2.68	2.77	2.78	2.82	2.81	2.82	2.91	2.95	2.92	2.87	2.89	2.91
1956	3.08	2.88	2.85	2.93	3.07	2.97	2.93	3.00	3.17	3.21	3.20	3.30	3.40
1957	3.47	3.34	3.22	3.26	3.32	3.40	3.58	3.60	3.63	3.66	3.73	3.57	3.30
1958	3.43	3.24	3.26	3.25	3.12	3.14	3.19	3.36	3.60	3.75	3.76	3.70	3.80
1959	4.07	3.90	3.92	3.92	4.01	4.08	4.09	4.11	4.10	4.26	4.11	4.12	4.27
1960	4.01	4.37	4.22	4.08	4.17	4.16	3.99	3.86	3.79	3.82	3.91	3.93	3.88
1961	3.90	3.89	3.81	3.78	3.80	3.73	3.88	3.90	4.00	4.02	3.98	3.98	4.06
1962	3.95	4.08	4.09	4.01	3.89	3.88	3.90	4.02	3.97	3.94	3.89	3.87	3.87
1963	4.00	3.88	3.92	3.93	3.97	3.97	4.00	4.01	3.99	4.04	4.07	4.10	4.14
1964	4.15	4.15	4.14	4.18	4.20	4.16	4.13	4.13	4.14	4.16	4.16	4.12	4.14
1965	4.21	4.14	4.16	4.15	4.15	4.14	4.14	4.15	4.19	4.25	4.28	4.34	4.43
1966	4.65	4.43	4.61	4.63	4.55	4.57	4.63	4.75	4.80	4.79	4.70	4.74	4.65
1967	4.85	4.40	4.47	4.45	4.51	4.76	4.86	4.86	4.95	4.98	5.18	5.43	5.36
1968	5.26	5.17	5.15	5.38	5.28	5.39	5.23	5.09	5.04	5.10	5.24	5.36	5.66
1969	6.12	5.74	5.86	6.05	5.86	5.85	6.06	6.07	6.02	6.32	6.27	6.51	6.81
1970	6.58	6.86	6.44	6.39	6.53	6.94	6.99	6.58	6.75	6.63	6.59	6.25	5.98
1971	5.70	5.93	5.85	5.73	5.77	6.00	5.88	5.80	5.68	5.47	5.36	5.40	5.53
1972	5.54	5.53	5.58	5.57	5.56	5.54	5.50	5.49	5.51	5.61	5.60	5.42	5.53
1973	6.21	5.80	5.99	6.11	6.02	5.18	6.24	6.45	6.76	6.32	6.16	6.24	6.25
1974	6.88	6.45	6.46	6.70	6.92	6.98	6.92	7.07	7.21	7.19	7.11	6.82	6.67
1975	6.96	6.58	6.61	6.65	6.99	6.94	6.85	6.93	7.13	7.29	7.28	7.20	7.16
1976	6.79	6.92	6.92	6.86	6.72	6.98	6.93	6.88	6.86	6.72	6.66	6.62	6.37
1977	7.53	7.35	7.53	7.57	7.50	7.57	7.43	7.45	7.50	7.45	7.60	7.60	7.77

continued

TABLE 17.3 continued

Year	Annual	Jan.	Feb.	Mar.	Apr.	May	June	July	Aug.	Sept.	Oct.	Nov.	Dec.
1978	8.40	8.02	8.10	8.10	8.22	8.37	8.45	8.61	8.38	8.37	8.60	8.68	8.84
1979	9.26	8.93	8.94	8.99	9.03	9.11	8.84	8.85	8.89	9.14	9.93	10.38	10.08
1980	11.23	10.54	12.01	12.26	11.22	10.15	9.74	10.20	10.94	11.34	11.63	12.30	12.35
1981	13.31	12.05	12.68	12.59	13.08	13.44	12.82	13.49	14.05	14.59	14.59	13.08	13.28
1982	12.61	14.16	14.07	14.37	13.24	13.05	13.75	13.40	12.84	11.86	10.84	10.46	10.60
1983	11.17	10.64	10.89	10.65	10.49	10.52	10.95	11.44	11.78	11.62	11.55	11.68	11.81
1984	12.36	11.65	11.81	12.28	12.58	13.32	13.43	13.24	12.68	12.34	12.00	11.55	11.51
1985	10.89	11.46	11.56	11.92	11.55	11.08	10.48	10.62	10.68	10.78	10.66	10.19	9.68

[1] Long term: Due or callable after 15 years.
SOURCE: Moody's *Municipal and Government Bond Manual*, vol. 1, 1986, p. a-7. Reprinted by permission.

TABLE 17.4 Williams & Associates
Business Cycles in the United States

Trough	Peak	Duration in Months (peak to peak)
1. November 1927	August 1929	34
2. March 1933	May 1937	93
3. June 1938	February 1945	93
4. October 1945	November 1948	45
5. October 1949	July 1953	56
6. May 1954	August 1957	49
7. April 1958	April 1960	32
8. February 1961	December 1969	116
9. November 1970	November 1973	47
10. March 1975	January 1980	61
11. July 1980	July 1981	18
12. November 1982	–	–

SOURCE: *Business Conditions Digest* (Washington, D.C.: U.S. Department of Commerce Bureau of Economic Analysis).

TABLE 17.5 | Williams & Associates
Yield-to-Maturity by Rating Class
for Peaks and Troughs of the Business Cycle (percent)

Date	Aaa	Aa	A	Baa
November 1927	4.49	4.65	4.94	5.35
August 1929	4.79	4.99	5.39	6.04
March 1933	4.68	5.61	6.64	8.91
May 1937	3.33	3.43	3.98	4.84
June 1938	3.26	3.68	4.41	6.25
February 1945	2.65	2.73	2.94	3.41
October 1945	2.62	2.70	2.84	3.20
November 1948	2.84	2.92	3.18	3.53
October 1949	2.61	2.70	2.94	3.36
July 1953	3.28	3.42	3.62	3.86
May 1954	2.88	3.03	3.15	3.47
August 1957	4.10	4.21	4.35	4.82
April 1958	3.60	3.78	4.01	4.67
April 1960	4.45	4.58	4.79	5.20
February 1961	4.27	4.40	4.63	5.07
December 1969	7.72	7.93	8.21	8.65
November 1970	8.05	8.42	8.74	9.38
November 1973	7.67	7.90	8.07	8.42
March 1975	8.67	8.92	9.37	10.48
January 1980	10.87	11.13	11.38	11.77
July 1980	10.52	10.72	11.15	11.67
July 1981	13.97	14.21	14.55	15.23
November 1982	10.70	11.12	11.85	13.60

SOURCE: Standard & Poor's *Bond Guide,* various issues. Reprinted by permission.

Gilda Sears
(Coupon and Maturity Effects)

Gilda Sears, a finance major, was enrolled in an introductory investments course. Her instructor had recently (and unexpectedly) announced that each student in the class would be responsible for a research project dealing with some aspect of the course.

Gilda had been annoyed when the project was initially assigned, but after some thought, she decided to make the best of a "bad deal." The class had just completed the section of the investments text dealing with corporate bonds, and Gilda was somewhat confused about bond price theorems. She was especially uncertain about the influence of coupon and maturity on bond price changes. Neither the text nor the instructor had provided any realistic numerical examples to illustrate the process.

After considerable thought, Gilda decided that a good project could be developed dealing with the bond price theorems. The two main theorems that she decided to illustrate dealt with coupon rate and term-to-maturity. Her sample, therefore, would have to include at least two bonds with the same rating and term but different coupon rates and at least two bonds with the same rating and coupon rate but different terms. Once the sample of bonds was identified, she would be able to calculate prices for each of the bonds based on different assumed interest-rate levels. The resulting price changes could then be associated with the differences in the terms or coupons.

Gilda spent a lot of time looking at the New York Stock Exchange bond quotations in the *Wall Street Journal* and the bond ratings in Standard & Poor's *Bond Guide* in an attempt to identify an appropriate sample. Although the *Wall Street Journal* typically reports approximately 1,500 bond quotations, Gilda had difficulty finding bonds with the desired characteristics because of the numerous combinations of rating, term, and coupon.

Her search for an appropriate sample finally resulted in the selection of four bonds. Gilda was concerned about the small sample but remembered the discussion in class about efficient capital markets. She thought that if the bond markets were efficient, bonds with similar characteristics would be priced so that there would be little difference in yields-to-maturity. Because of her ideas about bond market efficiency and the difficulty in finding appropriate bonds for the sample, she decided the sample was adequate.

In addition to Standard & Poor's *Bond Guide,* Gilda also consulted Moody's *Bond Record* to get the additional information she needed to illustrate bond price behavior. The exact dates for interest payments and the maturity dates were necessary in order to calculate the present value of future interest and principal receipts. Table 18.1 provides the information that Gilda collected for the bonds.

Gilda was aware of the dramatic increase in interest rates over the 1984–86 period. She thought that one way to illustrate the price behavior of the bonds would be to observe the actual yields-to-maturity at different points in time. By selecting November 1, 1984, 1985, and 1986, she was able to identify three periods with significant differences in yields-to-maturity. Gilda calculated the bond prices for those dates, net of accrued interest (see Table 18.2).

QUESTIONS

1. Using the prices given in Table 18.2, calculate the *percentage* price changes from November 1, 1984, to November 1, 1985; from November 1, 1985, to November 1, 1986; and from November 1, 1984, to November 1, 1986, for the Boston Edison and American Brands bonds. Explain the differences between the changes for the two bonds.

2. Using the prices given in Table 18.2, calculate the *percentage* price changes from November 1, 1984, to November 1, 1985; from November 1985, to November 1, 1986; and from November 1, 1984, to November 1, 1986, for the AT&T and Batimore Gas and Electric bonds. Explain the differences between the changes for the two bonds.

3. Assuming that you anticipate a significant decline in interest rates, which of the four bonds would provide the largest potential capital gain? Discuss.

TABLE | Gilda Sears
18.1 | Corporate Bond Sample

Bond	Coupon Rate	Interest Payment Date	Maturity Date	Standard & Poor's Rating	Yield-to-Maturity 11/1/84	11/1/85	11/1/86
1. Boston Edison	4¼%	June 1, Dec. 1	Sep. 15, 1992	A+	12.30%	10.78%	8.67%
2. AT&T	7	Feb. 15, Aug. 15	Feb. 15, 2001	AA	12.09	9.81	8.70
3. American Brands	5⅞	Jan. 1, July 1	July 1, 1992	A+	11.50	9.20	7.86
4. Baltimore Gas and Electric	7	June 15, Dec. 15	Dec. 15, 1998	AA	12.12	10.85	9.02

TABLE | Gilda Sears
18.2 | Calculated Prices Net of Accrued Interest

Bond	Prices for 11/1 1984	1985	1986
1. Boston Edison	$592.29	$679.79	$789.79
2. AT&T	626.67	699.17	847.92
3. American Brands	699.51	781.92	896.95
4. Baltimore Gas and Electric	631.25	707.50	826.25

CASE 19

First Coast Bank
(The Yield Curve)

Mike O'Neal graduated from college in June 1983 with a degree in finance and found a job with a major brokerage firm. Shortly after he was hired, Mike was sent to New York City to participate in a training program for new employees. The training program lasted for six months and had as its objective the preparation of new employees for a successful career as a retail broker with the firm.

After completing the training program in January 1984, Mike was assigned to a brokerage office in Orlando, Florida. He quickly began to develop a clientele by aggressively pursuing contacts and by calling on potential customers whose names were supplied by his firm. He established a reputation as a knowledgeable and hardworking broker and was quite successful.

Despite his success, Mike began to feel that the retail brokerage business did not offer the type of career that he wanted. His interest in investments had been primarily security analysis and portfolio management. His job as a broker, however, consisted entirely of dealing with clients and required very little analytical skill.

On several occasions, he had been very uncomfortable about accepting the analyses and recommendations supplied by the brokerage firm's research department. When this first occurred, he had discussed his feelings with the local office manager, who advised against taking a contrary opinion on any security that had been analyzed by the research department. Though he refrained from using his own opinions, Mike continued to follow the stock market in general and a number of stocks in particular. In several instances, he discovered that his analysis tended to be more accurate than that of the firm's research department. This reinforcement and his dissatisfaction with being a retail broker finally convinced Mike to look for a job as an analyst.

Since he and his family were quite happy living in Orlando, his job search was restricted to the central Florida region. He quickly discovered, however, that the number of positions as an analyst was extremely limited in the area; most of the large brokerage firms had their research staffs located in New York City and did little or no analysis locally. Essentially, the only available local positions were at some of the larger financial institutions, especially the banks, where analysts were primarily responsible for recommendations concerning the investment of bank funds.

Mike initially faced some resistance from the local banks in his attempt to make the transition from a retail broker to an "in-house" analyst. With his educational background and a strong recommendation from his office manager, however, he finally secured a position with the First National Bank of Oviedo in December 1986. The bank was relatively small, with less than $100 million in deposits, and was located in a community approximately twenty miles from Orlando. Oviedo, like much of central Florida, was growing very rapidly, and Mike was convinced that the bank would expand and provide him with a promising career.

Despite the small size of the First National Bank of Oviedo, the trust department was well known and had a good reputation. This reputation, combined with the presence of many retired people in the area, gave the bank over two hundred trust accounts, with assets in excess of $30 million to manage. The bank was conservative in its lending policies, for both individual and commercial loans. This conservatism resulted in a relatively low loan/deposit ratio, providing the bank with excess funds that were usually invested in short- and intermediate-term securities of the U.S. Treasury.

Mike was responsible for making investment recommendations to the head of the trust department for the trust accounts and to the president and chief executive officer for the bank's funds. He was the only analyst employed by the bank and consequently dealt with both equities and bonds.

After reviewing some of the bank's portfolios and a few trust portfolios, Mike realized that his job would require him to devote most of his time to analyzing fixed-income securities. His impression of the portfolios, however, was not entirely favorable. He noticed that both the trust portfolios and the bank's portfolios had little if any trading activity. The bank seemed to employ a "buy-and-hold" management strategy. Mike questioned whether this was an appropriate strategy, given the dramatic cycles in interest rates over the previous five years.

He decided, however, to be very cautious in recommending any dramatic changes in the bank's portfolio mangement strategy. He felt that his knowledge of fixed-income security prices was very limited and that he needed to do some research that would provide him with a basis for making such recommendations.

Since U.S. Treasury securities constituted such a large portion of the portfolios, Mike decided to gather some historical data on prices and yields-to-maturity for selected U.S. Treasury notes and bonds. Table 19.1 gives a sample of twenty-one Treasury securities with prices and yields-to-maturity in January and July, from 1982 through January 1987. To facilitate the analysis, Mike selected only the securities that matured in February of the year indicated. He planned to use the data to analyze the behavior of prices and yields over the period and to develop various portfolio strategies appropriate for the bank. This historical analysis could then be used to compare the current strategy to alternative strategies the bank might employ.

QUESTIONS

1. Use the data in Table 19.1 to plot separate "yield curves" for January 8, 1982; January 7, 1983; and January 6, 1984. For each of the three yield curves, plot the term-to-maturity on the horizontal axis and the yield-to-maturity on the vertical axis. Draw a curve through the points you plot. Comment on the three different shapes of the curves with regard to the factors that determine the relationship between term and yield.

2. Using the graphs that were constructed in Question 1, explain why some of the bonds do not plot close to the yield curves.

3. Calculate the holding period rates of return for the following portfolio strategies:

    a. *Strategy A: "Buy-and-hold"* Buy the 12 3/4s of 1987 on January 8, 1982, and hold this bond until January 9, 1987, at which time the bond is sold at the price that existed at that time. Calculate both the annual and semiannual return over the entire period. (Ignore commissions and accrued interest.)

    b. *Strategy B: "Rolling over" a long-term bond* Buy the 10 1/2s of 1995 on January 8, 1982, and hold until July 9, 1982. Buy the same bond on July 9, 1982, and hold until January 7, 1983, and continue to buy and sell the bond at six-month intervals until January 9, 1987. Calculate *each* of the 10 semiannual holding period returns that would result from this strategy, and calculate their average. (Ignore commissions and accrued interest, and assume that one semiannual interest payment is received at the end of each semiannual holding period.)

    c. *Strategy C: "Rolling over" with short-term notes* For each of the notes and time periods shown below, calculate the semiannual holding period returns and the average return. (Ignore commissions and accrued interest, and assume that one semiannual interest payment is received at the end of each semiannual holding period.)

Periods	Notes
1/8/82–7/9/82	8s of 1983
7/9/82–1/7/83	8s of 1983
1/7/83–7/1/83	7 1/4s of 1984
7/1/83–1/6/84	7 1/4s of 1984
1/6/84–6/29/84	8s of 1985
6/29/84–1/4/85	8s of 1985
1/4/85–7/2/85	13 1/2s of 1986
7/2/85–1/8/86	13 1/2s of 1986
1/8/86–6/3/86	12 3/4s of 1987
6/3/86–1/9/87	12 3/4s of 1987

4. Assume that $100,000 is available to invest on January 8, 1982. Using the semiannual holding period returns estimated above, calculate the terminal value of the $100,000 on January 9, 1987, for each of the three strategies. Do there appear to be significant differences in the terminal values?

5. Discuss any differences in the risks associated with the three strategies. Does there appear to be any relationship between risk levels and the holding period returns?

6. Briefly discuss the factors that determine whether an active strategy such as a "rollover" strategy will be successful and when it should be preferred to a "buy-and-hold" strategy. Do you think that Mike should attempt to change the strategy the bank is employing? Explain.

TABLE 19.1	First Coast Bank
	U.S. Treasury Securities

Bond		1/8/82		7/9/82		1/7/83		7/1/83	
Coupon[1]	Maturity Date[2]	Close[3]	Yield[4]	Close[3]	Yield[4]	Close[3]	Yield[4]	Close[3]	Yield[4]
1. $6\frac{3}{8}$	1982n	99−15	11.88	−	−	−	−	−	−
2. 8	1983n	94−24	13.32	97−10	13.35	100−10	7.43	−	−
3. $13\frac{7}{8}$	1983n	99−29	13.97	100−05	13.61	100−27	7.09	−	−
4. $7\frac{1}{4}$	1984n	85−21	14.03	91−18	13.30	98−18	8.66	98−24	9.40
5. 8	1985n	85−30	14.11	88−10	13.49	97−25	9.19	97−12	9.80
6. $13\frac{1}{2}$	1986n	97−17	14.32	98−18	14.11	109−12	9.92	106−29	10.41
7. 9	1987n	81−24	14.15	84−04	13.78	97−15	9.76	95−23	10.45
8. $12\frac{3}{4}$	1987n	94−16	14.28	95−23	14.05	106−18	10.14	106−00	10.70
9. $10\frac{1}{8}$	1988n	−	−	−	−	100−20	9.97	98−30	10.66
10. $11\frac{3}{8}$	1989n	−	−	−	−	−	−	−	−
11. 11	1990	−	−	−	−	−	−	−	−
12. $14\frac{5}{8}$	1992n	−	−	−	−	121−18	10.34	118−12	11.24
13. $6\frac{3}{4}$	1993	60−23	13.74	64−18	13.00	−	−	77−00	10.62
14. 9	1994	−	−	73−30	13.51	91−20	10.28	88−04	10.91
15. $10\frac{1}{2}$	1995	77−30	14.27	81−00	13.71	100−20	10.41	96−27	10.98
16. $11\frac{1}{4}$	1995p	−	−	−	−	−	−	−	−
17. $14\frac{1}{4}$	1996p	−	−	−	−	−	−	−	−
18. $11\frac{3}{4}$	2001	83−08	14.41	87−10	13.65	107−19	10.79	103−22	11.26
19. $14\frac{1}{4}$	2002	98−10	14.50	103−15	13.74	126−24	10.89	123−08	11.25
20. $7\frac{5}{8}$	2002-07	59−30	13.46	61−24	12.75	76−24	10.24	72−31	10.80
21. $11\frac{3}{4}$	2005-10	83−22	14.10	87−06	13.53	107−20	10.83	104−14	11.20

continued

TABLE 19.1 continued

	Bond	1/6/84		6/29/84		1/4/85		7/2/85	
Coupon[1]	Maturity Date[2]	Close[3]	Yield[4]	Close[3]	Yield[4]	Close[3]	Yield[4]	Close[3]	Yield[4]
1. 6⅜	1982n	–	–	–	–	–	–	–	–
2. 8	1983n	–	–	–	–	–	–	–	
3. 13⅞	1983n	–	–	–	–	–	–	–	–
4. 7¼	1984n	99–28	8.29	–	–	–	–	–	–
5. 8	1985n	98–07	9.75	98–20	11.32	100–20	7.16	–	–
6. 13½	1986n	105–05	10.69	100–25	12.95	104–06	9.42	103–19	7.49
7. 9	1987n	94–26	11.02	90–26	13.26	97–28	10.15	100–26	8.45
8. 12¾	1987n	104–12	11.05	98–29	13.26	104–22	10.22	106–08	8.55
9. 10⅛	1988n	96–07	11.30	90–17	13.52	98–28	10.56	102–12	9.09
10. 11⅜	1989n	99–22	11.45	92–13	13.64	100–31	11.07	105–17	9.53
11. 11	1990	–	–	–	–	99–07	11.19	104–11	9.81
12. 14⅝	1992n	114–11	11.82	103–25	13.81	114–10	11.67	120–22	10.25
13. 6¾	1993	74–21	11.28	66–25	13.35	76–28	11.16	84–11	9.70
14. 9	1994	84–16	11.65	74–31	13.77	85–22	11.59	93–09	10.19
15. 10½	1995	92–20	11.71	81–25	13.82	93–26	11.55	104–04	10.15
16. 11¼	1995p	–	–	–	–	–	–	105–28	10.27
17. 14¼	1996p	–	–	–	–	–	–	–	–
18. 11¾	2001	93–11	11.84	86–26	13.79	93–17	11.82	108–10	10.65
19. 14¼	2002	117–17	11.87	103–11	13.74	117–15	11.84	127–17	10.68
20. 7⅝	2002-07	68–21	11.53	58–19	13.53	69–17	11.52	76–07	10.41
21. 11¾	2005-10	99–24	11.78	86–05	13.71	99–26	11.77	113–00	10.53

continued

TABLE 19.1 | continued

Bond		1/8/86		6/3/86		1/9/87	
Coupon[1]	Maturity Date[2]	Close[3]	Yield[4]	Close[3]	Yield[4]	Close[3]	Yield[4]
1. 6⅜	1982n	–	–	–	–	–	–
2. 8	1983n	–	–	–	–	–	–
3. 13⅞	1983n	–	–	–	–	–	–
4. 7¼	1984n	–	–	–	–	–	–
5. 8	1985n	–	–	–	–	–	–
6. 13½	1986n	100–22	6.62	–	–	–	–
7. 9	1987n	101–10	7.74	101–20	6.23	110–11	4.97
8. 12¾	1987n	105–08	7.71	103–31	5.99	100–22	4.80
9. 10⅛	1988n	104–10	8.01	105–30	6.73	104–13	5.89
10. 11⅜	1989n	108–10	8.39	110–10	7.09	110–00	6.20
11. 11	1990	108–30	8.62	111–08	7.39	112–20	6.43
12. 14⅝	1992n	126–10	8.94	131–22	7.58	133–27	6.67
13. 6¾	1993	91–00	8.46	98–06	7.10	100–30	6.56
14. 9	1994	101–13	8.75	108–18	7.50	111–12	6.94
15. 10½	1995	108–30	9.09	119–10	7.58	121–04	7.03
16. 11¼	1995p	113–04	9.13	123–10	7.63	125–20	7.04
17. 14¼	1996p	–	–	109–30	7.41	112–00	7.06
18. 11¾	2001	118–00	9.48	134–00	7.81	137–04	7.45
19. 14¼	2002	138–17	9.52	156–10	7.93	159–22	7.55
20. 7⅝	2002-07	85–30	9.24	99–24	7.65	102–10	7.40
21. 11¾	2005-10	118–30	9.57	137–00	7.92	139–15	7.68

SOURCES of price and yield data: *Barron's,* selected issues.

[1] Interest on all securities in the table is paid semiannually on February 15 and August 15.

[2] All securities in the table mature on February 15 for the year indicated. The "n" following the year of maturity represents notes; "p" represents treasury note and non-U.S. citizen exempt from withholding taxes.

[3] Prices are quoted in terms of "points" and thirty-seconds of a point. For example, if the close is given as 85–30, the price is $859.375 (i.e., [85 + 30/32] × 10). The prices represent over-the-counter asked prices at the close of the week.

[4] The yield represents yield-to-maturity percentage.

Jonathan Edwards
(Bond Swaps)

In early August 1987, Jonathan Edwards had just returned from an intensive three-day training program sponsored by the brokerage house he had joined shortly after graduation from college. Although a number of sessions had been devoted to selling techniques, one session on bonds had been of particular interest to Jonathan. He had no funds available for investment, but his father had built a sizeable portfolio of bonds over the years. The senior Edwards owned a small retail business; though he was not wealthy, he had been fairly successful. Mr. Edwards had told his son on numerous occasions that since he was self-employed, it was his own responsibility to provide for supplemental retirement income. He had always thought that his Social Security benefits would be inadequate.

Jonathan had never discussed investments with his father but now thought it might be a good idea to assist him in managing the portfolio. He realized that his father was a conservative investor, and he considered this attitude was probably warranted. Mr. Edwards needed to allocate his savings to investments that had little chance of losing money. This dictated that his principal investment objective must be the preservation of capital, even at the expense of higher rates of return. His decision to devote most of his funds to high-quality bonds seemed consistent with this objective. Jonathan also knew that his father planned to retire within a few years. Because of these factors, he decided that it was appropriate to try to convince his father to consider other types of investments.

Jonathan decided that he would attempt to develop some recommendations for his father's bond portfolio. He knew that his father had always purchased high-quality long-term bonds, with the idea of holding them to maturity. Interest from the bonds was usually accumulated and used, along with additional funds, to acquire new bonds. Jonathan recalled from his training program that the dramatic change in interest rates and bond prices in recent years had provided an opportunity to profit from actively trading bonds rather than simply holding them to maturity. Many of these transactions, referred to as bond swaps, were feasible because of anticipated changes in yields or because of tax considerations. He decided to select a sample of bonds that could be used to illustrate the advantages of bond swaps to his father. Mr. Edwards was knowledgeable about cash flows and the time value of money, and would consider Jonathan's ideas and recommendations if they were logical and well presented.

The first example Jonathan analyzed involved a "substitution swap." This swap is designed to take advantage of temporary yield differentials between bonds having similar coupons, ratings, and maturities. After reviewing his father's portfolio and a current issue of the *Wall Street Journal*, Jonathan decided to analyze the possibility of swapping the ten bonds his father held in Duke Power Company for the same number of Commonwealth Edison bonds. Jonathan had discovered that the Commonwealth Edison bonds were currently selling 2 3/8 points ($23.75) below the Duke Power Company bonds. This suggested the possibility of a feasible substitution swap since the bonds had somewhat similar characteristics. (Details about both bonds are given in Table 20.1; Table 20.2 provides some data on the utilities that issued the bonds.)

The other two bonds that Jonathan identified for possible swaps were those issued by Philadelphia Electric and Consumer Power Company. His father currently owned five of the Philadelphia Electric bonds, which had a relatively low coupon of 7 3/4 percent. Since the Consumer Power Company bond had a coupon of 11 1/2 percent, Jonathan thought that it offered an opportunity for a "yield pick-up swap." This type of swap is designed to improve the cash flow and current yield of the bond portfolio. (See Tables 20.1 and 20.2).

Before Jonathan calculated the potential feasibility of the swaps, he realized that some additional information was needed. An important aspect of bond swap analysis is the tax effects of such a swap. He determined from his father that any additional income earned for the year would be taxed at 33 percent and that, according to the current tax code, the tax rate on long-term capital gains is the same as the rate on ordinary income.

Jonathan was also concerned about an appropriate reinvestment rate and the investment time horizon that should be used in the analysis. Realizing that the reinvestment rate should reflect the returns that could be earned on the cash flows over a specified investment time horizon, he decided to collect the yields-to-maturity given in Table 20.3 as an indication of recent yields on utilities and U.S. Treasury Bonds. Finally, Jonathan found that his father paid an average commission charge of $3.00 per bond.

QUESTIONS

1. Calculate the current yield and the yield-to-maturity on the Duke Power and Commonwealth Edison bonds, as of July 31, 1987. Estimate the holding period yields that would result from continuing to hold the Duke Power Company bonds and from swapping them for a similar number of Commonwealth Edison bonds. Assume that the reinvestment rate is 8 percent and that the time horizon is one year. Also, assume that both bonds will be selling to provide a yield-to-maturity of 8 percent at the end of the year.

2. Using the same assumptions given in Question 1, evaluate the "yield pick-up swap" of the Philadelphia Electric and Consumer Power Company bonds.

3. Do you think that the "substitution swap" and/or the "yield pick-up swap" are feasible from a risk-return standpoint? Discuss the risks that are involved in these types of transactions.

4. Do you think that Jonathan should recommend an "active" bond portfolio management strategy involving swaps? Discuss the pros and cons of such a strategy.

		Issuing Company		
TABLE 20.1 — Jonathan Edwards Bond Characteristics	Commonwealth Edison	Consumer Power Company	Duke Power Company	Philadelphia Electric
Moody's rating (August, 1987)	A	Baa	Aa	Baa
Standard & Poor's rating (August, 1987)	BBB+	BBB−	AA−	BBB−
Coupon	$ 81.25	$115.00	$ 81.25	$ 77.50
Maturity date	7/15/07	7/1/00	7/1/07	12/15/00
Closing price on July 31, 1987	$ 83	$102¾	$ 85⅜	$ 81¾
Interest dates	1/15 & 7/15	1/1 & 7/1	1/1 & 7/1	6/15 & 12/15
Current call price	$105.26	$105.75	$105.03	$103.50
1946–86:				
high	$101⅛	$118⅞	$ 96⅝	$107
low	$ 57½	$ 63	$ 51	$ 48
1986:				
high	$ 94⅛	$108⅜	$ 95⅜	$ 90½
low	$ 79	$ 94	$ 81	$ 74¾
1987 (Jan.–July):				
high	$ 94⅞	$106⅝	$ 98⅛	$ 92½
low	$ 88	$100⅛	$ 84	$ 81½
Amount outstanding (millions)	$180	$ 52.5	$119.5	$ 6.8
Cost for tax purposes	–	–	$ 90	$100
Date bonds acquired	–	–	3/78	1/78

SOURCES: Moody's *Bond Record*, August 1987; reprinted by permission; Standard & Poor's *Bond Guide*, August 1987; reprinted by permission.

TABLE 20.2 | Jonathan Edwards
Selected Financial Data for Years Ending 12/31

	Commonwealth Edison		Consumer Power Company	
	1985	1986	1985	1986
Operating revenues (000's)	$2,442,788	$2,720,922	$1,866,921	$2,003,374
Net income (000's)	$ 320,958	$ 296,678	$ 185,131	$ 203,787
EPS	$ 3.30	$ 2.51	$ 3.21	$ 3.24
Current assets (000's)	–	$ 621,200	$ 788,559	$ 749,147
Current liabilities (000's)	–	$1,027,000	$ 502,279	$ 912,453
Times interest earned	3.0	2.48	2.58	2.49
Sources of revenue:				
Residential	–	35%	–	30%
Commercial and industrial	–	55%	–	66%
Other	–	10%	–	4%
Source of energy for electrical output:[1]				
Coal	–	40%	–	69%
Nuclear	–	60%	–	24%
Oil	–	–	–	–
Natural gas	–	–	–	–
Hydro	–	–	–	3%
Geographic service areas	Northern and Central Illinois		Southern Michigan Peninsula (excluding Detroit)	

continued

TABLE 20.2 continued

	Duke Power Company		Philadelphia Electric	
	1985	1986	1985	1986
Operating revenues (000's)	$ 353,343	$ 386,056	$1,456,758	$1,578,505
Net income (000's)	$ 60,918	$ 69,530	$ 184,861	$ 194,471
EPS	$ .67	$ .71	$ 1.87	$ 1.86
Current assets (000's)	–	$ 283,700	$ 363,975	$ 439,569
Current liabilities (000's)	–	$ 334,600	$ 292,892	$ 483,575
Times interest earned	3.14	2.96	2.59	2.37
Sources of revenue:				
Residential	–	26%	–	39%
Commercial and industrial	–	59%	–	56%
Other	–	15%	–	5%
Source of energy for electrical output:[1]				
Coal	–	34%	–	25%
Nuclear	–	64%	–	56%
Oil	–	–	–	1%
Natural gas	–	–	–	–
Hydro	–	2%	–	6%
Geographic service areas	Central N. Carolina and Western S. Carolina		Philadelphia and surrounding area	

SOURCES: Moody's *Handbook of Common Stock*, Winter 1985–86, and *Public Utilities Manual*, 1987. Reprinted by permission.

[1] For Consumer Power Company, "pumped storage" accounts for 3 percent of electrical output. For Philadelphia Electric, "pumped storage" and "other sources" account for the remainder of the electrical output.

TABLE 20.3	Jonathan Edwards Yield-to-Maturity on Utility and U.S. Treasury Bonds (percent)						
	Public Utility Bonds				**U.S. Treasury Bonds**		
1985	Aaa	Aa	A	Baa	Long-term	Intermediate-term	Short-term
Jan.	12.47	12.68	12.99	13.36	11.36	11.31	10.18
Feb.	12.61	12.87	13.08	13.44	11.46	11.46	10.30
Mar.	13.08	13.50	13.87	14.19	11.62	11.86	10.78
Apr.	12.77	13.17	13.61	14.11	11.46	11.37	10.29
May	12.18	12.65	13.12	13.62	11.00	10.76	9.59
June	11.17	11.68	12.13	12.66	10.31	10.04	8.77
July	11.18	11.55	12.07	12.70	10.48	10.19	8.91
Aug.	11.23	11.65	12.13	12.73	10.54	10.22	8.98
Sep.	11.27	11.68	12.13	12.72	10.57	10.23	8.93
Oct.	11.23	11.61	12.01	12.52	10.44	10.10	8.93
Nov.	10.71	11.10	11.49	12.04	10.00	9.67	8.69
Dec.	10.24	10.57	10.97	11.48	9.43	9.08	8.24
1986							
Jan.	10.14	10.44	10.79	11.24	9.41	9.07	8.27
Feb.	9.65	9.98	10.26	10.74	8.94	8.69	8.03
Mar.	8.75	9.16	9.48	9.91	8.16	7.84	7.37
Apr.	8.45	8.87	9.14	9.63	7.58	7.35	6.93
May	9.07	9.38	9.59	10.02	8.05	7.84	7.43
June	9.02	9.36	9.62	10.03	8.29	8.04	7.55
July	8.66	9.05	9.37	9.69	7.89	7.52	7.03
Aug.	8.59	9.03	9.29	9.70	7.75	7.24	6.59
Sep.	8.91	9.28	9.52	9.96	7.99	7.35	6.58
Oct.	8.84	9.24	9.52	9.95	8.11	7.42	6.57
Nov.	8.59	9.01	9.28	9.69	7.85	7.22	6.43

SOURCE: Moody's *Bond Record*, January 1987. Reprinted by permission.

Other Investments

CASE 21

Nancy Garcia (Options)

In September 1987, Nancy Garcia held a portfolio of land and income properties worth over $250,000. Believing in the importance of spreading the risk over different assets, she decided to diversify her New Mexico real estate portfolio. Ms. Garcia, a college professor, was twenty-nine years old and had an annual income from all sources of approximately $45,000.

A number of Ms. Garcia's friends had advised her to include options in her portfolio. Since she had only a limited knowledge of options, Garcia asked Richard Elmswood, an account executive with a stock brokerage firm, to suggest a portfolio of approximately $100,000 involving options. Elmswood was a strong advocate of writing covered call options as a means of increasing income while reducing risk. He thought that the portfolio he designed for Garcia (see Table 21.1) provided diversification as well as a steady stream of option income. He considered Halliburton, Raytheon, Tandy, Bank America, and IBM growth stocks. Homestake Mining, a low beta stock, was included in the portfolio to reduce the risk.

To get a second point of view, Garcia asked J. F. Kusick, of the Kusick and Kusick investment firm, to develop a portfolio which included options. Mr. Kusick, stressing the highly speculative nature of an option strategy, suggested that Garcia invest only a portion of her $100,000 in options. In the portfolio that he developed (see Table 21.2), approximately one-third of the $100,000 was allocated for the purchase of call options which had striking prices fairly close to the current stock prices. The expiration dates of the options were staggered. Kusick recommended that the remaining two-thirds of the $100,000 be invested in six-month Treasury bills. Thus, the portfolio would provide a mix of one-third very high-risk options and two-thirds low-risk Treasury bills.

QUESTIONS

1. What are the main determinants of the price a buyer must pay for an option?

2. In Table 21.2, which of the options are "in-the-money," and which are "out-of-the-money"? How does being in-the-money or out-of-the-money relate to the minimum value for a call option? What is the maximum market price per share of a call option?

3. Compare the portfolios suggested by Elmswood and Kusick in terms of potential risks and returns.

TABLE 21.1 | Nancy Garcia
Suggested Option-Writing Portfolio as of 9/30/87

Stocks

No. of shares	Company	Price	Total investment after commissions	Dividend per share	Total yearly dividends
1,500	Bank America Corp.	$ 11⅛	$16,854	–	–
400	Halliburton	39⅛	15,807	$1.00	$ 400
400	Homestake Mining	45½	18,382	.20	80
100	IBM	150	15,150	4.40	440
200	Raytheon	83⅛	16,791	1.80	360
300	Tandy Corporation	51¼	15,832	.50	150
			$98,816		$1,430

Options

No. of options	Company	Striking price	Option price per share	Expiration month	Net proceeds after commissions
15	Bank America Corp.	$ 12½	$ ½	January	$ 668
4	Halliburton	40	¾	October	267
4	Homestake Mining	50	2¼	January	845
1	IBM	155	7¼	January	698
2	Raytheon	80	4⅞	November	932
3	Tandy Corporation	50	5⅜	January	1,566
					$4,976

TABLE	Nancy Garcia
21.2	Suggested Option-Buying Portfolio with Treasury Bills as of 9/30/87

Options

No. of options	Company	Striking price	Option price per share	Stock price	Expiration Month	Total cost after commissions
15	Delta Airlines	$ 55	$2¾	$ 52¼	January	$ 4,250
5	Dow Chemical	100	8½	105⅝	November	4,350
40	K Mart	45	4¼	48⅜	December	17,400
14	McDonalds	55	2¾	54	December	4,010
7	PepsiCo, Inc.	35	5⅜	39¾	November	3,878
8	Polaroid	30	4⅝	33⅛	January	3,820
5	Schlumberger	40	7½	46¾	November	3,850
7	Syntex	40	5⅜	43⅝	December	3,880
						$45,438

Treasury Bills

$68,000 par value, due May 12, 1988

Sold at a discount to yield 7.43% $ 66,880

Total Investment: $112,318

Stanford Investment Management Company (Convertible Bonds)

Specializing in personal and pension fund investment advisory services, the Palo Alto, California, firm of Stanford Investment Management has prospered since it was founded in 1972. Stanford's proprietors, Robert Kilpatrick and Ethel Grossman, seek to provide investment advice tailored to their clients' needs. The firm manages twenty-five accounts with assets totaling $60 million. In addition, Stanford publishes a monthly investment advisory letter which has approximately three hundred subscribers. Most of Stanford's clients tend to prefer investments with strong growth potential.

In April 1980, many of Stanford's clients were very concerned about unfavorable developments in the securities markets. During March, both stock and bond prices had declined substantially. These declines were due to a dramatic rise in interest rate levels and general investor nervousness. Given an environment of record-high interest rates (the prime rate was 20 percent in April 1980) and concern over an impending recession, many of Stanford's clients were seeking investments that could provide appreciation potential as well as preservation of existing capital. Kilpatrick and Grossman decided that convertible bonds might be appropriate for their clients.

Since a convertible bond is basically a combination of a common stock and a bond, it has many of the favorable characteristics of both investments. Because the convertible bond can be exchanged for the common share of the issuing company, the value of the convertible bond will normally increase when the stock rises in value. Thus, a convertible bond has the appreciation potential of the underlying stock into which it can be converted. This upside potential is normally greater than that of a nonconvertible (straight) bond.

Because it is a bond, a convertible bond also has a favorable risk-limiting feature—the bond will decline in value only until it reaches its value as a nonconvertible bond. This "price floor" offers more downside protection than the underlying common stock. Theoretically, a convertible bond's maximum decline in value is to its straight-bond value. Such price protection is not available with a common stock investment.

In analyzing a convertible bond investment, Stanford considered several factors. First, the price appreciation potential of the common stock was analyzed. Typically, Stanford preferred to recommend convertible bonds of those companies that appeared to have significant appreciation potential. Also, Stanford normally compared the common stock's dividend yield with the yield-to-maturity of the convertible bond. Stanford was more willing to buy a bond with a substantial conversion premium (20 percent, for example) if the bond's yield-to-maturity was much greater than the common stock's dividend yield. Stanford also considered other factors, such as the bond's straight value.

Several of Stanford's clients had mentioned the newly issued convertible subordinated debentures of Digital Equipment Corporation (DEC). In April 1980, the bonds were selling at par value of $1,000, carried an 8 7/8 percent coupon paid semiannually, matured in 25 years, and carried a conversion price of $72. DEC's common stock was selling for approximately $62 per share, and no cash dividend was paid on the common.

DEC was a computer manufacturer with a record of strong sales and earnings growth. For the fiscal year ending June 1979, DEC's sales rose to $1.8 billion, up 28.6 percent from the previous year's $1.4 billion. Earnings per share rose from $3.38 in fiscal 1978 to $4.10 in fiscal 1979, a gain of 21.3 percent. The company's strong growth continued in fiscal 1980. In the first six months of that year, sales increased to $1.041 billion, up 27.9 percent from sales of $813 million in the first six months of fiscal 1979. Earnings per share for the first six months of fiscal 1980 climbed to $2.23, up 36.8 percent from the $1.63 reported for the same period of 1979.

Stanford projected DEC's sales for all of fiscal 1980 to rise 25 percent from fiscal 1979 to $2.25 billion. Earnings per share for fiscal 1980 were projected at $5.00, up 22 percent from the previous fiscal year. Earnings were projected to rise at a slower rate than sales, mainly because of the diluting effect of the convertible bonds and the presence of heavy price competition in the computer mainframe market.

Kilpatrick computed DEC's beta, based upon 60 monthly returns; he found it to be 1.30, with an R^2 of the regression equation of .40. This level of systematic risk was judged to be compatible with the objectives of Stanford's clients.

QUESTIONS

1. Calculate the following for the DEC convertible bond:
   a. Conversion ratio
   b. Conversion premium
   c. Yield-to-maturity

2. Estimate the price floor on the DEC convertible bond if nonconvertible bonds of similar default risk and maturity are priced to provide a yield-to maturity of 16 percent.

3. Project a one-year holding period return for the convertible bond, assuming that DEC's common stock sells in one year for

    a. $100

    b. $50

4. Would you recommend the convertible bonds to Stanford's clients? Specifically, which of Stanford's cients do you think should consider investing in these bonds? Why?

Leanna Harris (Hedging in Convertible Bonds and Preferred Stocks)

Leanna Harris was a successful career woman; until recently, she had been actively involved in local and state politics. Over the years she had been appointed to a number of important positions at the state level. Unfortunately, the candidates she supported during the recent elections were not elected, and she had been asked to resign from her current position. While cleaning out her desk, she came across a 1971 article, "Riskless Reward? Skillful Traders May Reap One by Hedging in Convertible Bonds" (see Table 23.1).

She remembered reading the article and thinking that the approach suggested by the author made good sense. In fact, she had planned to wait a year and then to see how well she would have done by hedging in the convertible bonds suggested by the author. Because of her busy schedule, she had never been able to pursue the idea. Now that she had some free time, she decided to investigate the strategy.

In gathering the necessary price and dividend information as of March 27, 1972 (see Table 23.2), Leanna discovered that several of the companies had paid stock dividends over the period. However, the bond indenture agreements for those companies contained clauses indicating that the conversion privilege was protected against dilution. Further, two of the companies, Banister Continental and Crown Central Petroleum, had retired their bonds prior to March 27, 1972. She decided to eliminate these two bonds in calculating the average holding period returns. Although she realized that this might bias her results, a check of the March 27, 1972, prices for these stocks indicated that if these annualized holding period returns had been included, the results would not have been significantly different.

▌QUESTIONS

1. What is the logic underlying the convertible hedge strategy described in Table 23.1?

2. Why is it important for the investor to consider the convertible's premium over conversion value and current yield advantage before entering into a hedged position?

3. If Leanna had taken the author's recommendation and hedged the convertible bonds listed in the article (with the exception of the Banister Continental and Crown Central Petroleum), what would her average annual holding period return have been for the March 25, 1971–March 27, 1972, period? Use the stock and bond prices given in the article as the beginning prices, and assume the receipt of interest payments on the bonds for one year. Further, assume the purchase of one bond and the short sale of the equivalent number of common shares, rounded to the nearest whole share. Ignore commission costs and taxes.

4. What would Leanna's average holding period return over the March 25, 1971–March 27, 1972, period have been if she had taken only a long position in the convertible bonds or a short position in the common stocks? Would these investment alternatives have been more or less risky than hedging in the convertible bonds?

5. Identify one listed convertible bond that would currently be appropriate for a convertible hedge.

TABLE 23.1	Leanna Harris Riskless Reward? Skillful Traders May Reap One by Hedging in Convertible Bonds by Daniel Turov

Now that the bear market is over, many investors are wondering what to do with their spare cash. Although bonds are still offering high yields, they are no hedge against inflation. Many of the high-flying stocks are enjoying big gains, but they have done so before, only to plunge sharply. Various low-priced warrants are getting a play, but if the potentials are high, so are the risks. Some blue chips look cheap, but they have already risen impressively. In short, much of today's investment scene is characterized by either high risk or low potential.

However, there is a way an investor can obtain high income at little risk: by hedging in convertible bonds. In fact, he stands to make more money if prices fall.

Two Basics

The understanding of two basic factors is necessary to employ this technique. The first is that of convertible securities. A convertible bond is an interest-paying bond or debenture, convertible into common stock. For example, when a company's common stock is selling for about $10, it may issue a $1,000, 6% debenture, convertible into 100 shares of the common stock. Obviously, if the stock moves to $20, the bond will sell for $2,000. However, if the former sinks to $3, the latter will probably not sell down to $300, for at that price it is yielding a very high 20%. It may fall to say $500, where it returns 12%. But the fact that it has outperformed the common stock is little solace to the man who purchased it for $1,000. This is where the second idea becomes important: selling short, but doing so without the risks normally connected with this practice.

Selling short, of course, is borrowing somebody else's stock, selling it, and then buying it back some time later. Obviously, if the price falls after it is sold, there is a profit; if it rises, there is a loss—or exactly the opposite from what happens when a stock is bought. It is not necessary to actually arrange to borrow the security which you're shorting. Your broker will do it for you, generally at no cost.

Returning to the example of the aforementioned 6% convertible bond, for simplicity let's assume that the common stock paid no dividends and that when the bond sold for $1,000 the equity was selling at parity of $10. If an investor buys the bond for $1,000 and sells short 100 shares of common at $10, he is assured of a 6% yield. If the stock rises, the bond will rise at least as much; if the former falls, the latter will probably fall less. The investor not only obtained a 6% yield on the bond, but when the stock fell to $3 and the bond to $500, he also had a $700 profit on the short sale of the stock and a $500 loss on the bond, for a $200 net profit. This represents an additional 20% profit on the original investment of $1,000.

Owing to a quirk in federal margin regulations, only the long side of this transaction must be paid for. Section 220.3(d)(3) of Regulation T reads in part: ". . . [the] amount as the Board shall prescribe from time to time . . . as the margin required for short sales, except that such amount so prescribed . . . need not be included when there are held in the account securities exchangeable or convertible without restrictions other than the payment of money, into such securities sold short. . . ."

This means that you own a security, convertible into common stock within 90 days, the equity may be sold short without depositing any additional funds. Moreover, since there is no debit balance created on a short sale (which for technical reasons must be done in a margin account), there are no interest charges.

Here's an actual example: On September 25, 1970, it was possible to buy $5,000 face amount of Allied Artists Pictures Corp. 8.75% convertible debentures, each ex-

continued

**TABLE
23.1** | continued

changeable for 222.22 shares of common stock, for $1,280 per bond. The common stock (1,111 shares) could then be shorted for $6 each. This was a particularly attractive situation, for at these prices the convertible was actually selling 4% below its intrinsic worth or parity. On December 30 the hedge could have been dissolved, selling the bond at $950 for a loss of $1,650, covering the short position in the stock for 3⅝ for a profit of $2,637.25. After collecting $115.44 in interest and paying $334.47 in commissions and the like, the investor would have ended up with a net profit of $768.22. On a per-annum basis this profit is 44.5%.

Dual Advantages

Convertible hedging offers two advantages: the possibility of getting high income without worrying over fluctuating bond prices and the opportunities for capital gains caused by price fluctuations.

The obvious question is, What if the company goes bankrupt and stops paying interest entirely? If it is completely unsalvageable, the investor will dissolve the hedge, and if it was entered into at parity, will suffer no greater loss than his commission costs. However, if the company is still worth something, the debentures or preferred stock will probably sell above—and perhaps well above—parity since they have a prior claim on the assets in liquidation.

Best Opportunities

Lower-quality issues offer the best opportunities for hedging. There are several reasons; the most important is the share difference between the yield on the senior security and that of the common. The company, which most likely pays little or no dividends on its equity, will probably have to offer a substantial yield on its convertible bond or stock in order to attract this type of investor. Furthermore, such securities are most prone to wide price swings, which may enable the hedger to take his profit in a shorter time span. These volatile swings often lead to the placing of temporary excessive premiums on the preferred, which can be beneficial to the hedger if he takes advantage of them before other arbitrageurs do.

Normally, too, the investor would look for a convertible trading near or below par. A key reason is that the higher the price of the convertible, the lower will be its yield. Furthermore, if it is selling close enough to its investment value (i.e., where a bond of its quality would sell were it not convertible), this provides a deterrent to its falling in price even if the common does. This, of course, would tend to increase the premium placed in the senior security and lead to precisely the price divergence which the hedger seeks. Moreover, since a bond or preferred stock is often subject to call, the owner of such a security selling above this call price (which is usually close to par) would see the dissolution of its premium were it called. If, on the other hand, the security were selling below par, a call would be welcome to the owner. Finally, the hedger should seek the most liquid situations available, since many preferreds—including most traded over-the-counter—have wide spreads between the bid and offered quotations.

Despite the potential profits, there are several very important precautions to consider in hedging in convertibles. The most important one is the problem of simultaneous executions. By law, it is always necessary to sell a stock short on an uptick or zero uptick (i.e., at a price higher than the last different price). This may cause undesirable delays in getting an execution. It will also probably be necessary to buy the preferred in a market which does not have optimum liquidity.

continued

TABLE 23.1 | continued

In searching for available hedges, one often finds attractive situations which would be ill-advised to enter, owing to commission costs. For example, Walter Kidde preferred A, which often sells at parity, rarely rises far enough above it to both cover commissions and yield an adequate profit. The same is true of the Uris Buildings and Hilton Hotel hedges; in the latter two, it is necessary to create an artificial convertible by combining a warrant and a usable bond. Accordingly, unless one finds particularly attractive convertible preferred stock, it is generally better to choose attractive convertible bonds because of their very low commission costs.

Finally, a hedger should be very sure to ascertain the correct terms of the convertible in question. Two of the more reliable publications, for example, Standard & Poor's *Stock Guide* and the Kalb Voorhis *Convertible Fact Finder*, show different conversion terms for the preferred stock of Maremont Corp. and Western Union preferred A and B. In the accompanying table, the listed convertible bonds and convertible preferreds are currently selling at less than a 5% premium over conversion value and have a yield advantage over their equity of at least 5%. While they are not all currently hedging candidates, many may be in the weeks and months to come.

Listed Convertible Bonds

Company	Bond		Convertible into:		Market price:		Conv. Value of Bond	% Premium on Bond	Yield Adv.
			Shares	Price	Bond	Stock			
Alaska Airlines	6.88%	1987	94.25	$10.61	$ 65	$ 6.63	$ 62	4%	10.6%
Apco Oil	5.00%	1988	31.24	32.01	99	31.25	98	2%	5.0%
Banister Cont.	6.50%	1989	93.02	10.75	90	9.38	87	3%	7.2%
Cablecom Gen'l.	6.50%	1990	67.80	14.75	98	13.75	93	5%	6.6%
Crown Central Pet.	5.75%	1993	31.54	31.71	116	37.38	118	0%	5.0%
Fuqua Industries	7.63%	1995	76.92	13.00	125	16.00	123	2%	6.1%
Itel Corp.	7.00%	1995	54.05	18.50	93	16.50	89	5%	7.5%
Ozark Airlines	5.25%	1986	129.03	7.75	50	3.75	48	3%	10.5%
Sanitas Svcs.	9.00%	1990	125.00	8.00	117	9.00	113	4%	6.3%
Wilshire Oil	6.00%	1995	ª136.37	7.33	80	5.88	80	0%	7.5%

Listed Preferred Stock

Company and Series	Dividend	Cv. into # of shares	Market price		Cv. Value of Pref.	% Premium	Yield Adv.
			Pref.	Common			
APL Corp. pf. C	$1.06	0.80	$17.88	$21.50	$17.20	4%	5.9%
Bates Mfg. pf. A	1.00	1.25	18.75	14.25	17.81	0%	5.3%
Chris Craft pf. B	ᵇ1.40	2.11	16.00	8.25	17.40	0%	8.8%
Glen Alden pf. B	3.15	7.65	57.75	7.88	60.20	0%	5.5%
Glen Alden pf. N	3.00	7.00	54.00	7.88	55.09	0%	5.6%

ª Convertible after August 31, 1971.
ᵇ Dividends payable in cv. pr. stock of $1.40 value and 20 cents cash until March 1, 1973, thereafter $1.40 in cash.

| TABLE 23.2 | Leanna Harris
Price and Dividend Information as of 3/27/72 |

	Bond Price	Stock Price	Annual Cash Dividend/ Share ($)	Stock Dividend (%)	Payment Date
Alaska Airlines	$ 93	8.13	–	–	–
Apco Oil	82	20.13	–	4	12/27/71
Cablecom General	107	14.38	–	–	–
Fuqua Industries	198	24.88	–	2	6/29/71
				2	9/30/71
Itel	81	10.50	–	–	–
Ozark Air Lines	125	9.75	–	–	–
Sanitas Services	123	9.38	.12	–	–
Wilshire Oil	97	6.13	–	–	–

Amelia Investments Company (Precious Metals)

The investment advisory firm of Amelia Investments Company, headquartered in Amelia Island, Florida, offers investment advice to potential precious metal investors. Amelia's president, R. K. Jensen, believes that investors should consider a wide range of investment media and that a truly diverse portfolio should include precious metals like gold and silver in addition to other investments, such as stocks and bonds. He often cites the rather dismal performance record of stock and bond portfolios during the 1970s. Although some individual stocks and bonds had rates of return in excess of the inflation rate, the vast majority were unable to provide a return equivalent to the rate of inflation. In contrast, precious metals yielded very high returns, particularly during 1979.

In November 1987, Raj and Anita Patel visited Jensen's office to explore the idea of investing in precious metals. The Patels, both in their fifties, were from the Jacksonville area. Mr. Patel, retired, spent his time managing his large portfolio of stocks. Mrs. Patel was a successful real estate broker. Their combined income was approximately $100,000 per year, and their net worth was over $1 million. Their investment portfolio consisted of stocks, municipal bonds, and real estate holdings.

During their visit, Mr. Patel indicated that they wished to invest $120,000 in precious metals. He and Mrs. Patel understood the high risks and rewards of such an undertaking. They emphasized to Jensen that these funds were only a small portion of their net worth. Their other investments tended to be quality-oriented, low- to moderate-risk issues.

Jensen discussed the various types of precious metal investments that were available to the Patels. Gold could be purchased directly—in coin or bullion—or indirectly, through gold stocks, mutual funds, certificates, or futures contracts. Silver was available in coin or bullion, or in silver mining stocks and commodities futures. The Patels ruled out gold and silver futures because of the very high risk of these investments. They decided that they would like direct ownership of precious metals and shares of gold- or silver-mining stocks.

If the Patels purchased precious metals, they planned to take delivery. Jensen cautioned them to store the metals in a safe place; the storage area would have to be large, since a silver ingot is bulky and weighs approximately 83.3 pounds. The Patels could rent a large safe deposit box from their local bank for $80 per year.

Jensen thought that direct ownership of gold could best be accomplished by buying non-numismatic coins. (These are gold coins whose value is determined only by the price of gold. Numismatic coins, those prized by coin collectors, usually sell at a high premium over their gold value, making them less suitable as a precious metal investment.) Jensen considered the Canadian Maple Leaf, Austrian Corona, Mexican 50 Peso, and South African Krugerrand appropriate non-numismatic investments; another was the U.S. government gold medallions. However, he was somewhat hesitant about this investment because of the relatively cumbersome procedures used to buy the medallions. He recommended that the Patels include one hundred of the Canadian coins in their portfolio (see Table 24.1). Each of these coins contains one troy ounce of 99.9 percent pure gold.

Because of silver's large industrial demand, Jensen thought that a direct investment in silver should be a worthwhile long-term investment for the Patels. He suggested the purchase of five 1,000-ounce ingots. (Silver ingots, as well as silver and gold coins, are sold through stock brokers and precious metal dealers. Commissions on these items vary somewhat but are generally a function of the size of the order, with the commission percentage declining as the dollar amount of the purchase increases.)

Mr. Patel indicated that he wanted to buy only very speculative gold- or silver-mining stocks, since he already owned several good-quality, natural-resource-mining stocks in his equity portfolio. Jensen suggested 2,000 common shares of Echo Bay Mines, an over-the-counter issue. Echo Bay Mines owned the second largest gold mine in Canada, and had a 50 percent stake in the third largest gold mine in the United States. Jensen thought that these mines could be profitably operated as long as gold sold for over $300 per ounce. According to Jensen, the recent rise in gold and silver prices had dramatically improved Echo Bay's potential profit picture, which had been rather erratic to this point. He cautioned the Patels that investing in Echo Bay would be a very speculative undertaking with a great risk of loss.

█ QUESTIONS

1. Describe the form in which returns are received from direct investments in precious metals. What factors affect these potential returns? Have the risks associated with precious metals increased in the last few years? Why, or why not?

2. Comment on Mr. Jensen's philosophy that precious metals should be a part of most portfolios.

3. Comment on the pros and cons of Jensen's suggested portfolio. What modifications, if any, would you make to the portfolio?

TABLE 24.1	Amelia Investments Company Suggested Portfolio of Precious Metal Investments for the Patels as of 11/9/87

Investment	Price	Total Cost Including Commissions
100 Canadian Maple Leaf gold coins	$476.30/coin	$ 48,106
1,000-ounce silver ingots (5)	6.42/ounce	32,421
2,000 shares of Echo Bay Mines	19.50/share	39,585
		$120,112

Portfolio Management

Kelly Westbrook
(Personal Portfolio Management)

In early January 1988, Kelly Westbrook is looking forward to finishing her M.B.A. and starting a business career in the Atlanta area. Her salary will not be needed for current family expenses. Her husband, Claude, expects to receive a major raise this year, and municipal bonds, valued at $110,000, purchased after the sale of some land, are maturing shortly. Kelly wants to devise a plan for investing their surplus funds. In view of their changing financial situation and the present investment environment, she also wants to insure that their current investments fit their objectives.

Claude, who (like Kelly) is forty years old, is employed as director of site selection in the southeastern regional office of Valu-Mart, a worldwide retailing firm. During the nineteen years that Claude has worked for Valu-Mart, he has progressed from stock man to his present position, which pays $56,000 a year. Furthermore, this year he will receive a promotion that will result in an $11,200 annual raise.

The Westbrooks have two children. David, seventeen this past December, is a senior in high school; Richard, fourteen last June, is a freshman.

After David and Richard graduate from high school, they want to go to college, preferably a private one. Tuition, fees, room, board, books, supplies, personal expenses, and transportation for three academic quarters are estimated to cost $7,920 at a public university like Georgia State University for a student who is a state resident, lives in an apartment, and commutes by bus. Comparable expenses will be $14,150 at a private university like Emory University if the student lives on campus. Because of the boys' high-school achievements, the Westbrooks believe that some merit scholarships will be offered. If no aid is available, however, the Westbrooks plan to finance their children's college educations out of current income.

Claude is also partially responsible for the support of his seventy-eight-year-old mother. At present these expenses total about $1,680 a year and can be met out of current income. The Westbrooks have decided that to handle any emergency Claude's mother might have and to take care of their other responsibilities, they should maintain a reserve fund equal to one-half of their "bare-bones" annual expense budget.

The Westbrooks want to obtain returns from their investments large enough to offset inflation and increase their real (inflation-adjusted) value of their investments. Yet, the Westbrooks would not feel comfortable in taking a large amount of risk, an attitude they realize will limit their returns.

To help them devise and execute an appropriate investment strategy, the Westbrooks have consulted an investment counselor at the brokerage firm of Morgan, Lodge, Paine, Felton and Straus. In response to inquiries by the investment counselor, the Westbrooks have provided the following additional information about their financial circumstances and needs.

FINANCIAL STATEMENTS

The Westbrooks' income, taxes, expenses, and savings during 1987, and their balance sheet as of December 31, 1987, are shown in Tables 25.1 and 25.2.

Kelly is initially projecting income, taxes, expenses, and savings for this year on the basis of the following assumptions. She will start to work on April 1, at an annual salary of $25,200. Claude will receive an $11,200 raise, beginning July 1. Taxable investment income will be $1,540, and if the municipal bond principal is reinvested at 5%, nontaxable investment income will be $5,500. Thus, their income for the year will total $87,540. Accordingly, their Social Security, state income, and federal income taxes in 1988 will amount to $24,800. Their incremental U.S. and Georgia income tax rates will be 28 percent and 6 percent, respectively. Those expenses that were in last year's budget and are not fixed will rise, in line with inflation. In addition, on April 1, Kelly will begin to incur incremental expenses for transportation, lunches, and clothes of $125 per month; hiring a cleaning service will cost an extra $35 per week. As a result, the family expense budget this year will total $40,330, and $22,410 will be left for college expenses, savings, and investments.

PROPERTY SALE AND HOME OWNERSHIP

Ten years ago the Westbrooks bought an undeveloped lot in the northeast metropolitan area with the idea of building a house on it. As time passed, the Westbrooks changed their minds, and the area was rezoned for commercial development. Two years ago, a developer bought the Westbrooks' lot as part of a parcel of land for a shopping center. The Westbrooks invested the after-tax proceeds of $110,000 in Georgia municipal bonds paying 5 percent interest and maturing on January 15, 1988. The Westbrooks' house has a current market value of $77,000 and is subject to 7.5 percent mortgage with an unpaid balance of

$26,600. Their monthly payments—incuding princial, interest, taxes, and insurance—is $316. Although the Westbrooks could afford a more expensive home, they do not want to move in the near future. However, they are wondering if they should consider buying a second home for recreational purposes.

INSURANCE

Claude has $43,400 in a life insurance policy which will be fully paid up when he reaches the age of sixty-five. This policy has a current cash value of about $6,300 and permits him to borrow up to this amount from the life insurance company at an annual interest rate of 5 percent. Through Valu-Mart, Claude also has $106,000 in group term life insurance (which he can increase as his salary increases), $210,000 worth of business travel accident insurance (which his employer pays for), and comprehensive medical, long-term disability, and accident insurance.

SOCIAL SECURITY BENEFITS

If Claude should die, Kelly will receive a lump-sum payment of $255 for burial expenses; in addition, each surviving member of the family will receive monthly benefits of $604, based on Claude's earnings record and subject to a total maximum monthly family payment of $1,633. Each child will receive $604 monthly if he is in high school and under nineteen. Kelly will receive $604 monthly if she remains at home to care for two children who are under nineteen and in high school, and $425 monthly if she remains at home to care for one child who is under nineteen and in high school. These Social Security benefits are exempt from federal and state income taxes, and the monthly benefits (but not the lump-sum payment) usually increase as the cost of living rises. However, if Kelly, David, or Richard earns more than $5,400 per year, her or his benefit will be reduced $1 for each $2 of earnings in excess of $5,400.

OTHER INCOME FOR THE SURVIVING FAMILY

If Claude should die and Kelly works outside the home, she will earn about $25,200 per year and receive $7,040 in interest and dividends from the family's current investments. If she is taxed as a "head of household" and continues to live in her present home, she will pay $4,770 in federal income, Georgia income, and Social Security taxes. Any additional income from investing the proceeds from Claude's life insurance will be subject to incremental federal and state income tax rates of 15 percent and 6 percent respectively.

On the other hand, if Kelly should die, Claude will earn about $61,600 this year and receive $7,040 in interest and dividend income. If he is taxed as a head of household and continues to live in his present home, he will pay $18,600 annually in federal income, state income, and Social Security taxes. His incremental federal and state income tax rates will be 28 percent and 6 percent respectively.

RESERVES

The Westbrooks have $900 in a joint checking account at a commercial bank. In addition, they have $14,000 in a 6.3 percent ninety-day notice account and $5,600 in an 8 percent four-year savings certificate at a federally insured savings and loan association. If the Westbrooks withdraw funds from the ninety-day notice account without giving notice, interest for three days is forfeited. If the Westbrooks withdraw funds from the four-year certificate before it matures next December 31, interest for three months is forfeited. However, the Westbrooks can borrow up to 85 percent of the face value of the savings certificate, at 4 percent above the certificate's rate of interest.

INVESTMENTS

Over the years, Claude has purchased 125 shares of Value-Mart common stock through the employee purchase plan. Currenty, the stock sells for $28 per share and pays an annual cash dividend of $1.68. In addition, the company has given Claude an option to buy 200 shares, at $42 per share, at any time during the next three years. Finally, the Westbrooks have deposited $5,600 at the geriatric care center that manages the apartment in which Claude's mother lives. This obligatory deposit earns 3 percent interest and will be returned to the Westbrooks upon the death of Claude's mother.

RETIREMENT PLAN

The Westbrooks expect to receive pensions from three sources. First, Claude is fully vested in Valu-Mart's (noncontributing) pension plan. His annual pension will be about 50 percent of the average of the three largest yearly salaries he earns at Valu-Mart; thus, Claude's pension appears to be protected from inflation until he retires, but not afterward. Second, when Kelly becomes employed, she will probably have some type of retirement plan. Third, when retired, the Westbrooks will be eligible for Social Security benefits.

After analyzing these facts, the investment counselor recommends that Claude purchase $420,000 worth of term insurance and invest $110,000 in a 6 percent, six-year deferred annuity. The guaranteed rate on the annuity after the six years is 5 percent per annum, and 7 percent of the original principal may be withdrawn each year without a penalty. However, any amount withdrawn in excess of 7 percent is subject to a decreasing withdrawal penalty, ranging from 7 percent in the first year to 1 percent in the last year.

Kelly is wondering if this plan really meets their needs, and if not, what their investment strategy should be.

QUESTIONS

Solve the "Kelly Westbrook" case as of the beginning, and within the context, of the period described in "The 1988 Investment Environment" contained in the appendix of this case.

1. How large should the Westbrooks' emergency fund be, and how should it be invested?

2. How much life insurance do the Westbrooks need?

3. After providing for an emergency fund, how much principal do the Westbrooks currently have left for investment? What cash flows will they have available for investment from 1988 to 1995?

4. What are the Westbrooks' investment needs and constraints, and how intense are they? What are the Westbrooks' investment objectives?

5. How should the Westbrooks invest their present principal and future cash flows? Why?

Note: The U.S. government taxes the interest income from U.S. government issues, but not from municipal issues. The State of Georgia taxes the interest income from municipal securities issued by political subdivisions outside the state; however, Georgia does not tax interest income from U.S. government securities or Georgia municipal securities. Both the United States and Georgia tax capital gains from U.S. government notes and bonds and from municipal securities. The discount on a U.S. Treasury bill is considered to be interest income (rather than a capital gain).

TABLE 25.1	Kelly Westbrook Income and Expenditures	
Income during 1987		
Claude Westbrook's salary		$56,000
Taxable dividends and interest		1,470
Nontaxable interest		5,500
Total income		$62,970
Taxes, Expenses, and Savings during 1987		
Social security, Georgia income, and U.S. income taxes		$14,450
Food and clothing		8,400
Housing		3,800
Loan payments		1,900
Auto expenses		3,500
Utilities		2,600
Expenses for mother		1,680
Insurance		3,600
Savings and investments		12,040
Vacations and recreation		3,200
Gifts and contributions		2,100
Medical and dental expenses		1,100
Miscellaneous expenses		4,600
Total expenses		$62,970

TABLE 25.2	Kelly Westbrook Assets, Liabilities, and Net Worth as of December 31, 1987

Assets

Savings account and certificate	$ 19,600
Municipal bonds (maturing January 15, 1988)	110,000
Checking account	900
Investments	9,100
House	77,000
Home furnishings and personal effects	28,000
Two automobiles and a boat	11,200
Cash value of life insurance	6,300
Total assets	$262,100

Liabilities and Net Worth

Mortgage	$ 26,600
Automobile loan	3,100
Total liabilities	$ 29,700
Net worth	232,400
Total liabilities and net worth	$262,100

APPENDIX
KELLY WESTBROOK
THE 1988 INVESTMENT ENVIRONMENT

This appendix provides information about the 1988 investment environment. Table 25.1A presents selected current yields and price/earnings as of January 4, 1988. Table 25.2A presents the 1988 economic outlook, summarized from articles in the December 28, 1987, issue of *Business Week*. Tables 25.3A and 25.4A provide information about seven of the Vanguard Group of Mutual Funds.

TABLE 25.1A | The 1988 Investment Environment
Yields and Price/Earnings Ratios

**Yields on Certificates of Deposit
at a Representative Federally Insured Savings and Loan Association**

Maturity	Minimum Investment	Percentage Yield*
91 days	$500	6.30
182 days	500	6.80
12 months	500	7.50
18 months	500	7.80
24 months	500	8.00
36 months	500	8.30
48 months	500	8.45
60 months	500	8.55

*Penalty for early withdrawal. Regardless of the length of time the funds have remained on deposit, if a withdrawal is made from this account before maturity, the accountholder shall forfeit a penalty equal to: (1) one month's interest on the amount withdrawn, whether or not earned, if the original maturity of the account was greater than 31 days and less than 182 days; (2) three months' interest on the amount withdrawn, whether or not earned, if the original maturity of the account was greater than 181 days and less than or equal to 12 months; (3) six months' interest, whether or not earned, if the original maturity of the account was greater than 12 months and less than 48 months; or (4) nine months interest, whether or not earned, if the original maturity of the account was greater than or equal to 48 months. Penalty amounts shall be calculated using the nominal (simple) interest rate being paid on the account.

continued

TABLE 25.1A	continued

Standard & Poor's Bond Yield Averages (%)

Type	Jan. 4, 1988	1987 High	Low
Industrial			
AAA	9.48	10.74	8.37
AA	9.96	11.09	8.89
A	10.76	11.40	8.83
BBB	11.18	12.06	9.52
Utility			
AAA	N.A.	N.A.	N.A.
AA	9.89	10.96	8.59
A	10.13	11.27	8.89
BBB	10.53	11.78	9.13
U.S. Government			
Long-term	9.18	10.30	7.61
Intermediate-term	8.79	9.89	6.90
Short-term	7.67	8.90	6.26
Municipal	7.98	9.31	6.53

continued

TABLE 25.1A continued

Standard & Poor's Price Indices

Type	Jan. 4, 1988	1987 High	1987 Low
Preferred			
Yield (%)	9.23	9.20	7.50
Common			
500 Composite			
P/E Ratio	10.67	19.08	12.69
Yield (%)	3.73	3.86	2.64
20 Transportation			
P/E Ratio	10.15	19.05	11.65
Yield (%)	2.62	2.97	1.82
40 Utility			
P/E Ratio	8.84	11.33	8.38
Yield (%)	7.29	7.31	5.74
40 Financial			
P/E Ratio	5.99	N.M.	N.M.
Yield (%)	4.84	4.88	3.08
400 Industrial			
P/E Ratio	11.69	19.44	12.63
Yield (%)	3.20	3.33	2.22

N.A. = not available.
N.M. = not meaningful.

TABLE	The 1988 Investment Environment
25.2A	Economic Outlook

The consensus of fifty economists and econometric forecasting services is that the U.S. economy during 1988 will avoid a recession but show only sluggish growth. For the year, growth in real GNP (gross national product after adjustment for inflation) is expected to average 1.8%. In the first and second quarters, growth in GNP will be only 1.0 and 1.5%, as the effects of last October's stock market crash work their way through the economy. In the third and fourth quarters, growth in GNP is expected to pick up to 2.3%.

Interest rates are forecast to follow the path of the economy; that is, they will be flat or declining during early 1988 and then rise as growth rises. The unemployment rate will increase from 5.9% in the fourth quarter of 1987 to 6.2% in the fourth quarter of 1988. Inflation is expected to remain stable at 4.0%.

Underlying this consensus, however, is an unusually wide divergence of opinions. Ten of the fifty economists and econometric forecasting services predict real GNP for the year will grow from 3.0 to 5.5%; six others predict real GNP will decline by 0.1 to 3.5%. The quarterly forecasts are even more dispersed. The expected changes in real GNP range from +6.3% to −7.6% in the first quarter, +7.2% to −4.5% in the second, +6.5% to −4.0% in the third, and +7.2% to −2.0% in the fourth.

This wide divergence of forecasts stems importantly from disagreements over how much gains in exports can offset slowing consumer spending. Stimulated by a three-year decline in the dollar, foreign demand for exports is boosting industrial production. But exports account for only 11% of GNP, while consumer spending accounts for 67%. Moreover, as the economy enters its sixth year of expansion, consumers are already burdened by low savings, slowing income growth, and high debt. The key question, therefore, is how much the 1987 stock market crash will dampen consumer spending.

| **TABLE** | The 1988 Investment Environment |
| **25.3A** | Descriptions of Seven Vanguard Mutual Funds |

The Vanguard Group consists of over thirty mutual funds, most sold without a sales charge. There is no charge for exchanging shares of one fund for another. In addition, through the funds' jointly owned subsidiary, Vanguard Group, Inc., the funds obtain their executive management, accounting, legal services, shareholder account maintenance, and shareholder reporting and distribution services at cost.

The *Money Market Fund's* objective is to provide maximum current income consistent with the preservation of capital and liquidity. The fund's policy is to hold only short-term securities. The fund has three separate portfolios: "insured," "federal" (all U.S. Government securities), and "prime" (prime commercial paper, bankers' acceptances, and bank certificates of deposit). All or any portion of an account can be redeemed at any time by mail. Withdrawals of $500 or more can be made by writing checks, and withdrawals of $1,000 or more can be made by telegraph or telephone. The minimum initial investment is $3,000 per portfolio.

The *Bond Market Fund's* objective is to replicate the Salomon Brothers Broad Investment Grade Bond Index, a portfolio of over 4,000 government, corporate, and mortgage-backed bonds. The Salomon Index typically outperforms about 80% of managed bond funds. The minimum initial investment is $3,000.

The *Municipal Bond Fund's* objective is to provide the highest level of income exempt from federal income taxes, consistent with the conservation of capital. The fund's policy is to hold high-quality municipal bonds, with at least 95 percent in Moody's or Standard & Poor's three highest ratings. Separate portfolios in the fund include "money market," "short term," "limited term," "intermediate term," "long term," and "high yield." The minimum initial investment is $3,000 per portfolio.

The *Index Trust's* objective is to match the price and yield performance of the Standard & Poor's 500 Composite Stock Index. The fund's policy is to own all 500 stocks in proportion to their percentage weightings in the index. The minimum investment is $1,500 initially and $100 thereafter.

Windsor II's objective is to invest in undervalued companies with lower-than-market P/E ratios, high yields, and above-average growth prospects. Windsor II was started in 1985, to operate under the same general principles as the popular Windsor Fund when it closed to new purchases. Minimum investment is $1,500 initially and $100 afterwards.

The objective of the *World Fund's International Growth Portfolio* is to seek capital appreciation by investing in stocks outside the United States. Minimum investment is $1,500 initially and $100 thereafter.

TABLE	The 1988 Investment Environment
25.4A	Performance of Seven Vanguard Mutual Funds

Fund/Portfolio	Average Maturity	Jan. 4, 1988 Yield
Money Market		
"Insured"	25 days	6.14%
"Federal"	45 days	6.48
"Prime"	42 days	6.77
Municipal Bond		
"Money market"	64 days	4.58
"Short term"	427 days	5.10
"Limited term"	2.6 years	5.71
"Intermediate term"	8.7 years	6.43
"Long term"	21.1 years	7.18
"High yield"	21.2 years	7.29

% Change in Net Asset Value

Fund	Year 1987	Year 1986	5 years 1983–87	Beta[a]	Jan. 4, 1988 Yield
Bond Market	+1.0	N.A.	N.A.	N.A.	9.1%
Index Trust	+5.1	+16.9	106.3	1.00	2.8
Windsor Fund	+1.7	+19.9	137.9	0.77	7.8
Windsor II	−1.9	+21.3	N.A.	N.A.	5.7
World Fund-Intl Gr.	+14.6	+55.7	286.4	0.52	1.3

[a]Betas and percentage changes in net asset values were obtained from the December 15, 1987, and January 15, 1988, issues, respectively, of the *United Mutual Fund Selector*. Reprinted by permission of *United Mutual Fund Selector*, 212 Newbury St., Boston, MA 02116.

N.A. = not available

Trammell Jackson
(Personal Portfolio Analysis)

In early January 1988, after receiving a check for $84,400 in settlement of his father's estate, Trammell Jackson is considering how the check should be invested and whether his family's existing investments should be altered.

Trammell is presently employed as the regional sales manager of Plasform in Atlanta, Georgia. Plasform, a small division of Plastec Corporation, manufactures injection-molded stock and semicustom boxes such as typewriter cases and tool boxes. After working for five years with a small firm, Trammell switched three years ago to Plastec because of the growth opportunities available in this Fortune 200 corporation. In the eight years since his release from the Army, Trammell has progressed from salesman to district sales manager to his current position as regional sales manager. He is recognized as a manager with a bright future and expects to be promoted to national sales manager in two to three years. Trammell's medium-term career goal is to become vice president and general manager of Plasform, or a division of similar size, within six years.

Trammell and his wife, Ann, are both thirty-four years old and have two daughters. Ashley, nine last August, is in the fourth grade, and Courtney, six last June, is in the first grade.

One of Trammell and Ann's goals is a college education for their daughters. Tuition, fees, room, board, books, supplies, personal expenses, and transportation for an academic year are estimated currently to cost $14,150 at a private university like Emory if the student lives on campus. The cost will be $7,920 at a public university like Georgia State University if the student is a state resident, lives in an apartment, and commutes by bus. Trammell and Ann believe that a good state university will satisfy their goal. To help to insure its realization, they believe that they should save enough to pay 80 percent of their daughters' college expenses for four years and that to appreciate the value of a college education, their daughters should pay the rest.

Trammell has a B.B.A. in marketing and is finishing an M.B.A. in finance. He is currently taking an advanced course in security analysis and portfolio management, which has motivated him to reassess his personal investment situation. Several questions have come to mind. Although he presently has little need for investment income, he is wondering how he can insure a college education for his children and build financial security for his and his wife's later years. In addition, he is strongly motivated to seek higher investment returns and feels that he has the temperament for more speculative investments. But while he has started trading options and buying stocks on margin, a recent magazine article on the estimated future costs of a college education has given him some second thoughts about these speculative investments. Moreover, because the family's incremental federal and state income taxes this year will be 28 percent and 6 percent, respectively, he is wondering what part, if any, tax-exempt securities should play in their investment portfolio.

PERSONAL FINANCIAL STATEMENTS

The Jacksons' income and expenditures during 1987 are presented in Table 26.1; their assets, liabilities, and net worth as of December 31, 1987, in Table 26.2.

Not counting income to be earned by investing his inheritance, Trammell is initially projecting his family's income, taxes, expenses, and savings this year as follows: His salary will be $55,000; investment income, at least $1,830; and federal income, state income, and Social Security taxes, $14,650. Trammell estimates that those expenses that were in the budget last year and are not fixed will rise in line with inflation. Hence, family expenditures for food, clothing, housing, automobile expenses and loan payments, utilities, vacations and recreation, gifts and contributions, insurance, household improvements and furnishings, and medical and dental services will increase to $35,110. Consequently, $7,070 will be left for savings and investments.

INSURANCE

Trammell's life insurance program consists of the following:

Whole Life—$35,000. Trammell bought a $15,000 policy when he was twenty-one and recently added $20,000. Premiums total $56.00 per month. Trammell can borrow the cash value of the policies (currently $3,740) from the life insurance company at an annual interest rate of 6%.

Group Life—$160,000. This term life insurance is made available by Trammell's employer on a contributory basis. Trammell's portion of the premiums is $39.00 per month.

All-Risk Accident—$280,000. Available through his employer, this insurance costs $18.00 per month and insures against accidental death on a 24-hours-a-day basis.

Business Travel Accident—$150,000. Plastec provides this insurance at no cost to Trammell.

Long-term Disability and Medical—Available through Plastec, this insurance costs Trammell $27.00 per month.

SOCIAL SECURITY BENEFITS

If Trammell dies prematurely, Ann will receive a lump-sum payment of $255 for burial expenses. In addition, each surviving member of the family will receive monthly benefits of $537.50, based on Trammell's earnings record, subject to a maximum monthly family payment of $1,633. Each of the girls will receive $537.50 monthly if she is in high school and under nineteen. Ann will receive $537.50 monthly as long as she remains at home to care for a child under nineteen and in high school. These Social Security benefits are exempt from federal and state income taxes, and the monthly benefits (but not the lump-sum payment) usually increase as the cost of living rises. However, if Ann, Ashley, or Courtney earns more than $5,400 per year, her benefits will be reduced $1 for each $2 of earnings in excess of $5,400.

OTHER INCOME FOR THE SURVIVING FAMILY

Although Ann has worked as a homemaker for the past nine years, she previously worked as a practical nurse and has maintained her practical nurse's license. She could reasonably expect to find work at a hospital at about $6.00 per hour. If she works full-time, her fringe benefits will typically include a pension plan and group accident, disability, health, and life insurance. She will also receive $1,830 in interest and dividends from the family's current investments (not counting income from investing Trammell's inheritance). Thus, if she is taxed as the head of a household and continues to live in her present home, she will pay $1,420 in federal income, state income, and Social Security taxes on a gross annual income of $13,830; any additional income from investing the proceeds from Trammell's life insurance will be subject to incremental federal and state income taxes of 15 percent and 3 percent. However, if she works part-time, for $5,400 per year (the maximum earnings allowed before her Social Security benefits begin to be reduced), she will pay $399 in Social Security taxes but no federal or state income taxes on her gross annual income of $7,230.

On the other hand, if Ann dies prematurely, Trammell will earn about $55,000 this year. In addition, he will receive $1,830 in interest and dividend income from the family's current investments (excluding his inheritance). If he is taxed as head of a household and continues to live in his present home, he will pay $16,000 annually in federal income, state income, and Social Security taxes on a gross income of $56,830. His incremental federal and state income taxes will be 28% and 6%, respectively.

RETIREMENT PLAN

The plan provided by the company is noncontributory, with 100% vesting after five years of employment. The financial benefit at age sixty-five is based on a formula that includes the impact of Social Security benefits. Trammell has calculated that if he retires from Plastec after thirty years of service, his retirement income would approximate 60% of his annual salary at that time. Should he die soon after retirement, his wife's income from the plan is estimated at 30% of his final salary; but should Trammell die prior to age fifty-five, Ann will not receive a pension from the company. Trammell believes that if he stays with Plastec, he and his wife will not face any financial problems in their old age. Of some concern, however, are the probability of his changing jobs prior to retirement and the effect such a career change might have on pension benefits if he does not become vested in a plan.

HOME OWNERSHIP

Trammell and Ann own a three-year-old home having a current market value of about $93,400, subject to a 9% mortgage with an unpaid balance of $67,200. Principal, interest, taxes, and homeowners' insurance cost $630 per month.

LIQUID RESERVES

The Jacksons' goal is to maintain an emergency fund equal to one-half of Trammell's annual after-tax income. Currently they have $18,620 in a 6.5% ninety-day notice account at a federally insured savings and loan association. If they withdraw funds from the account without giving notice, they forfeit three days' interest.

SAVINGS AND INVESTMENT PLAN

Last year Plastec introduced a savings and investment plan that offers an attractive means of building financial security and sheltering savings from taxes. The plan allows an employee to make "basic contributions" of up to 6% of the employee's salary and "supplemental contributions" of up to an additional 6%. An employee can select a fixed-income fund, an equity fund, Plastec stock, or proportions thereof as the investment vehicle. The company contributes $1 of its common stock for each $2 of an employee's basic contribution, but the company makes no contribution to match an employee's supplemental contribution. Employee contributions are always fully vested, and company contributions are vested two years after they are made. The plan allows employees to suspend or change contribution rates and to withdraw vested contributions with no penalty other than suspension of participation for three months.

Trammell has chosen to contribute 6% of his salary, $3,300 per year, to the fixed-income fund because it guarantees to pay at least 10% interest annually over the next five years. He has not chosen to make any supplemental contributions; however, he has been pondering this decision in light of the plan's flexibility, interest rate, and tax-sheltering provisions. Specifically, Trammell is considering diverting the amount he currently invests in a mutual fund and Plastec common stock to the savings and investment plan.

Though Trammell is not entitled to income tax deductions for his own contributions, he is not taxed on Plastec's contributions or on the income and gains earned on his and Plastec's contributions, as long as they remain in the plan. If he makes a withdrawal while he is still working for Plastec, it is not taxable until it exceeds his own contributions; then the portion that exceeds the amount of his contributions, reduced by the sum of any prior withdrawals, is taxable as ordinary income. If when he retires Trammell makes a lump-sum withdrawal that exceeds the amount of his contributions not previously withdrawn, the withdrawal will be taxable; however, it will be taxable at the favorable rates applicable to lump-sum distributions from pension and profit-sharing plans. Moreover, if the lump-sum distribution includes Plastec common shares, any unrealized appreciation in their value over their cost to the plan will not be included in the amount then taxable to Trammell. Such unrealized capital gains will be taxable to Trammell as long-term capital gains if he later sells the shares, but will not result in income tax liability for Trammell if he retains the shares until his death.

MUTUAL FUND

Trammell has been purchasing shares in a mutual fund on a "dollar-cost-averaging" basis for the last eight years. His monthly investment is currently $90.00, and the fund retains all dividends and capital gains for reinvestment. This no-load fund's objective is long-term growth in capital and income. Trammell originally expected this investment to be a primary contributor to his daughters' college education costs, but now he has doubts since this mutual fund has not performed as well as the Standard & Poor's Composite Index during the past five years. At the close of last year, this investment had a market value of $7,450 and a current yield of 3 percent.

PLASTEC COMMON STOCK

Since joining Plastec, Trammell has been purchasing common stock through the company's employee stock purchase plan by having $50.00 per month deducted from his salary. All transaction costs are borne by the company, and all dividends are automatically reinvested. The current dividend yield is 7.1 percent, and including a one-time $1,570 purchase of shares two years ago, the market value of Trammell's investment on December 31 was $4,310.

OPTION TRADING AND MARGINING

Early last year Trammell decided to take a more aggressive posture with regard to investing. Reasoning that his financial situation and personal temperament could withstand the probability of realizing losses, Trammell decided to seek higher returns through margin trading and the buying and writing of call options. After establishing a margin account with $6,540 early last year, he has made short-term trades of common stocks on margin and has traded several options in the more volatile stocks. Last year he recorded capital gains of $2,060, a 31% return on his investment. At the close of last year, the market value of his portfolio was $13,820, with a margin balance of $5,950. This year, however, his losses on various options have already reduced his equity back to his initial investment of $6,540. Although Trammell has no immediate need for these funds, he is wondering if his investment posture should be more conservative.

PROPRIETORSHIP TYPES OF INVESTMENTS

Although Trammell currently has no proprietorship-type investments, he thinks that there may be attractive opportunities in this area. He has given some thought to real estate; however, because he is fully occupied with his own managerial responsibilities, he doubts that he has the necessary time and ability for selection and supervision of an income property.

ESTATE PLANNING

Other than having prepared a will, Trammell has conducted no other estate planning. He will not be the recipient of any other inheritances, and after reviewing the recent changes in the estate tax laws, he has concluded that his present financial situation does not warrant any in-depth estate planning.

Having analyzed his current situation, Trammell is now pondering what actions he should take.

QUESTIONS

Solve the Trammell Jackson case as of the beginning, and within the context of the period described in "The 1988 Investment Environment," included in the appendix to Case 25, "Kelly Westbrook."

1. How large should the Jacksons' emergency fund be, and how should it be invested?

2. How much life insurance do the Jacksons need?

3. After including the inheritance and providing for an emergency fund, how much principal do the Jacksons have left for investment? What cash flows will they have available for investment in the future?

4. What are the Jacksons' investment objectives? What are the Jacksons' investment needs and constraints, and how intense are they? (Note that the Jacksons' risk aversion relative to the college fund may differ from their risk aversion relative to other investments.)

5. How should the Jacksons invest their current principal and future cash flows?

TABLE	Trammell Jackson
26.1	Income and Expenditures

Income during 1987

Trammell Jackson's salary	$48,540
Capital gains	2,060
Dividends	530
Interest on savings	1,210
	$52,340

Expenditures during 1987

Social Security, Georgia income, and U.S. income taxes	$12,510
Food and clothing	7,840
Housing (principal, interest, real estate taxes, and insurance)	7,560
Loan payments (automobile)	3,360
Plastec savings and investment contributions, Plastec common stock purchases, mutual fund share purchases, and miscellaneous savings	5,950
Automobile expenses (e.g., insurance and repairs)	3,180
Utilities	2,800
Vacations and recreation	2,800
Gifts and contributions	2,240
Insurance (life, medical, and disability)	1,680
Household improvements and furnishings	1,120
Medical and dental expenses	920
Interest on margin account	380
Total expenditures	$52,340

TABLE 26.2	Trammell Jackson Assets, Liabilities, and Net Worth as of December 31, 1987

Assets

House	$ 93,400
Savings in savings and loan association	18,620
Home furnishings and personal effects	46,340
Brokerage account	13,820
Mutual fund shares	7,450
Two automobiles	6,300
Plastec common stock	4,310
Cash value of life insurance	3,740
Plastec savings and investment plan	1,500
Checking account	740
Total assets	$196,220

Liabilities and Net Worth

Mortgage	$ 67,200
Loan—margin account	5,950
Loan—automobile	2,800
Total liabilities	$ 75,950
Net worth	120,270
Total liabilities and net worth	$196,220

CASE

27

Robert Brown
(Beta Estimation and Components
of Risk)

Robert Brown, recently hired by a large regional brokerage house as a stock-broker, was participating, along with several other new brokers, in a company-instituted training program. The instructors were officers of the brokerage house and professors from a nearby university. The objectives of the training program were to familiarize the participants with the procedures of the brokerage house, develop selling skills, prepare for the New York Stock Exchange Registration Examination, and provide an introduction to investment analysis and management.

Before joining the brokerage house, Brown had been a successful salesman for a manufacturer of industrial chemicals. Despite his fascination with the stock market, Brown had had no formal training in investments. A psychology major in college, he had taken no business courses. Because of this lack of background, Brown was particularly interested in the investment training sessions.

At the first meeting dealing with investment analysis and management, the professor had indicated that his objective was to provide a basic background in traditional investments and risk-return concepts. He felt that many stock-brokers concentrated on selling individual securities and had no concern for the composition of the client's portfolio. Accordingly, his first lecture dealt with the importance of diversification.

Brown had been able to follow the general points of the lecture, but he thought that he had missed many of the details. The professor had used terms that were unfamiliar to him, such as *beta*, *systematic* and *unsystematic risk*, and *coefficient of determination*. At the end of the lecture, Brown asked the professor if he would provide him with some additional material, so that he could get a better feel for the terminology. The professor responded that he would provide Robert with additional reading material and a short exercise that would help familiarize him with the risk-return concepts.

Later that week, the professor gave Brown some selected readings from the *Financial Analysts Journal* dealing with portfolio management and capital market theory. He also gave him ten years of quarterly holding period returns for the common stock of Martin Marietta and the Standard & Poor's Composite Index of 500 stocks (see Table 27.1). He requested that Brown calculate the *characteristic line* for Martin Marietta's common stock, using the following regression model:

$$R_{st} = a_s + b_s R_{mt} + e_{st} \text{ for } t = 1, 2, \ldots, 40 \text{ quarters}$$

where R_{st} = quarterly holding period return for Martin Marietta stock in quarter t;

$\quad R_{mt}$ = quarterly holding period return for the Standard & Poor's Composite Index of 500 stocks in quarter t;

$\quad a_s$ = intercept of the regression;

$\quad b_s$ = slope coefficient of the regression = $\text{Cov}_{sm} / \sigma_m^2$;

$\quad e_{st}$ = random error term which occurs in quarter t.

The professor suggested that the data-processing staff at the brokerage house might be willing to let Brown use one of their statistical packages to estimate the characteristic line.

QUESTIONS

1. Using the information in Table 27.1, calculate and interpret the characteristic line for Martin Marietta's common stock.

2. Is the common stock of Martin Marietta an aggressive or defensive stock? Why?

3. Partition the total risk of Martin Marietta's common stock into its systematic and unsystematic components.

4. Calculate the systematic and unsystematic risk components as a percentage of total risk. Describe the relationship of these percentages to the coefficient of determination.

TABLE 27.1	Robert Brown Quarterly Holding Period Returns (HPRs)

Year	Quarter	Martin Marietta HPR (%)	S&P 500 HPR (%)
1977	1	−6.893	−7.438
	2	17.989	3.201
	3	−10.000	−2.812
	4	0.615	−0.271
1978	1	14.093	−4.932
	2	9.862	8.461
	3	9.106	8.652
	4	−3.715	−5.034
1979	1	10.250	7.054
	2	8.812	2.613
	3	12.500	7.568
	4	20.013	0.030
1980	1	−3.458	−4.076
	2	5.864	13.384
	3	29.793	11.150
	4	23.899	12.952
1981	1	−5.501	1.312
	2	0.926	−2.371
	3	9.933	10.241
	4	−25.169	6.893
1982	1	−22.625	−7.290
	2	−5.096	−0.601
	3	47.471	11.424
	4	19.138	18.211
1983	1	9.669	9.982
	2	28.379	11.031
	3	3.686	−0.180
	4	−13.048	0.371
1984	1	−5.706	−2.411
	2	−1.243	−2.643
	3	16.736	9.632
	4	18.768	1.801
1985	1	16.483	9.150
	2	9.234	7.253
	3	−10.067	−4.081
	4	7.519	17.113
1986	1	22.873	14.012
	2	0	5.840
	3	−9.855	−6.973
	4	0.647	5.581

Mrs. Wilford's Portfolio
(Portfolio Construction)

Jim Long was in the process of analyzing the portfolio of Carol Wilford. Mrs. Wilford, an elderly widow, had come to him with an unusual request. She owned a substantial number of shares of the common stocks of Exxon, General Mills, Minnesota Mining and Manufacturing (3M), and Sears, Roebuck & Company, and she wanted him to manage her portfolio. Her single requirement was that the portfolio contain one or more of these four securities and no others. During their thirty years of marriage, Wilford and her husband had held these four securities in their portfolio, and because of their portfolio's strong performance over this period, she was adamant that her portfolio comprise these securities.

Initially, Long had tried to convince Wilford of the benefit of adding additional securities, fixed-income and equity, to her portfolio. When she refused, he asked her why she needed professional help in managing the portfolio. She responded that although she was comfortable with the security composition of the portfolio, she thought that she needed professional advice on the proper proportions of the securities in the portfolio.

Long, vice president of a highly successful investment counseling firm in the Southeast, generally managed accounts containing a large number of securities. For this reason, his initial reaction had been to reject Wilford's business, but upon further consideration, he realized that the special nature of her request would allow him to try an approach that was unmanageable with his other clients.

While in graduate school, Long had been exposed to the concept of portfolio analysis using *Markowitz diversification*. Though this approach to portfolio construction appeared sound, Long realized that the number of computations required to implement the model made it impractical in most situations. Wilford's portfolio was the exception.

As an initial step, Long gathered the quarterly holding period returns of the four stocks for the 1981–1986 period (see Table 28.1) and estimated their correlation coefficients (see Table 28.2). Although Long planned to use the companies' fundamentals to estimate rates of return and risk, he decided to begin his analysis with historical data.

■ QUESTIONS

1. Why did Long try to convince Wilford of the need to add securities to her portfolio of four stocks?

2. Assuming an equal dollar investment in each stock, how many different combinations of portfolios can Long form with the four stocks? Without an equal dollar investment in each stock, how many portfolios can Long form? Why?

3. Using the historical data in Tables 28.1 and 28.2 and assuming an equal dollar investment in each stock, calculate the expected return and standard deviation for each portfolio.

4. Using your answer to Question 3, plot the expected return of each portfolio against its standard deviation. Determine the efficient frontier, and identify the portfolios on the efficient frontier.

5. What are the shortcomings in the approach suggested by Questions 3 and 4?

TABLE	Mrs. Wilford's Portfolio
28.1	Quarterly Holding Period Returns (%)

	EXXON	GENERAL MILLS	3M	SEARS, ROEBUCK & COMPANY
1981				
1	−13.023	24.981	8.263	22.721
2	1.639	14.592	−7.723	6.612
3	−6.593	−4.198	−11.739	−14.468
4	2.811	1.143	10.500	2.109
1982				
1	−7.600	8.460	1.468	19.938
2	1.333	9.831	0.826	3.763
3	3.604	7.069	20.986	17.239
4	8.929	10.896	19.136	36.156
1983				
1	6.303	8.636	5.267	17.859
2	11.741	6.114	8.256	18.875
3	10.519	−11.520	0.239	−10.864
4	4.589	9.065	0.241	2.753
1984				
1	5.485	−9.789	−10.718	−7.569
2	7.702	14.231	7.182	−2.760
3	11.902	5.327	0.843	7.892
4	2.458	8.064	5.091	−7.032
1985				
1	13.556	−0.323	5.723	8.866
2	8.905	10.426	−4.103	13.743
3	−2.135	−2.460	−1.442	−13.186
4	8.000	0.301	19.243	19.970
1986				
1	2.766	22.389	18.273	28.051
2	10.807	12.566	8.931	−1.131
3	11.951	−3.970	10.747	−16.619
4	5.613	9.814	16.795	1.107
1987				
1	23.565	19.003	11.730	29.245
2	9.796	9.696	10.284	0.491

TABLE | Mrs. Wilford's Portfolio
28.2 | Correlation Coefficients of Quarterly Holding Period Returns

	EXXON	GENERAL MILLS	3M	SEARS, ROEBUCK & COMPANY
Exxon	1.000	−0.147	−0.060	0.002
General Mills	−0.147	1.000	0.248	0.395
3M	−0.060	0.248	1.000	0.483
Sears	0.002	0.395	0.483	1.000

RD&I, INC.
(Portfolio Risk and Return)

RD&I, Inc. is an investment counseling firm headquartered in New York City with regional offices in Baltimore, Atlanta, and Washington. The firm is owned by five individuals who are active in its management. RD&I's primary activity is to provide portfolio management services to individuals and institutions with portfolios of $500,000 or more. The firm also provides related services, such as a custodial service for securities owned by clients and detailed quarterly reports on the status of each account. The firm's principal source of income is the fees paid by clients for portfolio management services. This annual fee is a percentage of the market value of the client's portfolio. Larger portfolios are charged a lower percentage; the typical fee is 1 percent per year.

Since RD&I's founding in 1950, the firm has enjoyed rapid growth. Today, with over $30 billion under management, it is one of the largest investment counseling firms in the country. A major portion of this success can be attributed to the firm's reputation for earning attractive rates of return on its clients' portfolios. This high return is due in part to the firm's fairly aggressive attitude toward portfolios of common stocks. The company's stated objective for equity portfolios is to achieve a 14–16 percent annual rate of return and, in achieving this goal, to limit the standard deviation of error to around 5–6 percent.

The professional staff and organizational structure are primary contributors to RD&I's success. The professional staff consists of financial and research analysts, information system processing personnel, and regional portfolio managers. Most of the analysts have earned the Chartered Financial Analyst (CFA) designation, and some have graduate degrees in fields such as finance, economics, and computer science. The primary financial and economic analysis is done at the New York City office; portfolio managers are located in the regional offices, established to provide close personal contact with clients.

Three top-level committees are involved in determining and carrying out RD&I's investment strategy. The Investment Policy Committee (IPC) develops economic forecasts. The IPC analyzes the economic and market data supplied by the research staff to construct scenarios of future returns available in the capital markets. The IPC relies on a staff of professional economists who use sophisticated computer-based econometric models and other forecasting techniques and procedures. The firm also retains a nationally known economic consultant to complement its own staff.

The Equity Selection Committee (ESC) uses the IPC recommendations in its selection of industries and individual companies to be analyzed. The major steps supervised and implemented by the ESC are

1. Develop recommended industry concentration levels that indicate how portfolio funds should be allocated by industry;
2. Complete a detailed fundamental analysis of promising companies;
3. Calculate an expected return for each security, under the various scenarios provided by the IPC;
4. Develop a final selection of stocks with an expected holding period return in the next three months of at least 50 percent more than the current yield-to-maturity on AAA-rated corporate bonds; and
5. Establish purchase price limits, price appreciation objectives, and downside review points for each issue included on the final selection list.

Another committee performs a similar analysis for fixed-income securities.

The Securities List Review Committee (SLRC) monitors the recommendations made by the IPC and the ESC. The SLRC meets at least once each week to monitor current economic developments or factors that may affect securities approved by the ESC. The SLRC can remove stocks from the approved list, adjust price appreciation objectives, and change downside review points—based on current developments. The committee also receives computer reports, automatically generated for any client's portfolio, that show a significant deviation from its established risk-return objective. If the committee thinks that the portfolio should be revised, the portfolio manager is notified to take the appropriate action.

Since several individuals serve on all three committees, considerable interaction between the committees is assured. The committees are always chaired and controlled by one of the firm's owners, and membership is usually restricted to senior-level employees.

The regional offices of the firm are staffed by portfolio managers, aided by clerical support personnel. The portfolio managers must solicit new clients in their geographic area and manage individual portfolios.

Henry Stone recently joined RD&I as a portfolio manager assigned to the Atlanta office. Prior to accepting his position, Stone had spent four years as a trust officer at a major Atlanta bank. One of Stone's first tasks in his new position was to study the organization and operating procedures relating to portfolio managers. He believed that he was capable and knowledgeable about the responsibilities of a portfolio manager, but he realized that RD&I operated differently than a bank trust department.

Stone began his study by carefully reading the most-recent reports and recommendations produced by the three major investment strategy committees. He was impressed by the quality of the macroeconomic analysis provided by the IPC and the detailed analyses of individual stocks provided by the ESC. He was also amazed by the recent performance record of the stocks identified by the ESC. Not only had these stocks appreciated more than stocks in general but their actual returns were remarkably close to their predicted returns.

Though Stone was impressed by the quality of support given the regional office, he was concerned about the high degree of flexibility given to individual portfolio managers. This concern stemmed from the lack of formal guidelines and procedures dealing with formulating and revising a client's portfolio. Portfolio managers were apparently expected to develop their own procedures for analyzing a client's goals and objectives and forming an appropriate portfolio. The only specific restriction imposed by the firm was that the portfolio must be formed from securities approved by the ESC. This lack of guidelines and procedures provided Henry considerably more latitude than he had enjoyed while working in the bank trust department.

In discussing this point with other portfolio managers, he was surprised to learn of a wide divergence in approaches to portfolio management. Some managers were traditional in their approach and simply saw to it that each portfolio consisted of enough stocks from several different industries to ensure diversification. Portfolios formed in this manner typically consisted of at least thirty securities, representing six to ten different industries.

Other portfolio managers used procedures that involved some of the concepts of modern portfolio theory. These managers paid considerable attention to the betas of individual securities and the resulting beta of the portfolio. They also frequently looked at other measures of risk, such as the price limits and downside review points supplied by the ESC.

After talking to the other portfolio managers, Stone was convinced that he should develop his own procedures for formulating and managing portfolios carefully. He had recently read several articles explaining how investment advisory firms were utilizing concepts from modern portfolio theory. He was aware that one of the most important developments in modern portfolio theory dealt with portfolio formation—specifically, how a list of acceptable securities should be combined into a portfolio to meet the desired risk-return objective.

As a first step, Stone decided to use the Markowitz variance-covariance technique and the Sharpe "simplified" procedure in an example. First, Stone identified two stocks on the approved list supplied by the ESC and compiled the data shown in Table 29.1. The return data were supplied by the New York office; the descriptive statistics in the table—such as the variances, covariances, and characteristic line statistics—were easily derived by using his desk calculator. (Table 29.2 contains estimated performances of the economy, the stock market, and the two stocks identified by Stone, for the second quarter of 1987. This table was also constructed from data supplied by the New York office.)

Although Stone was somewhat familiar with the Markowitz and Sharpe techniques, he had never been able to understand all of the similarities and differences between the two. He thought that an increased understanding of these portfolio models would benefit his clients and help him succeed in his new position. He also had a faint hope that if the techniques proved to be success-ful, other portfolio managers—and possibly even RD&I—would adopt these procedures.

To estimate the portfolio expected returns and variances, Stone decided on the equations shown below:

Markowitz: $E(r_p) = \sum_{j=1}^{n} X_j \, E(r_j)$

$\sigma_p^2 = \sum_{i=1}^{n} \sum_{j=1}^{n} X_i X_j \text{COV}(r_i, r_j)$

Sharpe: $E(r_p) = \sum_{j=1}^{n} X_j \hat{\alpha}_j + \left[\left\{ \sum_{j=1}^{n} X_j \hat{\beta}_j \right\} E(r_m) \right]$

$= \sum_{j=1}^{n} X_j [\hat{\alpha}_j + \hat{\beta}_j \, E(r_m)]$

$\sigma_p^2 = \sum_{j=1}^{n} X_j^2 \, \sigma_{e_j}^2 + \left[\left\{ \sum_{j=1}^{n} X_j \hat{\beta}_j \right\}^2 \sigma_m^2 \right]$

QUESTIONS

1. Using the Markowitz model and the data in Tables 29.1 and 29.2, calculate the expected portfolio return $(E(r_p))$ and variance (σ_p^2) for portfolios consisting of IBM and General Public Utilities stocks for the first quarter 1987. Let the pro-portion of funds invested in each security (X_j), vary from 0 to 1.0, by incre-ments of 0.1. For example, the weights in the first portfolio should be 1.0 and 0; in the second, .9 and .1; and so on. This will result in eleven different portfolios.

2. Using the Sharpe "simplified" approach, calculate the $E(r_p)$ and σ_p^2 for the eleven portfolios described in Question 1.

3. On a single graph, plot in risk-return space the two efficient frontiers identi-fied by the Markowitz and Sharpe models. Explain any differences in the two frontiers.

4. Compare and contrast the Markowitz and Sharpe models. Which model would be appropriate for RD&I? Explain.

TABLE 29.1 | RD&I, Inc.
Quarterly Returns and Descriptive Statistics

Year-Quarter	General Public Utilities (GPU)	International Business Machines (IBM)	Standard & Poor's 500 Stock Composite (Market)
1980-1	−.5072	−.1206	−.0476
-2	.3824	.0692	.1338
-3	−.1064	.1061	.1115
-4	−.0476	.0641	.1295
1981-1	−.1750	−.0614	.0131
-2	.2424	−.0584	−.0237
-3	−.0488	−.0499	.1024
-4	.3846	.0667	.0689
1982-1	−.3148	.0657	−.0729
-2	.0540	.0290	−.0060
-3	.1795	.2245	.1142
-4	.1739	.3235	.1821
1983-1	.1481	.0661	.0998
-2	.1774	.1912	.1103
-3	−.1096	.0630	−.0018
-4	−.0462	−.0309	.0037
1984-1	.0645	−.0578	−.0241
-2	.0909	−.0640	−.0264
-3	.1250	.1853	.0963
-4	.1358	−.0002	.0180
1985-1	.0435	.0404	.0915
-2	.1771	−.0169	.0725
-3	−.0265	.0099	−.0408
-4	.2364	.2642	.1711
1986-1	.1544	−.0186	.1401
-2	.0701	−.0257	.0584
-3	.0893	−.0744	−.0697
-4	−.0109	−.0996	.0558
Mean return	.0549	.0389	.0521
Alpha $(\hat{\alpha}_j)$	−.0106	.0131	
Beta $(\hat{\beta}_j)$	1.256	.9991	1.000
Coefficient of determination (R^2)	.2116	.4133	
Variance of residuals $(\sigma^2_{e_j})$	.0285	.0074	

continued

TABLE	
29.1	continued

Correlation Matrix

	GPU	IBM	Market
GPU	1.0000	.3770	.4908
IBM	.3770	1.0000	.6596
Market	.4908	.6596	1.000

Variance-Covariance Matrix

	GPU	IBM	Market
GPU	.0362	.0081	.0069
IBM	.0081	.0127	.0055
Market	.0069	.0055	.0055

TABLE	RD&I, Inc.
29.2	Economic, Stock Market, and Individual Security Forecasts for First Quarter 1987

Possible Economic Conditions	Probability	Expected Return on Standard & Poor's 500 Stock Composite
No growth	.1	−.05
Slow growth	.2	.01
Moderate growth	.5	.10
Rapid growth	.2	.25

	GPU	IBM	Market
Expected return, $E(r_j)$	.04	.10	.097
Variance of expected return, σ_j^2	.02	.03	.008
Standard deviation of expected return, σ_j	.141	.173	.089

Alex Urich
(Measures of Portfolio Performance)

In November 1987, Gus Kemp, vice president of Texas Investment Consultants (TIC), was considering possible responses to a request for a portfolio review from one of the firm's clients, Alex Urich. TIC, established in 1945, had long enjoyed a reputation as one of the finest investment counseling firms in the Southwest. Over the years, TIC had adopted the most modern techniques in the handling and processing of accounts and was considered a leader in adopting new quantitative investment techniques as they developed.

Urich had been a client for ten years and during that time had seemed to be generally pleased with the way his account had been handled. Although his personal situation changed after the account was opened, his investment objectives remained substantially the same as they had been in 1977 (see Table 30.1). At each review date TIC provided Urich with a portfolio evaluation that consisted of a complete breakdown of his holdings by category and data for each of the securities: date bought, unit cost, total cost, current market price, current market value, estimated annual income, and current yield. In addition, TIC provided several performance measures on a quarterly basis (see Table 30.2).

In October 1987, Urich met with Kemp and expressed some dissatisfaction with the portfolio performance measures he had been receiving from TIC. Although Urich did not indicate that he was dissatisfied with TIC's performance, Kemp got the distinct impression that Urich was looking for more details to evaluate the performance of his portfolio more accurately. Urich said that he had become friendly with a number of professors in the finance department at State University and had audited several courses in investments. As a result, he had read extensively in the areas of portfolio theory and portfolio performance measurement.

Urich had examined the performance measures of Sharpe, Treynor, and

Jensen.[1] Though the methods used in these studies represented great strides in developing risk-adjusted performance measures, Urich thought that they could not produce the type of performance-measuring system he wanted. In particular, he wanted to measure TIC's ability to maintain a portfolio consistent with a stated investment objective. He also wanted to measure TIC's ability to predict and take advantage of general market turns.

At the conclusion of their meeting, Kemp told Urich that he would look into the matter of a more extensive measure of portfolio performance and that he would get back in touch within a month. Kemp knew that TIC had been concerned with this problem for some time, and he wanted to find out what had been done before he responded to Urich's request. He was familiar with a number of companies that provided portfolio performance analysis on a commercial basis, but he thought that these performance measures might not be what Urich and other sophisticated clients wanted.

That afternoon Kemp had a meeting with a new employee, Thomas Todd. Tom had recently graduated from a large, well-known business school and had begun working for TIC in the area of portfolio performance measures. After outlining his conversation with Urich, Kemp requested that Tom examine possible alternatives, keeping in mind the cost factors involved and the sophistication of the firm's clients. He gave him a folder containing all the information relating to Urich's account.

In early November 1987, Tom wrote the following memorandum to Kemp:

> After our meeting in October, I began reviewing various techniques for evaluating portfolio performance. I agree with Mr. Urich that many of the existing techniques have serious shortcomings. As an alternative, I suggest that we explore a method of portfolio evaluation developed by Campanella that I have modified somewhat.[2] This method is not a complete evaluation technique, but it is fairly easy to calculate, and it provides the type of evaluation Mr. Urich and our other clients may desire.
>
> Campanella's technique has its basis in the single-index market model
>
> $$R_j = a_j + b_j R_m + e_j$$
>
> where R_m is the return on the market factor, a_j and b_j are parameters of the jth security, and e_j is a normally distributed random element. Since b_j is a measure of the responsiveness of the jth security's returns to the returns in the market, the responsiveness of a portfolio at any particular time, t, to the changes in the market (systematic risk of a portfolio, β_t) is the weighted sum of the systematic risk elements of its component securities. Thus,
>
> $$\beta_t = \sum_{j=1}^{n} X_{jt} b_{jt}$$
>
> where
> n = the number of securities in the portfolio;
> X_{jt} = the fraction of the portfolio invested in the jth security at time t; and
> b_{jt} = the systematic risk of the jth security at time t.

[1] For example, William F. Sharpe, "Mutual Fund Performance," *Journal of Business* 39, no. 1, pt. 2 (January 1966): 119–38; Jack L. Treynor, "How to Rate Management of Investment Funds," *Harvard Business Review* 43 (January–February 1965): 63–75; and Michael C. Jensen, "The Performance of Mutual Funds in the Period 1945–1965," *Journal of Finance* 23, no. 1 (May 1968): 389–419.
[2] Frank B. Campanella, *The Measurement of Portfolio Risk Exposure* (Toronto: Lexington Books, 1972).

The calculation of the portfolio's systematic risk can be done in the following manner: (1) identify the securities within a portfolio; (2) compute the systematic risk at each time interval, b_{jt}, for each security using the market model; (3) weight the risk factor for each security by the proportion of the portfolio it represents; and (4) sum the weighted risk factors. I have calculated the quarterly systematic risk factors for Mr. Urich's portfolio from January 1983 through October 1987 (see Table 30.3). Note that I have included the list of stocks and their individual betas for the first and last quarters. These quarterly systematic risk factors are calculated for the total portfolio as well as for the equity portion of the portfolio.

Since it has been shown that an individual security's systematic risk factor is not completely stationary over time, I have updated the quarterly values of b_{jt} for the equity securities in Mr. Urich's portfolio. The first time a security appeared, b_{jt} was obtained from a time series least squares regression of the form

$$R_{jt} = a_j + b_j R_{mt} + e_{jt}$$

where R_{jt} was the log of the wealth relatives for each of the previous 57 months for the jth security and R_{mt} was the log of the wealth relatives for each of the previous 57 months for the S&P 500 Composite Index. For each quarter after a security's initial appearance, inputs were calculated by successively removing the logs of the wealth relatives for the earliest three months. Other techniques, such as exponential smoothing, could be used to update values of b_j.

The measure of systematic risk for the near-cash securities in Mr. Urich's portfolio was assigned a value of zero, since they consisted of cash and treasury bills. The corporate bond section of Mr. Urich's portfolio was assigned a systematic risk value of .17 based upon a study by Reilly and Joehnk.[3]

According to Campanella, once the quarterly weighted average betas for the portfolio have been calculated:

> We can examine the behavior of portfolio risk levels over time in order to gain an insight into one aspect of a manager's performance, viz., his ability to predict market turns. If a portfolio manager is able to call major swings in the market successfully, we would expect that he would adjust the portfolio's risk level downward prior to market downturns and, conversely, increase it in anticipation of market upswings.
>
> By using the model to measure the volatility of a series of portfolios over time and relating the results to observed market action, we can comment on the portfolio manager's ability in this area.
>
> We can also observe the manager's particular strategy for adjusting the portfolio's risk exposure. It is possible to compute a B_t net of cash and other liquid assets held in the portfolio and from these data make inferences about specific strategies employed to alter risk exposure. . . .
>
> It is also possible now to determine if a portfolio manager is earning a rate of return consistent with the portfolio's level of systematic risk for short intervals of time, i.e., monthly, quarterly, or annually, in place of the ten-year period used to date. And we can examine the con-

[3] Frank K. Reilly and Michael D. Joehnk, "Association Between Market-Determined Risk Measures for Bonds and Bond Ratings," paper presented at the Financial Management Association Meetings, Atlanta, Georgia, October 12, 1973.

tinuing relationship between a portfolio's stated objective and its level of risk.[4]

Although I have not had the opportunity to evaluate Mr. Urich's portfolio along these lines, I know that you are anxious to respond to his request. Since I am leaving for two weeks of reserve duty tomorrow, I thought I should get this information to you as soon as possible. I will be glad to complete the evaluation upon my return.

Mr. Kemp felt that he could not wait for Tom's return, as it had been some time since Urich had made his request. Therefore, he decided to complete the evaluation himself and to make a critical examination of the technique.

QUESTIONS

1. Compare and contrast the composite measures of performance developed by Sharpe, Treynor, and Jensen. What, if any, are the shortcomings of these measures?

2. What are some of the possible ways of measuring ex-post portfolio yield? Do the quarterly measures of adjusted current value used by TIC properly take into account portfolio capital additions and withdrawals?

3. How has TIC adjusted the volatility of Urich's portfolio—by moving into more- or less-volatile equity issues or by changing the proportion of near-cash and bonds in the portfolio?

4. Has TIC been successful in adjusting the volatility of Urich's portfolio in anticipation of market movements?

5. Has TIC's management of Urich's portfolio been consistent with the stated objectives of the portfolio?

[4]Campanella, 58.

TABLE | Alex Urich
30.1 | Personal Information and Portfolio Objectives

October 30, 1977

MEMO TO: File
SUBJECT: Alex Urich

I. PERSONAL INFORMATION

Mr. Urich is an assistant professor of English at State University and holds master's and doctorate degrees in the same field. He is 39 years old, and his wife is 36. They have two children: Scott, age 15, and Danielle, age 14.

Mr. Urich currently receives an annual salary of $23,500; additional income from his investment portfolio and from the Tar Land Corporation appears likely to provide another $10,000–$15,000 per year. The Tar Land Corporation owns approximately 17,000 acres of land between Baton Rouge and New Orleans, Louisiana, and produces revenues for the corporation through oil leases, timber sales, various types of royalties, and other sources. The corporation has been managed by a bank in Houston. Mr. Urich and his brother are trying to retain the services of a professional real estate manager to exploit the full potential of this real estate. It is hoped, therefore, that this land will generate more income in the future than it does at present. Mr. Urich and his brother, who lives in Arizona, together own a controlling interest in the corporation's common shares, but there are also minority stockholders.

Mr. Urich has $100,000 of life insurance on himself and owes $10,000 on the policy as it was purchased on the minimum deposit plan. In addition to the securities he owns outright, Mr. Urich has a margin account with Merril Lynch with a $22,430 debit balance.

Mr. F. D. Schwartz of May Accounting Firm is Mr. Urich's accountant. We should call him for tax and capital gain information. Mr. Urich already has some capital gains in the current year; we should obtain the amount from Mr. Schwartz.

II. INVESTMENT OBJECTIVES

Mr. Urich's objectives for the portfolio emphasize preservation of capital. While he has a moderate amount of income from his job and outside income from the real estate, he will need additional funds from the portfolio. He estimates that he will need $21,000 to $22,000 of additional income each year. Mr. Urich recognizes that with this substantial cash draw from the portfolio and considering future inflation, the portfolio must emphasize some growth of principal above normal income generation if he is to maintain and increase the size of the account. In allowing for his withdrawals from the account, Mr. Urich does not require that the income meet his full requirements; he is looking at a total-return approach in future growth. We have indicated that we think the portfolio should do somewhere between 8 and 11 percent a year with his investment objectives.

Mr. Urich would like to withdraw approximately $1,800 per month from the portfolio, whether it comes from income or principal cash. We will maintain sufficient cash in the account so that he can call for withdrawals as required. The actual transfer of the funds to Mr. Urich can be worked out at a later time.

continued

TABLE 30.1	continued

III. ADMINISTRATION

CORRESPONDENCE should go to Mr. Urich's home.

1. Home address: 168 Sam Houston Way
                              Houston, TX 74985
   Home telephone: 993-4963
2. Office address: English Department
                              State University
                              Houston, TX 78886
   Office telephone: 355-9906, ext. 78

REGISTRATION OF
  SECURITIES: Alex Urich
                              168 Sam Houston Way
                              Houston, TX 74985

SOCIAL SECURITY NUMBER: 254–67–2179

EXECUTION OF TRANSACTIONS: We execute all transactions without prior approval from Mr. Urich. Mr. Urich asked to be regularly advised by telephone, however, when we have significant changes in the market outlook or our investment strategy.

TABLE 30.2	Alex Urich Quarterly Performance Measures

Since Urich periodically withdrew and added cash (and, on a few occasions, common stocks) to his managed funds, TIC elected to evaluate the account with the assumption that all adjustments took place at the beginning of the quarter, regardless of when they actually took place. This resulted in the calculation of an adjusted current value at the beginning of each quarter. Specifically, the adjusted current value was calculated as follows:

     Current value of account at previous quarterly reporting date
 + Cash added during the quarter
 − Cash withdrawn during the quarter
 + Stock added by client to the account (capital adjustment) during the quarter
 − Stock removed by client from the account (capital adjustment) during the quarter
     Adjusted current value at the beginning of the quarter

The appreciation in adjusted current value was calculated as the difference between the current value of the account at the quarterly review date and the adjusted current value at the beginning of that quarter. For example, as shown below, the current value of Urich's account on July 30, 1987, was $465,441 − $2,726, or $462,715. The only change made by Urich during the following quarter was a withdrawal of $5,200. Therefore, his adjusted current value at the beginning of the quarter was

continued

**TABLE
30.2** | continued

$457,515. The current value of his account on October 31, 1987, was $471,215, giving him an appreciation in adjusted current value of $13,700 or a quarterly percentage gain of 3 percent.

In addition, TIC provided Urich with two cumulative figures each quarter: invested capital and appreciation in invested capital. The invested capital figure was derived by taking the invested capital figure from the previous quarter and adding or subtracting any cash and capital adjustments. The appreciation in invested capital in any quarter was the sum of the appreciation in adjusted current values for all previous quarters, including the current quarter.

Quarterly Review Date	Adjusted Current Value at Beginning of Quarter	Appreciation In Adjusted Current Value	Percentage Gain (Loss)
1/31/83	$410,751	$ 5,722	1.5
4/30/83	381,683	24,841	6.5
7/30/83	405,226	1,879	.5
10/31/83	405,855	18,586	4.6
1/31/84	423,441	(6,293)	(1.5)
4/30/84	414,767	20,514	4.9
7/30/84	574,631	(41,273)	(7.2)
10/31/84	514,160	45,643	8.9
1/31/85	521,351	(43,861)	(8.4)
4/30/85	472,546	(36,550)	(7.7)
7/30/85	422,963	(20,756)	(4.9)
10/31/85	396,638	24,008	6.1
1/31/86	406,646	60,822	15.0
4/30/86	461,648	36,117	7.8
7/30/86	484,585	(26,912)	(5.6)
10/31/86	451,673	15,419	3.4
1/31/87	456,592	20,084	4.4
4/30/87	466,576	24,339	5.2
7/30/87	465,441	(2,726)	(.6)
10/31/87	457,515	13,700	3.0

TABLE	Alex Urich
30.3	Quarterly Report
	1/31/83

Stock	(1) **Market Value**	(2) **% of Stock Port.**	(3) **% of Total Port.**	(4) **Beta**	(5) **Weighted Beta** Stock	Total
General Motors	$ 15,650	.05	.04	0.95	.05	.04
General Electric	13,181	.04	.03	0.95	.04	.03
Honeywell	11,895	.04	.03	1.15	.05	.03
PepsiCo	15,800	.05	.04	0.90	.05	.04
IBM	28,536	.10	.07	0.95	.10	.07
Exxon	10,388	.03	.02	0.90	.03	.02
American Tel. & Tel.	20,327	.07	.05	0.65	.05	.03
Donalson, Lufkin & Jin.	14,454	.05	.03	1.70	.09	.05
Greyhound	10,685	.04	.03	0.95	.04	.03
Goodyear Tire & Rubber	15,525	.05	.04	0.85	.04	.03
Union Oil of Calif.	18,851	.06	.05	1.30	.08	.07
Anheuser Busch	20,325	.07	.05	0.90	.06	.05
Hughes Tool	23,400	.08	.06	1.50	.12	.09
Prime Computer	18,356	.06	.04	1.65	.10	.07
Georgia Pacific	16,761	.06	.04	1.20	.07	.05
U.S. Home	10,100	.03	.02	1.55	.05	.03
Black & Decker	8,274	.03	.02	1.20	.04	.02
Foote Cone Belding	6,000	.02	.01	0.80	.02	.01
Varco Int.	12,844	.04	.03	1.60	.06	.05
Sykes Datatronics	5,650	.02	.01	1.60	.03	.02
Total	$297,002	.99			1.17	
Near Cash	60,458		.15	.00		.00
Bonds	59,013		.14	.17		.02
Total	$416,473		1.00			.85

continued

Table 30.3 (cont.)
Quarterly Reports
4/30/83–7/31/84

Quarter Ended	Market Value	% of Total Portfolio	Weighted Beta	
			Stock	Total*
4/30/83				
Stocks	$325,033	.80	1.29	1.04
Near Cash	21,627	.05		.00
Bonds	59,864	.15		.03
Total	$406,524	1.00		1.07
7/31/83				
Stocks	$325,723	.80	1.20	.97
Near Cash	20,344	.05		.00
Bonds	61,038	.15		.03
Total	$407,105	1.00		1.00
10/31/83				
Stocks	$359,500	.85	1.20	1.01
Near Cash	3,853	.01		.00
Bonds	61,088	.14		.02
Total	$424,441	1.00		1.03
1/31/84				
Stocks	$355,428	.85	1.19	1.06
Near Cash	2,725	.01		.00
Bonds	58,995	.14		.02
Total	$417,148	1.00		1.08
4/30/84				
Stocks	$353,120	.84	1.19	1.01
Near Cash	8,476	.02		.00
Bonds	56,685	.14		.02
Total	$418,281	1.00		1.03
7/31/84				
Stocks	$448,485	.85	1.18	1.04
Near Cash	17,225	.03		.00
Bonds	59,448	.11		.02
Total	$525,158	.99		1.06

continued

Table 30.3 (cont.)
Quarterly Reports
10/31/84–1/31/86

Quarter Ended	Market Value	% of Total Portfolio	Weighted Beta	
			Stock	Total*
10/31/84				
Stocks	$485,161	.88	1.10	.94
Near Cash	4,363	.01		.00
Bonds	59,179	.11		.02
Total	$548,703	1.00		.96
1/31/85				
Stocks	$402,653	.86	1.09	.96
Near Cash	9,639	.02		.00
Bonds	55,600	.12		.02
Total	$467,892	1.00		.98
4/30/85				
Stocks	$360,648	.85	1.11	.96
Near Cash	7,200	.02		.00
Bonds	58,950	.14		.02
Total	$426,798	1.01		.98
7/31/85				
Stocks	$327,003	.84	1.07	.92
Near Cash	1,577	.00		.00
Bonds	62,628	.16		.03
Total	$391,208	1.00		.95
10/31/85				
Stocks	$319,441	.84	.99	.84
Near Cash	0	.00		.00
Bonds	60,718	.16		.03
Total	$380,159	1.00		.87
1/31/86				
Stocks	$366,573	.82	.98	.83
Near Cash	408	.00		.00
Bonds	80,489	.18		.03
Total	$447,470	1.00		.86

continued

Table 30.3 (cont.)
Quarterly Reports
4/30/86–7/31/87

Quarter Ended	Market Value	% of Total Portfolio	Weighted Beta	
			Stock	Total*
4/30/86				
Stocks	$396,554	.84	1.01	.81
Near Cash	391	.00		.00
Bonds	74,041	.16		.03
Total	$470,986	1.00		.84
7/31/86				
Stocks	$379,010	.85	.97	.82
Near Cash	129	.00		.00
Bonds	65,635	.15		.03
Total	$444,774	1.00		.85
10/31/86				
Stocks	$362,383	.81	.95	.77
Near Cash	11,793	.03		.00
Bonds	75,144	.17		.03
Total	$449,320	1.01		.80
1/31/87				
Stocks	$374,413	.81	.96	.79
Near Cash	567	.00		.00
Bonds	84,637	.18		.03
Total	$459,617	.99		.82
4/30/87				
Stocks	$408,964	.86	1.03	.88
Near Cash	206	.00		.00
Bonds	66,058	.14		.02
Total	$475,228	1.00		.90
7/31/87				
Stocks	$411,857	.89	1.04	.94
Near Cash	858	.00		.00
Bonds	50,000	.11		.02
Total	$462,715	1.00		.96

*The weighted beta for the bonds is the bonds' percentage of total portfolio times .17, the assumed bond beta.

Quarterly Report
10/31/87

Stock	(1) Market Value	(2) % of Stock Port.	(3) % of Total Port.	(4) Beta	(5) Weighted Beta Stock	Total
General Motors	$ 25,550	.06	.05	1.10	.07	.06
PepsiCo	33,400	.08	.07	1.10	.09	.08
IBM	37,008	.09	.08	1.00	.09	.08
American Tel. & Tel.	18,866	.05	.04	0.85	.07	.03
U.S. Home	22,575	.05	.05	1.45	.08	.07
Eastman Kodak	41,813	.10	.09	0.85	.09	.08
Dome Petroleum	53,794	.13	.11	0.60	.08	.07
Halliburton	38,250	.09	.08	1.25	.11	.10
Western Digital	18,100	.04	.04	1.55	.06	.06
Delta Airlines	21,900	.05	.05	1.10	.06	.06
Chubb	29,203	.07	.06	1.10	.08	.07
Koger Prop.	27,563	.07	.06	0.75	.05	.04
Avon	26,125	.06	.06	1.05	.06	.06
Limited	18,900	.05	.04	1.50	.08	.06
Total	$413,047	.99			1.07	
Near Cash	1,168		.00	0.00		.00
Bonds	57,000		.12	.17		.02
Total	$471,215		1.00			.94

TABLE	Alex Urich
30.4	Quarterly Level of S&P 500 Composite Index

Quarter Ending	S&P 500 Composite Index Value
1/31/83	141.54
4/30/83	160.71
7/31/83	167.59
10/31/83	165.38
1/31/84	164.84
4/30/84	158.65
7/31/84	148.83
10/31/84	167.20
1/31/85	177.30
4/30/85	182.26
7/31/85	191.58
10/31/85	189.09
1/31/86	210.29
4/30/86	241.76
7/31/86	238.67
10/31/86	240.94
1/31/87	267.84
4/30/87	287.19
7/31/87	308.47

CASE
31

Sigma Sigma Sigma*
(Portfolio Evaluation)

In early October 1987, Nancy Wait, the newly elected national treasurer of Sigma Sigma Sigma Fraternity, was faced with the task of evaluating the performance of the fraternity's endowment fund.

Since its founding in 1910, this honorary business fraternity has established chapters at many colleges of business throughout the United States. The purpose of the fraternity is to promote high academic standards for students of business. Only outstanding students are eligible for membership, and the fraternity awards full scholarships to several members each year. The fraternity's executive committee is composed of a president, vice president, secretary, and treasurer, all of whom are elected at the annual national convention in November. The fraternity currently has approximately two thousand active members.

Each chapter collects membership fees from new members and annual dues from all members. Part of these fees is forwarded to the national treasurer for deposit into a checking account which is used to pay all expenses incurred on the national level. Over the years, the fees have far exceeded national expenses. In 1920, this very favorable situation allowed the fraternity to create the Sigma Sigma Sigma Endowment Fund. At the end of each year the treasurer transfers any excess moneys to the endowment fund.

Table 31.1 presents a summary of the total market value of the fund for the four quarters ending September 29, 1987. As can be seen from the table, the fund's total current market value had grown to over $700,000. The fund's increase in value was attributed to the excess of membership fees and dues over expenses and the returns earned on investments.

---

*This case was written by Professors John M. Cheney and Wallace W. Reiff, of the University of Central Florida, to provide a basis for class discussion rather than to illustrate the effective or the ineffective handling of an administrative situation.

INVESTMENT OBJECTIVES

The national officers thought that the increasing size of the fund and the executive committee's lack of time and experience necessitated professional management. The committee had hoped that the fees charged by a professional investment advisor would be more than recovered by an improvement in the performance of the fund.

After lengthy discussion, the executive committee formulated an investment policy to be followd by the advisor. The following statement was adopted by the national convention on November 21, 1985:

> The primary purpose of this fund is to maintain and/or increase the purchasing power of the capital entrusted to it. These moneys are to be managed by professional investment managers and are to be invested in common stocks, preferred stocks, corporate indebtedness, or U.S. government instruments. The fund will normally maintain a ratio of 75 percent common stocks to 25 percent fixed-income securities. These amounts may vary as much as 15 percent. The investment manager may, under certain conditions, vary these commitments, depending on the manager's assessment of the general economic and market climate. Corporate indebtedness must be securities with a minimum Standard and Poor's rating of A. Common stocks must be of the quality generally considered "investment-grade."

The membership charged the executive committee with selecting the investment advisor, evaluating the advisor's performance, and reporting on the financial status of the endowment fund at each annual convention. Largely on the recommendation of the bank used by the fraternity, the executive committee appointed Harriman Ross and Associates, of Chicago, as investment advisor. Harriman Ross agreed to provide custodial services for the securities and to submit quarterly reports giving a detailed list of all securities held, acquisition prices, current market values, and current dividend or interest yields.

AN OVERVIEW OF PERFORMANCE EVALUATION

Shortly after Nancy's election, she began to familiarize herself with the fraternity's financial documents and records. Included in these records were the quarterly reports from Harriman Ross, still serving as investment advisor, and the executive committee's annual evaluations of the advisor's performance. These evaluations consisted primarily of the advisor's quarterly reports and a brief statement by the treasurer, highlighting figures given in the reports.

Nancy's initial review of the material left her unimpressed by the performance of Harriman Ross. She was particularly concerned that the endowment fund had increased its assets only from $685,006 to $704,654 over the past three quarters (see Table 31.1), while over the same period the stock market, as measured by the Standard & Poor's 500 Stock Composite Index, had shown significant appreciation (see Table 31.3).

Nancy thought that the executive committee had been negligent in evaluating the performance of the investment advisor. She wanted to develop a fair procedure for evaluating the advisor's performance and to present the completed evaluation at the executive committee's January 1988 meeting. At that time a decision could be made to retain Harrimon Ross or to investigate other advisors.

Nancy had recently completed a course in investments which covered investment performance evaluation. The instructor had repeatedly emphasized that a "risk-adjusted return" approach was essential.

Nancy decided to review her text and notes from the investments class before developing the procedure to be used in the analysis of the fund's performance. She summarized the material she thought relevant to the evaluation process as follows:

1. Holding period returns: $r_{jt} = (P_{t+1} - P_t + D_{t+1})/P_t$, where P_{t+1} and P_t represent the price of the security at the end and beginning of the period, respectively, and D_{t+1} represents the cash dividend paid during the period.

2. Characteristic lines:

$$r_{jt} = \hat{\alpha}_j + \hat{\beta}_j r_{mt} + e_t$$

where r_{jt} represents the holding-period return for security j in period t, r_{mt} is the holding period return for a market index such as the Standard & Poor's 500, a_j and β_j are parameters of the security developed by regression analysis, and e_t is a normally distributed random element.

3. Security risk measure: $\hat{\beta}_j$ = beta, found from estimating the characteristic line. It is a measure of the volatility or risk of security j in relation to the market portfolio.

4. Risk measure for a portfolio: β_p = the beta for the portfolio, calculated as

$$\beta_p = \sum_{j=1}^{n} w_j \beta_j$$

where n is the number of securities in the portfolio; w_j is the proportion of funds, measured by market values, invested in security j; and β_j is the beta for security j.

5. Return measure for a portfolio:

$$r_p = \sum_{j=1}^{n} w_j r_j$$

where r_j is the holding period return for security j, and w_j and n are as defined in 4, above.

6. Security market line (SML): $E(r_j) = r_f + \beta_j(E(r_m) - r_f)$, where $E(r_j)$ is the expected holding period return on security j, r_f is the holding period return available on a risk-free asset, β_j is the risk measure for security j, and $E(r_m)$ is the expected holding period return for the market portfolio. The SML expresses the relationship between security or portfolio return and systematic risk.

7. Jensen's portfolio evaluation model:[1]

$$J_j = \tilde{r}_j - [\tilde{r}_f + \beta_j(\tilde{r}_m - \tilde{r}_f)]$$

[1] Michael C. Jensen, "Risk, Pricing of Capital Assets, and the Evaluation of Investment Portfolios," *Journal of Business* 42 (April 1969): 167–247.

where J_j is the performance index for portfolio j, $\bar{r}_j$ is the historical or ex-post holding period return for portfolio j, and $\bar{r}_m$ is the ex-post holding period return for the market. This model considers both risk and returns in evaluating performance.

ANALYSIS OF SIGMA SIGMA SIGMA ENDOWMENT FUND

Armed with this information, Nancy began gathering the data she would need to complete the analysis. She decided to limit her evauation to the period beginning with the fourth quarter of 1986 and ending with the third quarter of 1987. She immediately discovered that the quarterly reports prepared by Harriman Ross and the executive committee's annual reports did not provide the quarterly holding period returns (r_{jt}) or measures of risk (β_j) for each security.

In an attempt to develop the necessary data, Nancy listed all the common stocks that the fund had held during the last four quarters. From the price and dividend data in the quarterly reports, she was able to calculate quarterly holding period returns for each security (see Table 31.2). Several factors, however, complicated these calculations. For those stocks sold or acquired during a quarter rather than at the beginning or end of the quarter, the holding period return should cover (1) the beginning of the quarter to the date the stock was sold or (2) the date the stock was acquired to the end of the quarter. To overcome this problem, Nancy converted these short holding period returns to quarterly holding period returns by assuming that funds from stock sales during the quarter were invested in other stocks providing the same return as the stock sold and that funds obtained to buy stocks during the quarter were obtained from stocks with returns equal to the stock purchased. With these adjustments, all returns were equivalent to full-quarter holding period returns.

Another problem was the possibility that the fund's quarterly values reflected additional contributions from the fraternity's checking account. After reviewing the quarterly reports and the checking account records, Nancy discovered that no contributions had been made over the last four quarters.

Nancy also needed to calculate a measure of risk (beta) for each security and determine the weight of each security in the portfolio. Rather than attempt to estimate the characteristic line for each security, Nancy elected to use the betas for common stocks published by Value Line. She also checked at the beginning and end of each quarter to be sure that the betas had not changed significantly over the period. There was no published list of betas for assets other than common stocks. Nancy knew that she could not apply the procedure without a risk measure for each asset. Since she preferred not to make the calculations herself, she decided to limit her analysis to the common stocks.

Nancy realized that her decision to consider only the common stocks was largely for convenience. She was concerned about the implications of this decision, especially in light of the rapid increase of money market instruments in the portfolio; by the end of the third quarter of 1987, common stocks represented only 46.8 percent of the value of the portfolio, compared to 64.3 percent for the quarter ending December 30, 1986 (see Table 31.1).

The weights given in Table 31.2 reflect the proportion of each stock's market value to the total market value of the common stocks in the portfolio. For example, Citicorp represents 3.4 percent of the total value of the common stocks for the quarter ending December 30, 1986.

Finally, Nancy gathered the return information for the market and for a risk-free security. She elected to use the Standard & Poor's 500 to represent the market, and short-term U.S. government bonds to represent the risk-free security. (Quarterly holding period returns for each of these assets are given in Tables 31.3 and 31.4.) Nancy was careful to note that since she had calculated quarterly holding period returns for each stock in the fund, she must also use quarterly returns for the market and the risk-free security.

QUESTIONS

1. Evaluate the checking account practices and other cash management policies followed by the fraternity.

2. What changes would you make in the fraternity's stated investment policy?

3. Does it appear that Harriman Ross and Associates is following the investment policy established for the fund?

4. Calculate the quarterly change in the total dollar value of the portfolio and the quarterly rate of change. Also calculate the rate of change in the total value of the portfolio over the three-quarter period from December 30, 1986, to September 30, 1987.

5. Use Jensen's portfolio evaluation model to assess the quarterly and annual performances of the equity portions of the endowment fund. Interpret the results.

6. How can cash, bonds, and money market instruments be included in a risk-return portfolio performance evaluation?

7. Should Harriman Ross and Associates be replaced as investment counsel?

TABLE 31.1	Sigma Sigma Sigma End-of-Quarter Portfolio Holdings (market values)		
Quarter Ending	**Asset**		
December 30, 1986	Cash	$ 45,410	6.6%
	Money market instruments	104,606	15.3
	Bonds	94,531	13.8
	Common Stocks	440,459	64.3
	Total	$685,006	100.0%
March 31, 1987	Cash	$ 50,932	7.8%
	Money market instruments	109,699	16.8
	Bonds	88,151	13.5
	Common Stocks	404,190	61.9
	Total	$652,972	100.0%
June 30, 1987	Cash	$ 45,055	6.5%
	Money market instruments	135,167	19.5
	Bonds	95,657	13.8
	Common Stocks	417,285	60.2
	Total	$693,164	100.0%
September 30, 1987	Cash	$ 37,346	5.3%
	Money market instruments	249,448	35.4
	Bonds	88,082	12.5
	Common Stocks	329,778	46.8
	Total	$704,654	100.0%

TABLE	Sigma Sigma Sigma
31.2	Beta and Quarterly Holding Period Returns for Indicated Quarters

	Beta	Quarter Ending 12/30/86		Quarter Ending 3/31/87	
		% Return	Weight	% Return	Weight
1. Citicorp ([1])	1.25	−6.9%	.034	−7.5%	.033
2. Ameritrust	0.80	1.5	.039	−4.4	.040
3. Mobil	0.95	1.2	.027	−8.8	.028
4. Weyerhauser	1.30	1.4	.054	−4.5	.056
5. McDonalds	1.20	8.0	.086	.5	.096
6. Diamond Shamrock ([1])	NM	1.2	.027	−22.2	.028
7. Federated Dept. Store	1.15	3.5	.018	−11.5	.019
8. Savannah Elec. & Pwr.	0.65	5.5	.059	−5.8	.064
9. General Electric ([2])	1.10	−4.8	.069	−	−
10. DuPont	1.20	−4.4	.023	−10.9	.023
11. Inland Steel ([1])	1.20	10.1	.041	−6.0	.046
12. IBM	1.00	5.6	.053	−12.5	.058
13. Deere	1.05	−10.3	.027	−38.3	.025
14. May Dept. Stores	1.05	5.0	.035	−13.6	.038
15. Motorola	1.35	−17.3	.056	−4.7	.048
16. Northwest Corp.	1.00	8.9	.060	−4.0	.067
17. PepsiCo, Inc. ([3])	1.10	−	−	−2.9	.026
18. Phillips Petroleum	0.90	.8	.070	−5.6	.073
19. Quaker Oats	0.95	5.7	.035	−3.2	.038
20. Nabisco	1.05	−3.5	.042	−3.6	.042
21. Rockwell Int'l. ([1])	1.15	1.8	.041	−4.8	.042
22. Sante Fe So. Pac.	1.15	6.7	.060	−11.1	.066
23. Tenneco	0.85	−1.6	.044	−1.6	.044
			1.000		1.000

([1]) Sold during quarter ending June 30, 1987.
([2]) Sold during quarter ending December 30, 1986.
([3]) Acquired during quarter ending March 31, 1987.
NM = not meaningful.

TABLE 31.2	Sigma Sigma Sigma Beta and Quarterly Holding Period Returns for Indicated Quarters (cont.)

	Beta	Quarter Ending 6/30/87		Quarter Ending 9/29/87	
		% Return	Weight	% Return	Weight
1. Citicorp ([1])	1.25	18.6%	.032	—	—
2. Ameritrust	0.80	18.4	.041	4.0	.058
3. Mobil	0.95	−1.0	.027	13.2	.033
4. Weyerhauser	1.30	.7	.057	9.4	.069
5. McDonalds	1.20	11.7	.103	−4.4	.139
6. Diamond Shamrock ([1])	NM	21.1	.023	—	—
7. Federated Dept. Store	1.15	6.9	.018	−5.0	.023
8. Savannah Elec. & Pwr.	0.65	11.3	.064	5.6	.084
9. General Electric ([2])	1.10	—	—	—	—
10. DuPont	1.20	4.5	.021	18.3	.027
11. Inland Steel ([1])	1.20	5.3	.046	—	—
12. IBM	1.00	10.2	.054	8.8	.071
13. Deere	1.05	23.6	.016	—	—
14. May Dept. Stores	1.05	7.4	.035	7.0	.045
15. Motorola	1.35	18.6	.055	−1.9	.078
16. Northwest Corp.	1.00	24.0	.069	—	—
17. PepsiCo, Inc. ([3])	1.10	15.3	.026	3.4	.037
18. Phillips Petroleum	0.90	11.8	.074	8.7	.099
19. Quaker Oats	0.95	13.7	.039	4.9	.053
20. Nabisco	1.05	3.6	.043	10.7	.052
21. Rockwell Int'l. ([1])	1.15	−5.8	.049	—	—
22. Sante Fe So. Pac.	1.15	1.2	.062	−.9	.075
23. Tenneco	0.85	3.8	.046	1.2	.057
			1.000		1.000

([1]) Sold during quarter ending June 30, 1987.
([2]) Sold during quarter ending December 30, 1986.
([3]) Acquired during quarter ending March 31, 1987.
NM = not meaningful.

TABLE 31.3 | Sigma Sigma Sigma
Standard & Poor's 500 Stock Composite Index
Quarterly Holding Period Returns

	S&P 500 Index Ending Value	Change from Previous Quarter (%)	Effective Quarterly Dividend	Quarterly Dividend Yield (%)	Quarterly Holding Period Return (%)
September 29, 1986	250.84				
December 30, 1986	242.17	4.690	2.08	0.899	5.589
March 31, 1987	291.70	20.453	2.11	0.871	21.324
June 30, 1987	304.00	4.217	2.18	0.747	4.964
September 29, 1987	321.83	4.670	2.21	0.727	5.397

TABLE 31.4 | Sigma Sigma Sigma
Holding Period Returns on Short-term U.S. Government Bonds

Quarter Ending	Quarterly Holding Period Return (%)
December 30, 1986	1.71
March 31, 1987	1.81
June 30, 1987	1.89
September 29, 1987	2.08

Stock Price Behavior

PART SIX

Richard Green
(General Market Analysis)

Richard Green was a member of an investment club called The Technicians. The club had been formed in 1985 for the purpose of using technical analysis as a vehicle for investing in the stock market. Each of the initial twelve members had contributed $5,000 when the club was started. The current market value of the club's portfolio was approximately $78,000.

Although the club was partially social, the organization of the club was quite formal. The elected officers and the description of their responsibilities were as follows:

Head Technician: Preside over bimonthly meetings, call emergency meetings as needed, and provide the meeting place and refreshments.

Market Technician: Forecast market movements.

Industry Technician: Identify industries with favorable trends.

Stock Technician: Using information from the market and industry technicians, provide technical analysis of individual securities.

Treasurer: Maintain the financial records of the club.

The head technician and the treasurer were elected for two-year terms; the other officers' terms were one year. The market and industry technicians were each allowed to hire a graduate student on a part-time basis from the local university. The stock technician was authorized to hire two graduate students. The club had purchased a minicomputer with a printer to maintain the financial records and analyze market, industry, and stock data.

At the beginning of their terms, the market, industry, and stock technicians were required to present their proposed techniques of technical analysis to the other members. In addition to a detailed description, an illustration of each technique's performance over at least the previous two years was required.

Richard was recently elected the market technician. His predecessor had used a version of the Dow theory; in Richard's opinion, it had been only moderately successful. His main complaint was the length of time it took for a primary trend to be confirmed. Because of this delay, Richard thought, several turns in the market had been missed.

Richard decided to test two procedures for his presentation: the odd-lot theory and *Barron's* Confidence Index—the "dumb money" and "smart money" approaches. He viewed the two approaches as leading indicators. He had asked the graduate student to gather the data shown in Table 32.1.

QUESTIONS

1. What is the basic philosophy of technical analysis?

2. Prepare a description, including the underlying philosophy, of the odd-lot theory and the Confidence Index.

3. From the data in Table 32.1, plot on the same graph the Monday values for the odd-lot sales-to-purchases ratio and the Standard & Poor's 500 Composite. Would the odd-lot theory have been a successful predictor of market movements over the 1986–1987 period?

4. From the data in Table 32.1, prepare a point-and-figure chart of the Confidence Index. Let each block on the vertical axis represent 0.5 percent. Consider a change of 1 percentage points a significant reversal. With each significant reversal start a new column. Compare the signals from the point-and-figure chart with the subsequent movements in the Standard & Poor's 500 Composite.

5. Would the odd-lot theory or *Barron's* Confidence Index have provided a warning about the steep market decline in October 1987?

TABLE	Richard Green
32.1	Odd-Lot Sales-to-Purchases Ratio and Barron's Confidence Index

Date [1]	S&P 500	Odd-Lot Sales-to-Purchases Ratio	Barron's Confidence Index (%) [2]
1986			
1/03	207.97	252.50	90.60
1/10	208.26	243.10	90.90
1/17	203.49	221.20	92.30
1/24	210.29	238.50	91.90
1/31	212.96	215.60	91.50
2/07	215.97	220.10	91.30
2/14	219.76	245.20	91.80
2/21	224.04	241.10	90.70
2/28	224.34	258.50	90.40
3/07	232.54	161.10	91.60
3/14	235.60	196.80	92.10
3/21	237.30	204.80	92.50
3/28	235.71	167.40	90.60
4/04	233.75	253.50	90.60
4/11	242.22	185.20	90.40
4/18	241.76	189.90	91.10
4/25	235.52	206.10	92.10
5/02	236.08	180.90	93.00
5/09	237.54	194.50	91.90
5/16	235.46	282.60	92.10
5/23	246.63	176.80	92.70
5/30	243.94	156.70	93.40
6/06	241.13	169.40	93.30
6/13	244.99	126.50	93.70
6/20	248.93	175.30	93.50
6/27	252.70	196.10	92.40
7/04	242.82	228.30	93.20
7/11	235.01	165.40	92.20
7/18	238.67	168.70	92.60
7/25	236.59	202.30	92.40
8/01	236.84	238.90	92.30
8/08	245.67	169.00	91.60
8/15	249.77	120.70	90.00
8/22	253.00	230.50	92.20
8/29	250.08	195.30	92.10

continued

TABLE 32.1

Date[1]	S&P 500	Odd-Lot Sales-to-Purchases Ratio	Barron's Confidence Index (%)[2]
1986 (cont.)			
9/05	247.06	205.70	92.00
9/12	231.68	316.80	93.40
9/19	236.28	109.90	93.00
9/26	235.60	94.60	92.50
10/03	236.68	228.70	92.20
10/10	238.80	219.00	91.90
10/17	236.26	190.40	92.00
10/24	240.94	219.70	92.00
10/31	246.58	198.40	91.80
11/07	246.64	247.70	92.60
11/14	237.66	240.30	91.90
11/21	248.77	189.20	89.90
11/28	253.83	277.70	90.50
12/5	250.96	214.20	90.80
12/12	247.57	268.50	91.10
12/19	246.75	115.10	92.10
12/26	242.17	278.90	91.30
1987			
1/02	255.33	80.10	91.70
1/09	262.64	165.10	91.90
1/16	267.84	208.20	92.10
1/23	275.40	192.40	92.70
1/30	279.64	206.50	92.80
2/06	277.54	194.00	93.60
2/13	285.42	136.50	93.10
2/20	284.80	134.90	93.00
2/27	280.62	183.90	93.50
3/06	290.31	203.50	92.80
3/13	292.78	173.20	93.10
3/20	300.38	208.40	93.60
3/27	292.39	170.60	93.90
4/03	297.26	151.10	94.10
4/10	284.44	141.60	95.90
4/17	287.19	106.40	95.20

continued

TABLE 32.1

Date[1]	S&P 500	Odd-Lot Sales-to-Purchases Ratio	Barron's Confidence Index (%)[2]
1987 (cont.)			
4/24	284.57	203.90	94.90
5/01	295.47	163.90	95.00
5/08	293.98	165.80	94.40
5/15	278.21	185.60	95.40
5/22	288.73	155.90	93.10
5/29	293.47	170.40	94.40
6/05	297.47	180.50	94.30
6/12	304.81	153.40	94.50
6/19	306.86	157.80	94.30
6/26	302.94	173.50	94.80
7/03	308.29	176.90	94.40
7/10	310.42	167.70	94.10
7/17	308.47	171.90	94.10
7/24	315.65	159.80	94.30
7/31	318.45	162.20	95.10
8/07	332.39	153.60	94.90
8/14	329.83	144.80	95.40
8/21	334.57	131.10	96.20
8/28	321.68	173.40	96.20
9/04	312.92	169.90	96.50
9/11	314.86	157.00	95.20
9/18	321.19	183.40	95.90
9/25	321.83	169.90	94.60
10/02	318.54	167.80	95.20
10/09	315.23	211.20	96.90
10/16	258.38	238.70	93.90
10/23	233.28	57.10	92.50

[1] If the market was closed on a Monday, the dates and data are from Tuesday's market activity.
[2] Although the values for *Barron's* Confidence Index appear on Monday, they are based on the previous week's bond yields.

David Dobbs
(Filter Rules)

On a hot and humid Saturday in late August 1988, David Dobbs sat in his study at home, analyzing the price data he had gathered on the common stock of Apple Computer, Inc. (see Table 33.1). Because of the volatility of this stock's price over the past year, David thought that it would be a good candidate for a technical system of trading.

David was a graduate of a very prestigious engineering school. His educational background, coupled with years of serious study of stock market prices, had convinced him that the security markets were not efficient. He firmly believed that stock prices moved in trends and that the astute observer of these movements could earn a rate of return in excess of a simple buy-and-hold strategy.

For the past several years David had employed a number of technical tools. For overall market analysis, he used the weekly ratio of odd-lot sales to odd-lot purchases, *Barron's* Confidence Index, breadth-of-market indicators, and the cash position of mutual funds. David developed a composite indicator of these measures and thought that it provided him with a reasonable forecast of turns in the market.

David was less satisfied with his technical tools for analyzing individual securities. For each security he followed, he calculated two measures of relative strength: (1) the ratio of the security's monthly rate of return to the monthly rate of return of the firm's industry, and (2) the ratio of the security's monthly rate of return to the market's monthly rate of return as measured by the Standard & Poor's 500. David thought that the industry ratio was not very meaningful because so many of the companies he followed were diversified across industry lines. Though he had enjoyed some success with the market ratio, he did not think that the ratio had any significant advantage over using the security's beta coefficient in combination with his overall market analysis.

In addition to relative strength analysis, David maintained bar charts of each security's daily price movements and corresponding bar graphs along the bottom of the charts indicating the volume of shares traded. David thought that these charts were consistent with the underlying philosophy of technical analysis; however, he had great difficulty interpreting the price patterns to predict future price movements. After a significant price movement, the formations in the charts were relatively easy to interpret.

Given his dissatisfaction, David began looking for other technical tools that would embrace the basic philosophy of technical analysis, but require less judgment on the part of the user. After examining several alternatives, he decided to investigate a trading technique using a filter rule. Using a predetermined filter, the buy and sell decisions would become automatic. David considered the size of the filter critical: a purchase or sale and short sale would occur whenever the price of the security moved by the size of the filter from a previously established low or high. If the filter was set too low, the number of transactions would become excessive; If set too high, the filter would be relatively insensitive to the trend in the stock's price.

David decided to familiarize himself with this mechanical trading rule by simulating trading in the stock of Apple Computer, Inc. during 1987–88. His simulation procedure was as follows:

> Use the October 20, 1987 price of $34.50 for Apple Computer as a base price. If the price rises (or declines) from the base price by the size of the filter or more, buy and hold (sell short) the stock until the price drops (rises) by at least the size of the filter from a subsequent high (low). When this price decrease (increase) occurs, liquidate the long position (cover the short position) and sell the stock short (assume a long position) until the price rises (declines) from a subsequent low (high) by the size of the filter or more. Repeat this process as often as indicated by the price movements of the stock.

QUESTIONS

1. Define and explain the rationale for the technical techniques previously used by David.

2. Why did David think that the relative strength market ratio was equivalent to using a security's beta coefficient in combination with technical market analysis?

3. Using filters of 1 percent, 2 percent, and 5 percent, calculate the dollar and percentage gain or loss per transaction (ignore transaction costs). Estimate the mean percentage gain for each filter.

4. Assuming a 2 percent commission cost for each transaction, what is the mean percentage gain for each filter?

5. What are the advantages and disadvantages of the filter rule approach?

TABLE 33.1	David Dobbs Daily Closing Prices for Apple Computer, 1987–1988						

Date	Price	Date	Price	Date	Price	Date	Price
1987		12/10	34.25	2/1	41.50	3/24	40.75
10/20	34.50	12/11	34.00	2/2	41.00	3/25	40.00
10/21	40.25	12/14	37.00	2/3	39.50	3/28	41.25
10/22	36.50	12/15	37.50	2/4	39.50	3/29	40.75
10/23	35.25	12/16	39.25	2/5	38.50	3/30	39.50
10/26	27.75	12/17	39.25	2/8	38.50	3/31	40.00
10/27	30.50	12/18	40.25	2/9	39.50	4/4	38.50
10/28	33.25	12/21	41.50	2/10	40.75	4/5	39.00
10/29	39.25	12/22	41.25	2/11	40.50	4/6	41.50
10/30	38.50	12/23	42.00	2/12	40.75	4/7	40.75
11/2	38.75	12/24	42.50	2/16	41.00	4/8	41.00
11/3	36.25	12/28	40.25	2/17	41.75	4/11	41.50
11/4	36.00	12/29	42.00	2/18	41.50	4/12	41.75
11/5	38.00	12/30	43.25	2/19	41.50	4/13	41.25
11/6	37.50	12/31	42.00	2/22	43.25	4/14	39.50
11/9	37.00			2/23	42.50	4/15	39.50
11/10	36.25	**1988**		2/24	42.00	4/18	40.00
11/11	37.25	1/4	44.50	2/25	41.75	4/19	40.25
11/12	38.75	1/5	44.50	2/26	41.50	4/20	39.50
11/13	37.00	1/6	44.00	2/29	43.00	4/21	39.50
11/16	36.75	1/7	44.25	3/1	43.00	4/22	40.00
11/17	35.00	1/8	39.75	3/2	44.50	4/25	40.75
11/18	36.25	1/11	42.25	3/3	46.25	4/26	41.50
11/19	34.25	1/12	42.00	3/4	46.75	4/27	41.75
11/20	35.50	1/13	42.00	3/7	46.75	4/28	41.25
11/23	36.00	1/14	42.00	3/8	46.25	4/29	40.75
11/24	36.75	1/15	42.75	3/9	46.75	5/2	41.00
11/25	36.25	1/18	42.50	3/10	45.25	5/3	41.75
11/27	34.75	1/19	42.75	3/11	45.50	5/4	42.00
11/30	32.75	1/20	39.50	3/14	46.00	5/5	41.75
12/1	33.00	1/21	40.00	3/15	44.75	5/6	41.25
12/2	32.50	1/22	39.25	3/16	46.00	5/9	40.75
12/3	30.25	1/25	40.75	3/17	44.75	5/10	40.75
12/4	30.50	1/26	39.50	3/18	44.50	5/11	39.50
12/7	33.00	1/27	39.50	3/21	43.75	5/12	39.75
12/8	34.50	1/28	41.00	3/22	43.75	5/13	40.25
12/9	34.75	1/29	41.25	3/23	42.50	5/16	41.00

continued

TABLE 33.1	David Dobbs Daily Closing Prices for Apple Computer, 1987–1988

Date	Price	Date	Price	Date	Price	Date	Price
1988		6/13	44.75	7/11	45.00	8/5	44.25
5/17	40.50	6/14	45.25	7/12	44.75	8/8	44.00
5/18	39.50	6/15	45.50	7/13	44.75	8/9	43.50
5/19	39.00	6/16	44.50	7/14	45.00	8/10	41.75
5/20	38.75	6/17	44.50	7/15	44.88	8/11	43.00
5/23	37.75	6/20	44.00	7/18	45.25	8/12	42.25
5/24	38.75	6/21	44.75	7/19	44.50	8/15	41.25
5/25	38.50	6/22	45.50	7/20	44.00	8/16	42.25
5/26	39.25	6/23	45.00	7/21	43.00	8/17	41.75
5/27	39.75	6/24	44.75	7/22	42.50	8/18	42.25
5/31	41.25	6/27	44.50	7/25	42.75	8/19	40.50
6/1	42.25	6/28	46.00	7/26	42.50	8/22	39.50
6/2	41.75	6/29	46.25	7/27	42.50	8/23	39.50
6/3	42.75	6/30	46.25	7/28	42.75	8/24	40.50
6/6	43.75	7/1	46.25	7/29	44.25	8/25	40.00
6/7	44.00	7/5	47.00	8/1	45.00	8/26	40.25
6/8	44.75	7/6	46.25	8/2	44.50	8/29	40.75
6/9	43.25	7/7	45.75	8/3	44.50		
6/10	44.50	7/8	45.25	8/4	44.50		

Index of Cases